FIRST REPUBLIC BANK
It's a privilege to serve you®

THE POWER *of*
a CLIENT-FOCUSED HERITAGE
and CULTURE

EXCEPTIONAL PEOPLE
EXTRAORDINARY SERVICE

COPYRIGHT ©2015 BY FIRST REPUBLIC BANK

FIRST EDITION
ISBN 9781882771417
LIBRARY OF CONGRESS CONTROL NUMBER 2014941570

WRITTEN BY SCOTT MCMURRAY
WRITTEN AND EDITED BY SHANNON HOUSTON, WITH KIMBERLY SHANNON

PRODUCED BY THE HISTORY FACTORY
1200 NEW HAMPSHIRE AVENUE NW, SUITE 500
WASHINGTON, DC 20036
WWW.HISTORYFACTORY.COM

PRODUCTION MANAGEMENT BY HOWRY DESIGN ASSOCIATES
354 PINE STREET, 6TH FLOOR
SAN FRANCISCO, CALIFORNIA 94104
WWW.HOWRY.COM

PUBLISHED BY FIRST REPUBLIC BANK
111 PINE STREET
SAN FRANCISCO, CALIFORNIA 94111
WWW.FIRSTREPUBLIC.COM

While every effort has been made to verify the information included in this publication, some sections do reflect personal recollection of associated individuals. Please forward comments and questions to livingheritage@firstrepublic.com.

This presentation may contain forward-looking statements. You are cautioned not to place undue reliance on such statements, which are only predictions and involve estimates, known and unknown risks, assumptions, and uncertainties that could cause actual results to differ materially. For a discussion of these and other risks and uncertainties, see First Republic's FDIC filings, available in the Investor Relations section of www.firstrepublic.com.

The information provided herein may include certain non-GAAP financial measures. The reconciliation of such measures to the comparable GAAP figures are included in First Republic's Annual Report on Form 10-K, Quarterly Reports on Form 10-Q and Current Reports on Form 8-K.

TABLE *of* CONTENTS

"There are no businesses,

only

people."

JIM HERBERT

Chairman and Chief Executive Officer (Founding)
First Republic Bank

How did First Republic grow, organically,
from a single storefront in San Francisco to a bicoastal bank
among the 30 largest in the country?

Work hard. Stay humble. Keep it simple.
And always focus on the client.

This is the 30-year story of exceptional people providing
extraordinary service to remarkable clients.

TOTAL ENTERPRISE VALUE

March 2015
$8.1 Billion

MARCH 2015

With expansion to the East Coast, and into wealth management and business banking, First Republic continues to grow with its clients over time.

Associates:	2,574
Offices:	73
Total bank assets:	$ 51.1 Billion
Total wealth mgmt assets:	$ 56.4 Billion
Total capital:	$ 5.1 Billion

JULY 1985

First Republic Bancorp opened its doors in July 1985, focused on credit quality and providing the highest level of client service.

Associates:	10
Offices:	1
Total capital:	$ 8.8 Million

July 1985
$8.8 Million

Sept. 2007 - June 2010: Bank was not an independent entity

"I will do

almost

anything

to get trial."

JIM HERBERT

Chairman and Chief Executive Officer (Founding)
First Republic Bank

PART ONE

The Road to First Republic

LORAIN

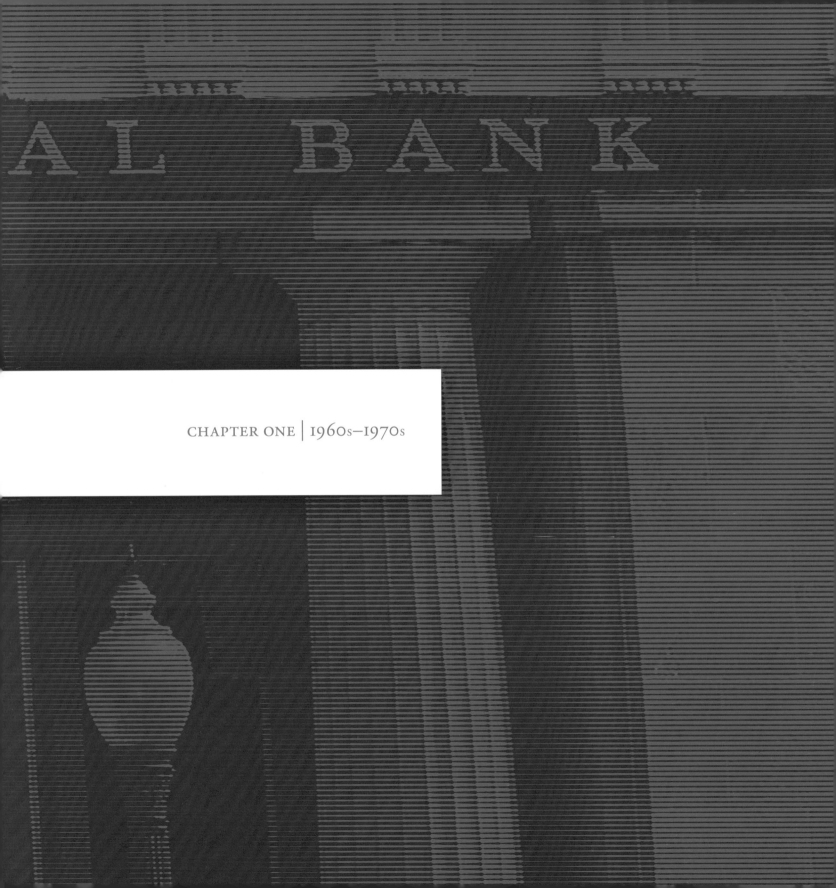

CHAPTER ONE | 1960s–1970s

TRYING

New Things

Community Banking

Jim Herbert first learned the banking business around the family dinner table in the 1950s. His father and namesake devoted his career to community banking among the small- to medium-sized towns straddling the rivers of central Ohio and the shores of Lake Erie. He was respected in the communities where he worked, including Coshocton, where he served as the Vice President of Coshocton National Bank, and Canton, where he was the Vice President of the Harter Bank & Trust Company. In 1962, Herbert's father became President of the Lorain National Bank – the same year his son, President of his high school student government, was about to head off to college. By then, Herbert's father had earned the esteem of his banking industry peers and would go on to serve as President of the Ohio Bankers Association in 1972.[1]

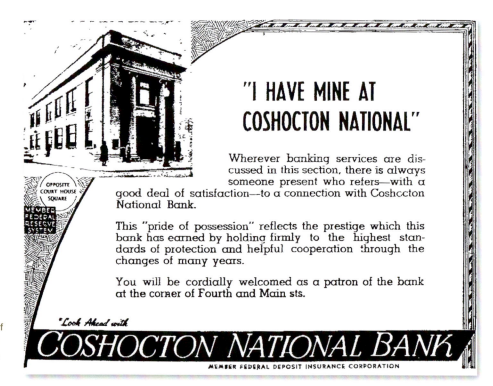

Jim Herbert's father served as Vice President of Coshocton National Bank in the 1950s, as well as Chairman of the Coshocton County Savings Bond Committee.

Established in 1905, Lorain National Bank, the result of the merger of The Lorain Banking Company and Lorain National, has a long history of dedicated service to its local communities and businesses. Herbert's father, James Herbert, President of The Lorain Banking Company in 1958, merged the two in 1961 and continued this legacy of community service as he expanded the bank's offerings and capabilities.

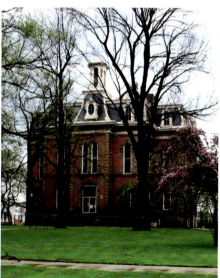

The small Ohio towns of Herbert's youth – Coshocton, Canton and Amherst – instilled in him an appreciation for relationship-based service and businesses with a community feel and focus.

Just before he graduated from Babson College in 1966, Jim Herbert was offered a position in Chase Manhattan Bank's Special Training Program.

America's manufacturing prowess during the early 1960s was second to none in most sectors, especially within the steel industry. Known as "Steel City" for its steel mills and shipyards, Lorain was a predominantly blue-collar, multicultural, immigrant town. Area bankers were trusted members of the community, working hard to extend credit to promising businesses and residents looking to capture a piece of the American dream.

Herbert remembers his father continually working to increase efficiency, responsiveness and profitability. Lorain National, for instance, was the first bank in Ohio to utilize federal funds as a low-risk way of generating additional income. And it was one of the first banks in the Buckeye State to install a state-of-the-art IBM 360 computer to speed its transaction processing and recordkeeping. "He was always trying new things, very carefully," Herbert recalled.[2]

BABSON COLLEGE

Herbert transferred to Babson College in Wellesley, MA, in 1963, after spending a year at Miami University in Oxford, OH. Known for its business and economics-oriented curriculum, this proved to be a life-changing step for Herbert, expanding his horizons and providing an extraordinary academic foundation for the burgeoning entrepreneur. He took 20 credits per semester, thriving in its analytical culture, and graduated in 1966. While at Babson, he served as President of Alpha Kappa Psi, a professional business fraternity, and gained overseas experience, living and working on a farm in Denmark.

New York City was a different world than the towns of Herbert's childhood. Though the scale of banking at Chase Manhattan also felt worlds away, the principles Herbert learned from his father's community bank – good service and attention to detail – provided an excellent foundation.

In 1962, Herbert attended Miami University in Oxford, OH, for a year, before transferring to Babson College in Wellesley, MA. While at Miami University, Herbert joined the U.S. Marine Corps and completed his basic training. He continued to serve as a reservist while a student, from 1963 to 1966, in the active Marine Corps reserve air wing, assigned to South Weymouth Naval Air Station. He moved to New York in 1966, following his graduation, and served through 1969 at Floyd Bennett Naval Air Station in Brooklyn, to complete six years of Marine Corps service.

"Best on the Street" Training from Chase

During his senior year at Babson, Herbert jumped at the chance to sign up for a prestigious training program offered by Chase Manhattan Bank. The bank, headed by Rockefeller family scion David Rockefeller, typically took students who had already earned advanced degrees but began inviting promising undergraduates, as well, in the mid-1960s. Chase included Babson on its short list of schools known for producing graduates with a solid business and economics education, and Herbert secured a spot in the firm's program at a starting salary of $6,000 per year.

David Rockefeller became President of Chase Manhattan in 1961 and its Chief Executive Officer in 1969.

Moving to New York City and enrolling in the program was like entering another world for the small-town Ohioan who had only been out of state three times before attending Babson. The program attracted young aspiring bankers from across the country and from just about every walk of life. Herbert could not help thinking it likely that more people lived on his block in Manhattan than in his entire hometown of Coshocton.

The Chase program was an "old-fashioned, best on the street" training regimen. The bank selected its applicants carefully and assiduously trained them. Most had earned MBAs or served full-time in the military, and all were older than Herbert, who, at 21, had just completed his undergraduate degree. This intensive basic training in credit analysis served the future Chairman and founding Chief Executive Officer of First Republic Bank well. "That core credit training I still use every day," he said.[3]

While in Chase's program, which ran six and seven days per week, Herbert enrolled in New York University's evening MBA program. Majoring in finance, he took classes two to three nights a week, balancing the grueling schedules of both institutions.

"If You Can't Do Better Than This …"

Working in Chase's training program at its One Chase Manhattan Plaza headquarters, Herbert was challenged in a way that would have a lasting impact. A few weeks into the program, Herbert was charged with creating a credit report for his then-superior, David Davies. Davies called Herbert into his office for a talk.

True to the level of talent Chase committed to its training, Davies was a relatively young but already established banker from England who had studied at University of Oxford and Harvard Business School – an industry leader later knighted for his service to British banking and commerce.[4] But on that afternoon the stern expression on Davies' face tipped Herbert off that he was not going to receive the positive response he had hoped for. The carefully typed report that Herbert had submitted was handed back to him, barely legible beneath a sea of red-inked commentary. "James," Davies said succinctly, "if you can't do better than this, you should work somewhere else."

It was precisely the wake-up call that the aspiring banker needed. "My standards shot up, and I never looked back," Herbert recalled. "I think one of the best things that can happen to younger people is to set very clear, high standards for them early. They don't know how good they can be until you test them."[5] It was a lesson that would reverberate throughout Herbert's career and become a foundation for his future approach toward leadership.

Completed in 1964, sculptor Isamu Noguchi's sunken garden was the centerpiece of One Chase Manhattan Plaza's main floor.

One Chase Manhattan Plaza rises 813 feet high and was the world's sixth tallest building when it opened in 1961.

MARTY GIBBS

Not long into the training program, Herbert signed a lease to share an apartment in Manhattan with a young Englishman working in advertising named Malcolm Turner. Turner was part of a regular poker game that attracted a rotating selection of young professionals.

One evening in 1966, Herbert found himself seated across the table from a corporate attorney a few years older than himself, named L. Martin Gibbs, known as Marty to his friends. After being born in Manhattan and growing up on Long Island, Gibbs had attended Brown University, earned a law degree at Columbia Law School and later worked at the prestigious law firms of Rogers & Wells and White & Case. "He was a young lawyer, and I was a young banker, and neither one of us could afford the quarter

raise, quite literally," Herbert said. "We met and we've been friends ever since."[6]

Gibbs recalled, "Jim was just starting out as a young man at Chase in their training program. I presume I may have been Jim's first guest to have lunch in the corporate dining room at Chase as a potential client."[7] It was the beginning of a lifelong business as well as personal relationship, as Herbert would turn to Gibbs for legal expertise on every business deal he would work on moving forward. And it would be Gibbs who would later serve as Lead Outside Director of First Republic Bank.

Trying New Things

Following his completion of the training program, Herbert continued his employment with Chase, which took him to Puerto Rico for a year as section leader and a training officer in the bank's credit training program. Herbert completed his MBA at New York University with the submission of his thesis on the Puerto Rican sugar industry. Upon returning to New York, he was promoted to calling officer and Assistant Treasurer in the Latin America area, covering Venezuela and Chile. Determined to broaden and deepen his expertise, however, he decided to look at other opportunities in the finance sector.

His credit analysis skills proved attractive to Wall Street, securing him an investment banking position with the Wall Street firm, Newburger, Loeb & Company, in 1970. The firm asked him to undertake an assignment back in his home state of Ohio, assuming operating control of a small, struggling start-up company, which serviced the steel industry, in which Newburger's clients had invested. Once investors were made whole on their investment, and with Herbert's interest in financing real estate heightened, he stayed in Cleveland, accepting a position with Citizens Financial Corporation that allowed him to explore this renewed interest.

Citizens Financial hired Herbert in its operations and planning division, later moving him into mortgage banking. By his 28th birthday, Herbert was charged with oversight of mortgage banking, the liability side of two real estate investment trusts, and management of over 100 people. With a passion for financing real estate fueled by his time at Citizens Financial, and valuable credit, operating and deal-making skills under his belt, as Herbert's 29th birthday approached he reflected upon his career path and concluded his experiences to date had not yet let him fully realize his entrepreneurial desire – it was time to run his own shop.

In August 1969, Jim Herbert and Marty Gibbs traveled to a music festival in upstate New York and found themselves at a historic and storied event – Woodstock.

"No Gasoline" was a common sight along highways, as a gasoline shortage hit the nation in the wake of the Arab-Israeli War of 1973.

Herbert and Associates

Herbert learned of a financing opportunity in the rapidly expanding Texas real estate market; he resigned from Citizens Financial, moved to Arlington, TX, and opened for business as Herbert and Associates. In truth, "Associates" was just for show: He was a one-man operation.

Herbert struck a deal with a developer who built motels mainly in Texas and other Southwestern states. Herbert's office was in the developer's building, and he functioned as its banker. "I would take a motel in Allen or Austin, TX, and go to New York or Boston and syndicate the equity," Herbert said. "I'd get paid as a percentage of the equity raised."[8] He closed on about 20 such deals until world events intruded.

At first glance, the Arab-Israeli War of 1973 did not appear to affect the motel business in Texas. But the global oil embargo and soaring gas prices that followed certainly did. With Americans dramatically cutting back on car trips, even in oil-rich Texas, the demand for motel rooms dried up. And so did the need to raise capital for new projects.

Jim Herbert, Jim Joy and David Dunlop met at J.G. Melon for lunch to discuss the possibility of buying the bottling plant in Richmond, VA. A few hours later, a rough sketch of the deal was in place.

A Burgeoning Entrepreneur

Herbert left Texas for good in early 1975 and returned to New York, where he maintained an apartment and had developed a significant network of business and finance contacts. His career definitely was a work in progress. "I kind of retired in New York for about four or five months and hung around and figured out what else to do," he said.[9] He knew his path would not follow a more traditional route, and so he did not pursue a position in one of New York's financial institutions. Instead, the burgeoning entrepreneur sought his next venture.

Herbert received a call from a friend, Jim Joy, who was working in investment banking at WE Hutton & Co. Joy proposed they meet for lunch at J.G. Melon, a Third Avenue bar and restaurant known for its burgers that remains a favorite to this day. Joy was going to bring along a business contact he thought Herbert should meet.

David Dunlop was a Canadian businessman in the soft drink bottling business. He was interested in selling his bottling plant and franchise in Richmond, VA, that was on the verge of bankruptcy. Joy thought that Herbert, given his track record of success in a variety of business ventures and locales, might be an interested buyer. He was right, and by the end of their three-hour lunch, they had agreed on the outlines of a deal.[10]

The Pop Shoppe

Herbert moved into a Holiday Inn for several months near the Richmond bottling plant he and Joy had purchased and set about learning the soft drink bottling, sales and distribution business. The franchise was for a Canadian brand of soda called The Pop Shoppe. The brand offered 26 flavors, sold only by the case, in returnable, redeemable bottles. Operating in 11 states in the United States, the company was among the first "green" soda manufacturers. Its slogan: "You'll find our plants all over the country … never our bottles."[11]

The quality of the product was not the problem; it was on par with leading brands sold across the country. Nor were profit margins. It cost $1 to produce a case of soda that sold for $3. The biggest challenge Herbert faced was gaining traction in a market that was dominated by some of the best-known and heavily advertised consumer brands in the business. As he would remind colleagues in years to follow, "If you can sell pop against Coca-Cola and Pepsi in the summer, in the South, you can sell anything."[12]

Herbert upgraded the very limited staff with people he thought were up to the challenges that lay ahead. In the process, he hired Linda Moulds as his Controller, the same position she had held at a small Philadelphia savings and loan. Over the next two decades, Moulds would join him three times and play a critical role as he built one new business after another.[13]

"Get Trial at Any Cost"

To revitalize sales, Herbert turned to a brand new ad agency to design eye-catching coupons redeemable for a free case of soda, provided customers made the $3 deposit for the case and bottles. Herbert distributed the coupons to the public through as many channels as possible, including local Boy Scout troops. When customers finished their pop, they returned the case and hopefully took another, leaving their deposit with the company. This cash flow provided the working capital to turn the business around.

The promotion drew the ire of the franchisor in Canada, who thought it was denigrating the image of the product, but Herbert argued that he had to get the pop in the hands of consumers to "get trial" and kick-start demand in the region. After the free-case coupon campaign, which was very successful, Herbert experimented with lowering the price of a case of soda from $3 to $2.50, still making a $1.50 profit per case. The case and bottle inventory in the factory warehouse was drawn down, cash came in, people tried and liked the product, and the business turned a profit within months.

The Pop Shoppe brand featured 26 flavors of soda and was sold by the case, in returnable bottles.

In August 1978, while at the Bank of Virginia and as her career also gained significant momentum, Cecilia Herbert was featured on the cover of *Fortune* magazine – just the second woman to have graced the periodical's cover.

While in Richmond, the Herberts lived in one of the first renovated homes in the Church Hill neighborhood.

CECILIA ANNE HEALY

Herbert's path as an entrepreneur had taken root. His personal life also reached a pivotal moment, when he met Cecilia Healy, his future wife. Healy was a young banker with J.P. Morgan at the time. Raised in Tacoma, WA, she held an undergraduate degree from Stanford University and an MBA from Harvard Business School, where she was one of approximately 20 women in the group of about 700 students who comprised the Class of 1973. Though based in New York, she sometimes traveled to Texas for business, where Herbert based his venture, Herbert and Associates. After being introduced in New York by a mutual friend, the two discovered they shared much in common, and a romantic relationship blossomed.

While Herbert was in the midst of turning around The Pop Shoppe, he and Healy married. She joined him in Richmond, accepting a job as Vice President with the Corporate Banking Division of Bank of Virginia. In August 1978, while at the Bank of Virginia and as her career also gained significant momentum, Cecilia was featured on the cover of *Fortune* magazine – just the second woman to have graced the periodical's cover.

As the newlyweds were house-hunting, they were drawn to the historic Church Hill neighborhood of Richmond near St. John's Church. At that time, much of the area had fallen into disrepair. But as luck would have it, the local historical society had renovated a Federalist mansion, originally built in 1849, at 2300 East Grace Street, not long before the Herberts' arrival. The society and its backers were seeking a tenant, and the Herberts were thrilled to oblige.

They took up sailing, which Herbert learned on Long Island Sound, and spent many weekends on the water. Only later did they fully appreciate the uniqueness of their move and the small part they had played in the rejuvenation of what would become a vibrant urban area. "We had a great time. We made friends there. It was wonderful," Herbert recalled.[14]

On March 23rd, 1775, Patrick Henry delivered one of the most famous lines of the American Revolution, "Give me liberty or give me death," from the sanctuary of St. John's Church in Richmond, VA. When the Herberts arrived in Richmond 200 years later, the building still anchored the Church Hill neighborhood.

"Don't be confused by the new returnable bottle law," declared this Pop Shoppe ad in *The Washington Post*. Customers could visit any of the six Fairfax County locations listed in the ad to buy Pop Shoppe soft drinks. "All by the case. All returnable. All guaranteed."

Sale.
10¢ a bottle. All 26 flavors, including 9 diet, tonic and soda.

Don't be confused by the new returnable bottle law. Come to the PoP Shoppe. We sell 26 flavors of the best tasting soft drinks and mixers you ever put in your mouth. All by the case. All returnable. All guaranteed. Now through October 2nd mix and match a case of 24 ten ounce bottles for just $2.39 plus deposit. And if you don't agree it's every bit as good as what you're drinking now, we'll give you your money back.

All 26 flavors on sale through October 2nd
The PoP Shoppe.

Belle View/Alexandria
The PoP Shoppe Belle View
Shopping Center
1610 Belle View Blvd.

Manassas
Battlefield Exxon/The PoP Shoppe
7113 Sudley Rd.

McLean
McLean Exxon Car Care Center/The PoP Shoppe
Old Dominion Drive and Chain Bridge Road

Woodbridge/Dale City
Shirley Exxon/The PoP Shoppe
Jefferson Davis Highway (Rt. 1) and Gordon Blvd.

Falls Church/Arlington
Washington & Lee Exxon
Car Care Center/The PoP Shoppe
6730 Lee Highway

Springfield
The PoP Shoppe, Springfield Tower Ct
6412 Brandon Ave.

Encouraged by these early successes, Herbert soon found another opportunity to get his product in people's hands. In 1977, Fairfax County, VA, just outside Washington, DC, tried to reduce roadside trash by requiring all distributors to institute a bottle deposit fee. When leading soda manufacturers balked at the law and refused to deliver to retail outlets in the county, Herbert rushed in.

He took his turn behind the wheel of pickup trucks and semi-trailers, as he and his team rushed their cases of pop up Interstate 95. "I drove in and opened business up – like crazy," Herbert recalled. "I just went in and got a lot of gas stations to put my pop in their empty bays, and we cleaned up." By the time the county repealed the deposit-fee requirement three years later, The Pop Shoppe had gained significant market share in the region.

The experience of turning around the soda business underscored the importance of moving quickly to seize opportunities at the critical step of getting initial trial of a good product. It was an invaluable lesson that continues to influence Herbert to this day. "If you have a good product, your number-one marketing barrier all the time, always, is to get trial," he said. "That's what we're doing. We're getting trial … I will do almost anything to get trial."[15]

A Golden Opportunity

The Pop Shoppe parent company was so pleased with the turnaround in Richmond that it wanted to buy back the franchise. Herbert and Joy were interested if the price reflected their hard work in resuscitating the operation. In 1978, they agreed on a selling price, and at the same time, as a quid pro quo, agreed to buy the struggling Pop Shoppe franchise in the San Francisco Bay Area.

Moving west, the Herberts settled into San Francisco's Russian Hill neighborhood in the fall of 1978. Cecilia, with fond memories of the region from her undergraduate years at Stanford, reunited with her former employer J.P. Morgan, while Jim commuted each day to the Newark, CA, bottling factory site in the East Bay.

Herbert owned one of three Pop Shoppe franchises in the Bay Area, along with the bottling plant for the region. The parent company agreed with Herbert that it had erred in creating three entities – in effect, splitting the same marketing area – but the owners of the other two were initially not interested in selling. Despite this and other obstacles, Herbert applied many of the lessons learned in Virginia, and in little more than a year, he had turned the plant around and was making a profit. He ended up buying the other two franchises, and then successfully sold the combined three operations as a single package back to the parent company in early 1980.

The experience was gratifying, but Herbert had come to a crossroads in his career. He was not sure what was next, but he was sure of one thing: "I had done enough pop."[16]

"How Fast Can You Move?"

Herbert would wonder aloud when talking with his friend and attorney Marty Gibbs, with whom he kept in touch with regularly, if it was time for him to get back into the banking business. In many ways, his first dozen years in business and his family background had all been pointing toward a career in banking. But he did not want to work for a bank as his father had; he wanted to establish and own one.

Gibbs contacted Robert Thompson, an attorney in his law firm's Los Angeles office, and let him know of Herbert's interest. Thompson alerted Herbert to another kind of deposit-taking institution in California. "You know, there's a license that's easier than a bank, called a 'thrift and loan,' and you only need a million and a quarter to start it," Herbert recalled Thompson telling him. Herbert said he was interested but put the thought on hold for the moment. He and Cecilia were already quite busy, passionately renovating their first home, a duplex they converted into two condominiums, in the Russian Hill neighborhood of San Francisco. Herbert also was looking forward to participating in the Singlehanded TransPacific Yacht Race to Hawaii, for which he had begun training with his 39-foot Freya sailboat.

When the Herberts moved to San Francisco in 1978, they settled in Russian Hill, home to one of the city's most famous sites. Lombard Street, known as America's crookedest street, runs through the neighborhood's center.

While Herbert contemplated his future, he prepared for entering the Singlehanded TransPacific Yacht Race, which began at the Golden Gate Bridge and ended in Hawaii.

The startup mentality was beginning to reign supreme in Silicon Valley in the late 1970s and '80s, especially near Stanford University, making Silicon Valley an ideal location for Herbert's first thrift and loan. The valley, once filled with farms, was now growing companies such as Hewlett-Packard, Intel, Apple and Adobe.

A few weeks later, in March 1980, Thompson was back on the phone. "How fast can you move?" he asked Herbert. "I think pretty fast, depending on the situation," Herbert replied. "There's an approved charter in Sunnyvale, CA, 40 miles south of San Francisco," Thompson said. "You can't move it. It has to be open within two miles of this location, and it has to be opened by the end of August."[17]

Back to Banking

Herbert paid a quick visit to the middle-class community of Sunnyvale, in Silicon Valley. He liked what he saw and decided to purchase the thrift and loan charter, but he needed additional capital in order to put the plan into action. Joy had just the man in mind. He arranged a meeting with Roger Walther, an accomplished entrepreneur and longtime associate.

ROGER WALTHER

Roger Walther, nearly 10 years older than Herbert, had spent four years in marketing with Procter & Gamble after graduating from the Coast Guard Academy and the Wharton School of the University of Pennsylvania. Also an entrepreneur, Walther co-founded the American Institute for Foreign Study, AIFS, in 1964, with Cyril Taylor, a British colleague at P&G and Harvard Business School graduate.

Building on the wave of enthusiasm for international projects created by the Peace Corps and similar 1960s-era initiatives, AIFS offered academic programs for international high school and college students with offices in Greenwich, CT, and London, England. In the years leading up to his meeting with Herbert, however, Walther had the feeling that the company had become as much of a bank as a foreign study organization.

Ever since President Richard Nixon had untethered the value of the dollar from the price of gold in August 1971, causing currency values to fluctuate dramatically,[18] a great deal of Walther's time had been spent managing the currency risk of AIFS. The dollar and other global currencies now floated in value, based largely on the economic outlook and financial soundness of the issuing country, not the price of gold. AIFS was buying currency futures and taking other steps to try to insulate itself from the impact of erratic currency prices.

The soaring inflation and interest rates of the late 1970s, in part a result of the combined heavy U.S. government spending on the Vietnam War and social programs at home, had made it ever more difficult to manage the company's finances.

Years earlier, Walther had brought his friend Joy on board as a Director of AIFS. In 1979, the two were having a conversation, and Walther said to Joy, "You know, Jimmy, we are a bank." When Walther then declared, "I think we ought to go into the banking business!" Joy reminded him of his friend, Jim Herbert, and insisted they reconnect.[19]

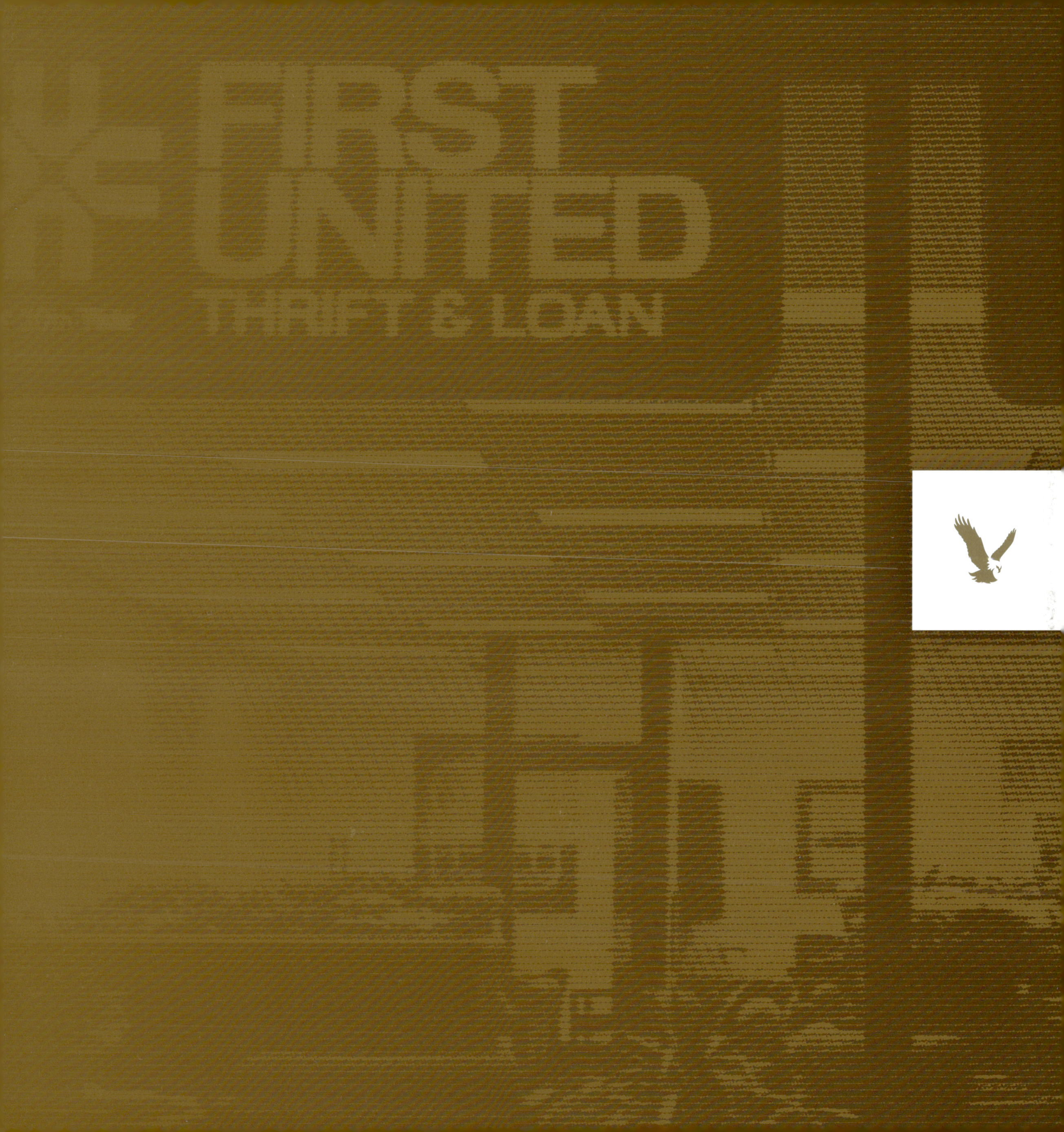
FIRST
UNITED
THRIFT & LOAN

CHAPTER TWO | 1980–1984

A KEY INNOVATION—

The Jumbo Mortgage

THRIFT AND LOANS

In 1910, Arthur J. Morris, a lawyer, founded Fidelity Savings & Trust Company in Norfolk, VA, launching a banking model and movement that took root in the Mid-Atlantic states over the next few years. His model was based on a set of lending principles:[3]

1) Character, plus earning power, is a proper basis for extending credit;

2) Loans made on this basis of credit may provide for the privilege of repayment over a period long enough to match the earning power of the borrower; and

3) Money so borrowed should always be for some constructive and useful purpose.

Institutions that subscribed to Morris' principles and lending strategy were referred to as "Morris Plan banks" or "industrial banks." By 1914, the Industrial Finance Corporation owned the majority of these institutions. The industrial banks were at the forefront of a national transition toward mass access to consumer credit, and by 1931 there were 109 Morris Plan companies and banks operating in 142 cities with an annual loan volume of about $220,000,000. However, by the end of the Great Depression, the number of industrial banks had declined and commercial banks had begun to adopt Morris' lending practices.[4]

Thrift and loans are a derivative of the Morris Plan bank, or industrial bank, model. Like their predecessors, thrift and loans are small, community-focused financial institutions that offer a narrower scope of services than commercial banks. They emphasize lending and savings options for individuals and small businesses.[5]

Federal legislation passed in the decades following the Great Depression and the related 1930s mortgage crisis extended deposit insurance to the thrift industry and promoted the full-term amortized home loan model. Thrift and loans, equipped for deposit-taking and with lending practices that already integrated an installment-based approach to loan repayment, grew in popularity.[6]

Financing by Fax

Green not only provided Herbert with invaluable advice based on his years of operating experience in the thrift business, he also introduced Herbert to automobile lending. Herbert quickly grasped the basics and then added his own innovation – financing by fax.

When consumers bought cars in 1980, they typically went shopping over the weekend. But if they wanted financing, which most did, they often would not know if their purchase contracts and financing had been approved until Tuesday or even Wednesday of the following week. Car dealers would show their sale contracts to banks or other financial institutions on Monday morning, and the lenders would then either move forward or decline the requests. The goal among lenders was to offer loans to only those clients with the best credit and let their rivals divvy up the rest.

Herbert bet that if Westcoast purchased and installed facsimile machines – in this case, hulking black machines that Herbert and his team dubbed "Darth Vaders" – in the finance offices of a few car dealerships, they could get these dealers to fax financing requests to Westcoast throughout the weekend. Modern fax machines, as

By furnishing car dealerships with fax machines, Westcoast Thrift & Loan got first pick, and therefore the best credits, of the financing requests from interested buyers.

BILL TRACY

Bill Tracy presented Jim Herbert with a commemorative keepsake in 1996, highlighting the first mailer they worked on together in 1981.

As he had with The Pop Shoppe, Herbert was anxious to "get trial" with clients, beginning with getting them to visit the office. Walther asked a designer in the art department at *San Francisco Magazine*, a periodical he owned, for a graphic designer she could recommend. Bill Tracy, who had just submitted the most sophisticated ad layout the designer had ever seen, got the nod. Tracy came to meet with Herbert at his home one weekend and found him in a T-shirt and jeans, working in his backyard. "I later learned that was very Jim," Tracy said.[7]

Instead of mailing free coupons as he had in Virginia, Herbert wanted a mailer with a key. Tracy's design was straightforward and to the point – also "very Jim." It was

sent to residents in the area, and if they brought in the key and used it to open a treasure chest in the lobby, they would receive a gift. "This was corny, but it worked," Herbert said, as he held one of the mailers years later. "What I wanted to do was get people to come in the front door. Find out where we were and who we were. If you have a superior product and superior people, the main challenge is getting trial. Word of mouth then takes over."[8]

The campaign was a big success with clients. It was also the start of a decades-long relationship between the designer and Herbert that would culminate in First Republic Bank's signature eye-catching color and imagery scheme.

of 1980, were relatively new and expensive, cutting-edge business technology. Each page of a car sales contract took a then-speedy four minutes to transmit.

Herbert and Green would come in on Sunday or early Monday and cherry-pick the best applications from each weekend's contracts. "As a result, we had a great business," Herbert said. "The difference was we would spend the money on the machine and no other bank would. By the time the other banks came around on Monday, the best contracts were gone."[9] This innovation succeeded in setting Westcoast apart from rival lending institutions, not only through building relationships with local car dealers, but with its demonstrated ability to institute change in a "move forward, move fast" style.

A Proposal for Change

One of Herbert's many tasks was to represent Westcoast at thrift and loan meetings and conferences. Herbert and Walther had jumped at the chance to buy the thrift and loan license in Sunnyvale. But as a newly opened institution, Westcoast was required by state law to limit its total loan portfolio to only three times its equity for several years. More established thrifts, on the other hand, were able to leverage approximately eight times their equity, and thereby boost their income. This law was based on the assumption that established lenders would be more prudent than newcomers entering the field.

This presented some challenges to newer institutions like Westcoast. In the fall of 1980, Herbert attended his first meeting of the California Association of Thrift & Loan Companies. Standing before the trade group, Herbert suggested that the law, in practice, protected the industry veterans' established markets and shielded them from competing with newcomers. He surmised that he had considerable support from many of the other younger faces in the room, but was too outnumbered by the thrift and loan establishment to engender immediate change.

Even before Herbert could return to his seat, an industry veteran rebuked him from his position in the front of the room, where he and a few others presided over the meeting. "Young man," he said, "you don't know what you're talking about. There's a big risk here."[10]

TROUBLED ECONOMIC TIMES

In early 1980, the U.S. economy entered a recession, following the Great Society program spending, the cost of the Vietnam War and the increase in oil prices, which led to inflation. Paul Volcker was appointed Chairman of the Board of Governors for the Federal Reserve System, "the Fed," and would serve an eight-year term under both Democratic President Jimmy Carter and Republican President Ronald Reagan.

In an effort to curb inflation, the Fed began raising interest rates in 1977. The federal funds rate, which had reached 11 percent in 1979, peaked at nearly 20 percent by 1981.

Westcoast Thrift & Loan, in line with the market, issued thrift certificates at over 15 percent. With unemployment and inflation in the U.S. around 10 percent at the same time, economic conditions were extremely challenging for many industries, especially the financial services sector.[13]

First United Thrift & Loan

By the late 1940s, Weiner had teamed up with his brother and Ingram to run a profitable escrow business in Southern California, working with banks to facilitate lines of credit, collections and other activities. In 1953, Weiner and Ingram learned that a license for a thrift and loan based in Los Angeles was available for purchase as part of an out-of-state bankruptcy proceeding. They pulled together the requisite amount of cash and bought the license for First United Thrift & Loan on the spot.

First United had only five employees at the time of purchase, but it had a solid book of business catering to the restaurant supply trade and the business of financing pinball games to restaurants and bars. Over the next few decades, First United would develop a lucrative business lending to liquor-related establishments, including bars, restaurants and liquor stores. Weiner and Ingram developed a well-deserved reputation as smart operators.

Weiner became an especially active advocate for the thrift and loan industry, over time assuming the leadership role of the California Association of Thrift & Loan

Companies.[14] By 1980, First United was clearing $750,000 to $1 million in profits annually on about $10 million in loans, with hardly a bad loan on the books. "They didn't know how to lose money," Herbert marveled.[15]

Closing the Deal

Herbert and Walther met Weiner and Ingram for lunch at the landmark Fior d'Italia restaurant in San Francisco's North Beach neighborhood in the spring of 1981. The young entrepreneurs had to admit they were impressed with Weiner and Ingram's experience and what they had accomplished. Herbert and Walther had considered expanding into Southern California. The question was whether to build their own operation or buy an existing one. In this case, it made a lot of sense to buy an established business with a very good reputation.

Weiner and Ingram were impressed, in turn, and realized they were being offered an opportunity to take equity out of their business on favorable terms. They were not getting any younger, and with interest rates continuing to soar and loan demand headed in the opposite direction, the challenges facing the financial industry were looking more formidable by the day. Besides, the personalities seemed to be a good fit. "I think they got a kick out of us and thought, 'Hell, this could be some fun,'" Walther said.[16]

A last-minute snag almost killed the deal. Both parties had initially proposed an all-cash transaction. But in the face of the staggering economy and record high rates, Herbert and Walther were unable to raise the full price in cash. They came back with an offer of half the purchase price in cash, with the balance in the form of an interest-bearing note. Weiner initially balked, but within a few days, he and Ingram agreed to accept the combination of cash and paper for First United.

Weiner and Ingram stayed on to run the Los Angeles thrift and loan. Herbert visited the Wilshire Boulevard location frequently and adopted several of its best practices for the Westcoast operation in Sunnyvale. With Westcoast now merged into the 1953 First United charter, both businesses were able to operate with greater leverage, allowing for further growth. "We could take off," Herbert said, and so could profits.[17]

Jim Herbert and Roger Walther met Steve Weiner and Jack Ingram at Fior d'Italia, which has served San Francisco diners since 1886, to discuss a partnership.

Jack Ingram (seated) stayed on as the Senior Vice President of First United
Thrift & Loan and also served as a Director of San Francisco Bancorp.

First United Thrift & Loan advertises its latest rates in 1983.

San Francisco Bancorp

In early 1980, Herbert and Walther had created San Francisco Bancorp as the holding company through which they would operate their expanding business.[18] Walther was the founding Chairman of the Board and Herbert the founding President, Chief Executive Officer and a board member. Later, in 1983, the enterprise would open a new office in San Francisco's business district, at 140 Battery Street, from which Herbert would operate the growing franchise. Albeit a modest space, the San Francisco address was intended as a signal to the Northern California community that their enterprise had "arrived."

Emboldened by their innovative intrastate deal in California, Herbert and Walther were keen on continuing to pursue their growth strategy. If they could make an intrastate deal work, why not find a way to build an interstate banking business, which was quite unique at the time?

Legislation at the time prohibited multi-state banks and savings and loans, but not thrift and loans. "We were building a multi-state bank, which had not yet been done," Herbert said. "I perceived that there might be unique value in multi-state. The only way you could get through the multi-state barriers was to go the thrift and loan route."[19]

SAN FRANCISCO BANCORP

FRANK FAHRENKOPF

Frank Fahrenkopf, a Brooklyn native who had moved to Reno as a child, received his law degree from the University of California at Berkeley during the mid-1960s free speech movement and later worked as a trial lawyer for several years in Reno. He had long been active in Republican politics – in a few years, Ronald Reagan would call him to Washington to chair the Republican National Committee for six years – and he enjoyed a friendly relationship with Nevada Governor Robert List, a Republican he helped elect in 1979.

Fahrenkopf had just the background Jim Herbert was looking for, having worked for years with Nevada's thrift and loan legislation. When Fahrenkopf heard that Herbert wanted to enlist him to try a different path, he agreed and joined the team.[20]

Fahrenkopf would become a Director of San Francisco Bancorp and later First Republic. He went on to found the American Gaming Association, in Washington, D.C., which he led for 18 years, retiring in June 2013. In 1987, he also co-founded the Commission on Presidential Debates, which he continues to co-chair.

Betting on Nevada

Herbert saw just such an opportunity next door in Nevada, where there was only a single thrift and loan in operation. Unfortunately, the law was written in such a manner that it would be very difficult, if not impossible, for a second thrift and loan license to be issued. The state legislature also only met every other year, leaving the entrepreneurs to wait an entire year to try to get the law amended. There had to be a better way.

Herbert talked to two major law firms in Las Vegas about representing the thrift and loan. Either one would have been a safe choice. His instinct, however, told him to go with an attorney in Reno named Frank Fahrenkopf, whom he decided to meet in person after a brief call from a Las Vegas phone booth.[21]

Opening in Las Vegas

Fahrenkopf developed a strategy for Herbert. They would propose that San Francisco Bancorp should be granted a license to operate in Nevada. The law, as written, prohibited a license from being granted to bank holding companies or savings and loan holding companies – but it did not say anything about a thrift and loan holding company. They met in person to make their case to Nevada Governor Robert List. He agreed with their logic that granting San Francisco Bancorp a license would not violate Nevada law. In turn, it would offer the added advantage of providing more borrowing options for Nevada consumers.[22]

Within a few months, Herbert and Walther were open for business in Las Vegas as First United Thrift & Loan, the Nevada operating subsidiary of San Francisco Bancorp. Governor List helped Herbert cut the ribbon at the opening ceremony, as Fahrenkopf, who would soon join the board of San Francisco Bancorp, looked on. Neon signs in the windows advertised the attractive interest rate, more than 9 percent at the time, which First United was paying on certificates of deposit. Herbert then recruited Jim Baumberger to join First United and establish the enterprise's presence in the region.[23]

By 1982, San Francisco Bancorp was a multi-state thrift and loan, operating in California, Nevada and Utah.

Jim Herbert (center) and Roger Walther (right) welcomed Gordon Taubenheim (left) aboard the leadership team as Executive Vice President and Chief Operating Officer of San Francisco Bancorp.

In short order, Herbert became aware of another expansion opportunity. He learned that Overland Thrift and Loan in Salt Lake City, UT, was for sale. It was a well-regarded one-office thrift specializing in mortgages and consumer finance. He scooped it up and included it under the San Francisco Bancorp umbrella, which, as of 1983, served clients in Sunnyvale, San Francisco and Los Angeles, CA, along with Las Vegas, NV, and Salt Lake City, UT. Their commitment to service, expanding loyal client base and industry reputation inspired confidence in the future growth potential of the enterprise.

A Key Innovation – The Jumbo Mortgage

The entrepreneurs were now in five markets in three states. Tight operating controls and quality assets produced profits from day one for San Francisco Bancorp. And the source of the thrift and loan holding company's success would increasingly be summed up in two words: jumbo mortgages.[24]

While still spending much of his time working out of the Sunnyvale office of Westcoast Thrift & Loan in 1981, Herbert noticed an intriguing trend. One Silicon Valley entrepreneur or corporate officer after another was coming in and looking for a home mortgage, despite the fact that rates hovered around 20 percent during this inflation-plagued period. But instead of seeking the typical mortgage size at the time, which usually topped out at under $90,000, they wanted to borrow around $250,000. Though larger than the typical size, often that was only 50 percent of the appraised value of their homes.

Herbert and Green rejected the first few requests out of hand. Then Herbert had a change of heart. "What are we missing here?" he asked Green. "Why don't we do a couple of these and see how they go? Can't bankrupt the whole bank." At the same time, Westcoast encouraged this new crop of clients to buy certificates of deposit through the thrift and loan, which bolstered its deposit base.[25]

Jeanne Forster Gutsche (left) and Linda Moulds (right) were part of Herbert's exceptional team.

It was a new world for the small lender, and not everyone was comfortable with the transition. Sensing that his area of expertise, the car loan business, was in permanent eclipse and having little interest in jumbo mortgages, Green retired within a few months. Herbert assumed Green's role as President of Westcoast. Shortly after, Herbert also hired Gordon Taubenheim, a colleague from his Citizens Financial days in Cleveland, as Executive Vice President and Chief Operating Officer.[26]

Herbert realized they needed to write an entirely new set of rules to cover jumbo home loans of this magnitude. He decided to focus on two things: borrower liquidity and loan-to-value ratios. Healthy liquidity ensured that loan payments would

The secret to San Francisco Bancorp's quick success was its employees, who worked quickly and efficiently serving clients.

continue to be made on schedule during good times and bad, while low loan-to-value ratios ultimately provided protection against loss in case of defaults. "I wanted three years of liquidity times the monthly mortgage payment in the bank, provable, or I didn't make the loan and we topped out at 50 percent loan-to-value ratio," he said.[27]

"We Knew We Were onto Something"

The jumbo mortgage business was a phenomenal success. "Jim discovered that jumbo home loans on primary residences were pretty damn good," Walther recalled. "We knew we were onto something."[28]

Herbert and Walther benefited from the fact that they did not have much competition in the jumbo market for several years. By the early 1980s, many existing savings and loans found themselves burdened with an excessive amount of fixed-rate mortgages on their books, while the cost of funding was rising, and they struggled just to stay afloat. Few others were willing to risk the relatively untested jumbo mortgage market on top of everything else. Westcoast, on the other hand, did not have a legacy book of mortgage loans and originated only adjustable-rate business.

At the same time, Herbert and Walther passed all but unnoticed by San Francisco's banking giants. These larger institutions seemed to show little interest in the jumbo mortgage market. And if anything, they seemed to back away from home loans in general, reacting perhaps to rising loan losses during the recession of the early 1980s.

The downturn also sparked continued consolidation in the banking sector, which encouraged banks to look for products that benefited from economies of scale, not high-service offerings such as jumbo mortgages. Herbert seized the opportunity.

As many of these Silicon Valley entrepreneurs were purchasing their first home, Herbert could see that this mortgage was not just a product, but a gateway to building a full client banking relationship. "Purchasing a home isn't a transaction," Herbert said. "It's helping a person or a family build their future. There is a highly emotional quality to that. If we do it well, and we take excellent care of this client, then it will lead to a much more robust banking relationship that will develop and grow over time." Though providing such levels of extraordinary service may cost a bit more, he knew the opportunity was in developing the relationship, not just in executing the transaction.[29]

The demand certainly existed. "We did a half a billion dollars of that business in the next three years at a quarter-million dollars a chunk with virtually no losses," Herbert said.[30]

Going Public

San Francisco Bancorp turned to the public markets in 1983 to help fund its burgeoning jumbo mortgage business and interstate expansion. Attorney and friend Marty Gibbs oversaw the preparation for an initial public offering, and everyone from Herbert to the newest hire pitched in.

While writing their stock-offering prospectus, Gibbs and others worked hard to capture the essence of the young enterprise: What San Francisco Bancorp was really selling was its people, culture and the client-centered service dynamic they created.[31]

"I think that was always the idea, that we were there because we had a client, not the other way around," recalled Linda Moulds. "When we first started, whoever answered the phone quoted rates for CDs or for accounts. You didn't get a client on the phone and let them get off until they were satisfied."[32]

Employee education and training were important, but there was more to Herbert's vision of success. As Moulds said, "It's not just their knowledge and smarts. It's their personality and their whole being and their attitude of how they want to treat others and how they want to get the job done." [33]

If the Bank was going to be a success, it would have to be from the bottom up, not just the top down. "Jim would hire very good people, put them in charge, and then let them go for it and expect them to get the job done," Moulds said. "I think Jim never got angry with somebody if they made a mistake. To cover it up, that was a good way to end your career. Admit you made a mistake, learn from it, and move on." [34]

JEANNE FORSTER GUTSCHE

When Jeanne Forster Gutsche interviewed to be Herbert's assistant in December 1982, there were all of 10 employees in San Francisco Bancorp's corporate office. She had worked at very structured major corporations, including Clorox, Booz Allen Hamilton and Aetna Life & Casualty, but she soon took to the open floor plan and team environment. No one let a phone ring for long, and everybody pitched in if there was a problem to be solved or an opportunity to be pursued. On Gutsche's first day at work, she was surprised to find that she would be working at a desk directly beside Herbert's. [35] The push was on shortly thereafter to prepare for the initial public offering. She recalled working long days, with Herbert there most days when the staff arrived, and there after many had left. Gutsche continued as Herbert's assistant from 1982 through 1994.

Prospectus

1,350,000 Shares

SAN FRANCISCO BANCORP

Common Stock

San Francisco Bancorp (the "Company") is selling 1,350,000 shares of Common Stock through the Underwriters of which 277,830 shares are reserved for sale to Atlantic Financial Federal. Prior to this offering, there has been no public market for the Common Stock of the Company. See "Underwriting," with respect to the method of determining the initial public offering price.

The Company does not conduct commercial banking operations, nor does it have any interest in a commercial bank.

See "Risk Factors" for a Discussion of Various Matters Relating to the Company.

THESE SECURITIES HAVE NOT BEEN APPROVED OR DISAPPROVED BY THE SECURITIES AND EXCHANGE COMMISSION NOR HAS THE COMMISSION PASSED UPON THE ACCURACY OR ADEQUACY OF THIS PROSPECTUS. ANY REPRESENTATION TO THE CONTRARY IS A CRIMINAL OFFENSE.

	Price to Public	Underwriting Discounts and Commissions(1)	Proceeds to Company(2)
Per share	$7.50	$.54	$6.96
Total (3)(4)	$10,125,000	$729,000	$9,396,000

(1) The Underwriters are being indemnified against certain liabilities, including liabilities under the Securities Act of 1933. See "Underwriting."

(2) Before deducting expenses payable by the Company estimated at $328,000.

(3) Includes 277,830 shares to be sold by the Underwriters to Atlantic Financial Federal. See "Underwriting."

(4) The Company has granted to the Underwriters a 30-day option to purchase up to 135,000 additional shares of Common Stock solely to cover over-allotments of which up to 27,783 shares are reserved for sale to Atlantic Financial Federal. If such option is exercised in full, the total price to the public, underwriting discounts and commissions and proceeds to the Company will be $11,137,500, $801,900 and $10,335,600, respectively. See "Underwriting."

Bateman Eichler, Hill Richards
INCORPORATED

The date of this Prospectus is July 25, 1983.

San Francisco Bancorp went public in July 1983.

Every employee was on duty to help clients in the thrift and loan's early days, quoting rates and answering questions.

San Francisco Bancorp went public in July 1983, offering 1.35 million shares of common stock at $7.50 a share. The underwriting was handled by the regional investment bank Bateman Eichler, Hill Richards.[36] In just under three years, the venture that began with $1.25 million of initial capital had grown to a total enterprise valuation of about $25.5 million.[37]

Atlantic Financial Federal

The capital raised through the stock offering helped support the growth of the business, but it was not enough. San Francisco Bancorp needed more capital on its books if it was going to continue to expand its jumbo mortgage operation. Herbert reached out to Donald Caldwell, a longtime friend. Caldwell and his wife, Judy, had introduced Herbert to his wife, Cecilia, whom they knew from their time at Harvard Business School; he and Don served as each other's best man in their respective weddings.

Caldwell had been a consultant to the savings and loan industry while at the accounting firm Arthur Young & Co. In May 1983, he joined Atlantic Financial Federal as Executive Vice President and Chief Operating Officer. Caldwell had put Herbert in touch, albeit a year earlier, with the firm's President and Chief Executive Officer, Raymond F. Strecker.

Atlantic Financial had been created out of four savings and loans in the Philadelphia and Pittsburgh, PA, regions that needed restructuring. Herbert described the adjustable-rate jumbo mortgage business to Strecker, and Strecker recognized it as just the sort of

high-quality, high-return asset his savings and loan had been unable to put on its books, given the nature of the relatively staid East Coast mortgage market.

The true value of the San Francisco Bancorp franchise was brought home to Strecker and his leadership team during a visit to the Bay Area. There, they saw block after block of homes valued at $1 million, $1.5 million and $2 million, which in their home market of Philadelphia would have sold for a few hundred thousand dollars at most. "So they thought, 'Boy, this is fantastic,'" Walther said. "'We'll gather the deposits, you guys get the product, and we're going to have a great marriage!'"[38]

Strecker told Herbert and Walther that he wanted to participate in as much of their jumbo mortgage loan business as was available. Herbert said if they were going to have what amounted to an exclusive arrangement with Atlantic Financial, then he wanted the savings and loan to invest capital in San Francisco Bancorp and Strecker to serve on the Board of Directors. An agreement was reached, and Atlantic Federal bought an issue of zero-coupon, convertible subordinated debt that on conversion would equal about 21 percent of the holding company's common stock.[39]

San Francisco Bancorp's jumbo mortgages created a high-quality, high-return asset for Atlantic Financial.

Thrift Unit Mer

SAN FRANCISCO, May 9
ers) — San Francisco Bancorp
had agreed in principle to be ac
by Atlantic Financial Feder
$8.50 a share. Atlantic currentl
about 21 percent of San Fra
Bancorp's common shares ou
ing. San Francisco Bancorp,
ings and loan company, had as
$108.4 million as of March 31

Atlantic Financial purchased the remainder of
San Francisco Bancorp in May 1984, freeing
Herbert and Walther to pursue their vision of a
banking model built around the jumbo mortgage.

Selling the Business

Even though the Atlantic Financial investment gave them room to grow, Herbert
was getting restless. He was convinced that the jumbo mortgage business was the
key to building the kind of relationship-based, service focused business he wanted to
lead. He was less convinced that San Francisco Bancorp was the right vehicle to get
him where he wanted to go. Its multi-state structure made it a valuable franchise, but
Herbert was concerned about the impact of troubles appearing on the horizon of the
savings and loan industry. It might make more sense to sell the business while it was
highly valued by the market and make a fresh start.

In the spring of 1984, Herbert conveyed to the San Francisco Bancorp Board of
Directors that he was interested in testing the market to see if there were any potential
buyers for the company. Herbert had lunch with Strecker as a courtesy, to give him
first look. Strecker immediately said that Atlantic Financial would make a bid for the
whole business.[40] On May 9th, 1984, less than a year after going public, San Francisco
Bancorp announced that it had agreed to be purchased by Atlantic Financial. The
transaction returned to the original investors over 10 times their initial investment in
less than 4 years.[41]

For the first few months after the buyout, the founders remained in charge of the
business they created, but reported to Strecker in Philadelphia. They were not sure
which path to take going forward, and noncompete clauses limited their options.
The situation was further complicated that September, when Strecker, only 55, died
suddenly of a heart attack, leaving Caldwell as Chief Executive Officer.[42]

An Amicable Split

Caldwell was focused on agency mortgages and expressed little interest in originating jumbo mortgage loans. Herbert, however, was convinced that the opportunity to use the jumbo home mortgage as a very high quality asset class and a lead-in to developing a full banking relationship was too good to pass up.

With friendly but differing opinions on strategic direction, they eventually decided that their friendship was more important than their business relationship, and that Herbert could leave the company to form a new entity focused on jumbo mortgages. Caldwell released Herbert from his noncompete clause and agreed to sell him the First United Thrift & Loan charter, which Caldwell no longer needed. He also agreed that Herbert could take a small team with him when he left.[43]

Over the past few years, with Westcoast Thrift & Loan and then San Francisco Bancorp, Herbert had refined his focus, zeroing in on jumbo mortgages for successful clients. He believed the emotional nature of the home purchase was key to growing a client banking relationship and differentiating his enterprise from the rest. In addition, providing an unusually high level of customer service at a time when industry consolidation left many clients feeling abandoned by the mega-banks was paramount, increasing client satisfaction, loyalty and subsequent referrals.

Herbert was ready to launch the next new company. He had the charter, team, strategy and initial location. All that was needed was capital and a name. ❖

Jim Herbert and Don Caldwell celebrate the departure of Herbert from San Francisco Bancorp in the fall of 1984.

"It's all about quick decisions,

customized

solutions,

and extraordinary service."

PART TWO

First Republic Bank — The First 30 Years

CHAPTER THREE | 1985–1989

I LIKE

'First' Anything

Jim Herbert and Roger Walther felt optimistic in early January 1985 as they stepped off the elevator onto the 52nd floor of the Bank of America Center in San Francisco for lunch at the Bankers Club. Joined by their wives, Cecilia and Anne, they enjoyed the panoramic views of the Bay Area while they deliberated their next step. Herbert and Walther, having spent the past five years refining their focus, discussed the simple business model for their next venture: jumbo mortgages for clients who met strict credit standards, coupled with certificates of deposit and passbook savings accounts to fund lending activities, delivered with unrivaled customer service. The entrepreneurs agreed they were on to a great idea – now they needed a name.[1]

Using San Francisco in their company's name felt too regional for their latest ambitions. Herbert, in particular, wanted a name that had the potential to be national in scope. He liked the name of then-prominent Republic National Bank and wanted to include "Republic" in the name of their enterprise. The word "First" topped Walther's list. "I like 'first' anything, First National, First City, first anything," Walther recalled. "It just puts you in a special category. And so we said, 'First Republic sounds like a hell of an idea.'"[2]

***

"We Hardly Missed a Beat"

First Republic Bancorp, while legally formed on February 5th, 1985, actually took wing over breakfast at San Francisco's quaint La Cucina earlier, in December 1984.[3] Following the sale of San Francisco Bancorp and Herbert's agreed-upon departure, he asked Walther, "Do you have another one in you?" With a resounding yes, the pair moved forward fast – Herbert as President and Chief Executive Officer and Walther as Chairman. The founders raised commitments for $8.8 million of capital in a few days, with more than 25 percent coming from themselves and other Officers and Directors. The initial private placement of stock was arranged by E.F. Hutton & Co. and The English Trust Group PLC, a British merchant banking firm that had invested in San Francisco Bancorp through an affiliate. Then, Herbert and Walther raised an additional $5 million in a private placement of debt securities with institutional investors, all by March of 1985.

They were determined to let as little time as possible elapse between the sale of San Francisco Bancorp to Atlantic Financial, closing in May of 1984, and the launch of First Republic. In June 1985, the thrift and loan holding company First Republic Bancorp formally bought the First United Thrift & Loan charter, which Atlantic Financial had agreed to sell to Herbert after acquiring San Francisco Bancorp.[4] On July 1st, 1985, with less than 10 employees, First Republic opened for business. Its renamed subsidiary, First Republic Thrift & Loan, welcomed clients in its comfortably furnished, sole storefront office at 201 Pine Street, in San Francisco's financial district.[5] Many early depositors came from San Francisco's Chinatown, which was only a few blocks away.

"We hardly missed a beat with several of the clients" who carried over from San Francisco Bancorp, Herbert recalled.[6]

Only five months after the formation of First Republic Bancorp in February 1985, it opened its first banking office at 201 Pine Street, on the corner of Battery, in San Francisco.

From day one, First Republic was established to provide meaningful personal banking service, and its offices would reflect this mission. It began with the Bank's ground-level retail spaces. The busy, entrepreneurial Bay Area clients would not have to travel to some upper floor – where many other banks housed their private banking operations – to receive extraordinary service at First Republic. They also would not have to wait in a traditional teller line: Clients would be greeted at the door of 201 Pine Street and escorted directly to a personal banker's desk, initiating what would become, for many, a lifetime relationship.

Herbert considered First Republic's banking offices key to enhancing the client experience and providing unparalleled service. He also viewed them as marketing vehicles, spending countless hours personally choosing the locations that provided the right visibility and fit. Operating in San Francisco's financial district – an urban, coastal market with the vertical density of a city, rather than the horizontal spread of a more suburban area – he understood the value of a highly visible corner. First Republic's 201 Pine Street location, at the corner of Battery, would benefit from a high volume of auto and foot traffic in an area ripe with prospective clients.

FLY LIKE AN EAGLE

The distinctive eagle logo has been part of the First Republic brand since the enterprise's founding in 1985. The first version of the iconic image was developed by graphic artist Dick Carroll, one of Walther's associates. Carroll did not initially use an eagle, but the California state bird, a condor – one with extended talons that added an unintended predatory touch. "We all looked at it," Walther said. "It looked like the condor was foreclosing; let's get the claws out of there," he recalled the group concluding. With the talons retracted, and the shape altered to resemble an eagle in flight, a private banking icon was born.[7]

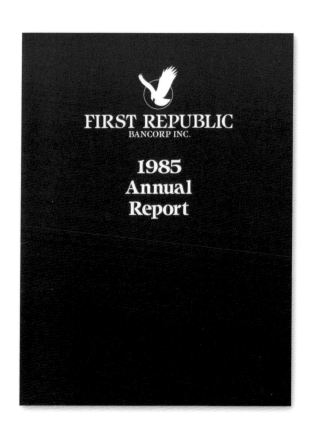

The message Herbert and Walther shared with their stockholders in First Republic's debut 1985 annual report still rings true today:

"We believe that narrowly targeted operations and strong capitalization will prove in the long run to be the proper format for a most successful banking enterprise."

"A Most Successful Banking Enterprise"

First Republic was funded and launched at a time of tremendous opportunity for an emerging financial services company, though it was the beginning of the savings and loan crisis. It would build further on its jumbo mortgage business, which was well-developed from the prior bank already, with sound financial management and lending practices, committed professionals and outstanding service, all of which had distinguished San Francisco Bancorp. But by decade's end, First Republic would be tested by the 1989 Loma Prieta earthquake that caused widespread damage in the Bay Area. In addition, the thrift and savings and loan industries that had given rise to First Republic would also be shaken to their core by the collapse of hundreds of such financial institutions nationwide.

Through it all, First Republic adhered to its high-quality assets and service principles, and it continued to grow by meeting its clients' needs. The message Herbert and Walther shared with their stockholders in First Republic's debut 1985 annual report still rings true today: "We believe that narrowly targeted operations and strong capitalization will prove in the long run to be the proper format for a most successful banking enterprise."[8]

In 1985, First Republic Bancorp's first annual report highlighted the enterprise's signature green color, eagle logo, and the strategic focus on strength, stability and service.

KATHERINE AUGUST-DEWILDE

In the process of parting company with Atlantic Financial in late 1984, Herbert led the search to quietly find his replacement. Herbert retained the search firm of Russell Reynolds in the spring of 1985 to find a new Executive Vice President of First United Thrift & Loan. Donald Caldwell, Chief Executive Officer of Atlantic Financial, and Herbert agreed not to advertise that they were looking for Herbert's successor, but for an Executive Vice President position.

Herbert interviewed several candidates and recommended Katherine August-deWilde, the Senior Vice President and Chief Financial Officer of PMI Mortgage Insurance Co., a mortgage insurance subsidiary of Sears / Allstate. Caldwell went with another candidate, however, which left Herbert to call August-deWilde to deliver the bad news.

She and Herbert talked on the phone, and in the process, Herbert admitted that he had been looking for his own replacement. She asked what he was going to do, and he sketched out the details for First Republic.

The two met in person, and August-deWilde met with Walther as well. Both agreed that she was a good fit as a member of the First Republic team, even though there was not a job for her in the business plan.[9]

She was intrigued by the entrepreneurial opportunity and impressed with the founders and their focus on the under-serviced, burgeoning jumbo mortgage market. She agreed to join as Chief Financial Officer. She was hired on July 15th, 1985 – one of the last few members to join the initial team – just after First Republic opened its doors.[10]

August-deWilde brought valuable perspective to the thrift. She had an MBA from Stanford University, and in addition to her time at PMI she had served as a consultant at McKinsey & Co. and as the Director of Finance for Itel. "I brought a bit more structure than the other people had, and because we were regulated, some of that structure was important," she said.[11]

Open Houses

First Republic got off to a strong start, with many clients of the previous bank eager to establish a relationship with the new enterprise. Just like San Francisco Bancorp, "We opened our doors with no federal insurance. Single location, ground floor and upstairs," Herbert recalled. Linda Moulds, who worked with Herbert at The Pop Shoppe, later joined him at San Francisco Bancorp and would be an invaluable contributor to this new venture. Moulds worked in the back of the ground-floor office space, as Controller of First Republic Bancorp. Herbert, Katherine August-deWilde and Gordon Taubenheim were upstairs, along with a few others, including Herbert's assistant, Jeanne Forster Gutsche. The team was busy tending to the flow of new clients, and by the end of 1985, this modest group had grown to 13 employees and set First Republic on its path to future success.[12]

With Taubenheim as the second in command and Chief Operating Officer, focused on internal issues, Herbert and August-deWilde quickly became the public faces of First Republic. She and Herbert would soon be on a first-name basis with dozens of real estate agents and home buyers in Pacific Heights, Nob Hill, the Presidio and other upscale neighborhoods in the Bay Area. They did not simply run ads and wait for the phone to ring. The two started that summer of 1985 by combing the *San Francisco Chronicle's* Sunday open house section and each attending multiple open houses that featured high-end homes.

Their goal was to make contacts within the San Francisco real estate agent community as well as with potential clients. They encouraged agents to call them directly concerning jumbo mortgages for their clients. "That was powerful. A senior executive will talk to you about your client's mortgage loan," August-deWilde said. The First Republic approach represented a level of service that agents did not get from the big banks in town.

Among clients, Herbert, Taubenheim and August-deWilde presented themselves as the decision-makers who could deliver a yes or no quickly on a mortgage – if not for the property being showcased at the open house, then for the next home they would be looking at. "They met us, they took our card, and we said, 'Call us, we'll help you, we'll give you a quick answer,'" August-deWilde said.[13] They helped finance housing for a broad range of consumers by making loans to owners of small

Jim Herbert and Katherine August-deWilde attended open houses on Sundays during First Republic Bancorp's early years, connecting with the broker community and prospective clients.

A DOLLAR SHORT

Herbert and Controller Linda Moulds attended the closing for the purchase of El Camino Thrift & Loan. The token $1 purchase price had been agreed upon for legal reasons, even though First Republic was getting the troubled thrift, effectively, for nothing. Still, the buyer had to pay up. After all the attention paid to El Camino's loan portfolio, its locations and staffing, Herbert had assumed he would have a dollar bill in his wallet when the time came to close on the deal. He did not. Herbert borrowed the dollar from Moulds so First Republic could take ownership of El Camino.[18]

First Republic Bancorp purchased El Camino Thrift & Loan for $1, which Jim Herbert had to borrow from Controller Linda Moulds.

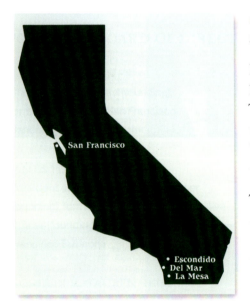

By the end of 1985, First Republic Bancorp, through the acquisition of El Camino Thrift & Loan, was serving clients in four cities in California.

million into the bailout of the thrift, with First Republic contributing an additional $1.5 million of new capital.[19]

Herbert and Taubenheim spent a great deal of time in Southern California in early 1986, as they revamped El Camino's operations in Escondido, Del Mar and La Mesa. The two shared an oceanside apartment in Del Mar, though they were rarely there at the same time. "We learned a lot about what not to do" while reviewing El Camino's books and restructuring its finances, Herbert said. "The importance of focusing on the highest possible credit quality was magnified."[20]

The reconstituted thrift was making a modest contribution to First Republic's operating profit by the end of 1986.[21] But it would take a few years, and an investment of additional capital from the Thrift Guaranty of California, to work off the bulk of the problem loans. The El Camino takeover was "a lot of work, and I wouldn't do it again in retrospect, but it turned out okay," Herbert said.[22]

"An Unexpected Bonus"

As time-consuming as the takeover of El Camino turned out to be, it did produce near-term benefits for First Republic. With Herbert and Taubenheim spending so much time away from San Francisco, August-deWilde began to play a more hands-on role in the management of First Republic Thrift & Loan in San Francisco, particularly in its sales effort. It was clear to Herbert and the rest of the First Republic

El Camino Thrift & Loan in Escondido, La Mesa and Del Mar became First Republic Thrift & Loan. The Southern California towns still house First Republic Bank offices.

team that her role at the company was more client-facing than that of the traditional Chief Financial Officer.

"I think that was probably quite interesting for the development of the whole place," Herbert said. "Because with us out of town, she had to expand her area of activities very dramatically, very quickly, which I think, in retrospect, was an unexpected bonus that came out of that situation."[23] August-deWilde later turned her attention to El Camino, and in December 1988, following the workout, was named President and Chief Executive Officer of the San Diego-area thrift.[24]

The addition of El Camino gave First Republic an overnight foothold in the rapidly growing market surrounding San Diego. It also added heft to First Republic, in terms of locations and assets, growth that provided reassurance to potential investors. "It got us critical mass fairly quickly," Herbert said. "I think if we had not been that big, we probably would not have been a candidate for going public."[25]

Even though a public offering was not on Herbert's to-do list at the start of 1986, First Republic would soon avail itself of just such an opportunity to raise additional capital to support its growing business. But having spent significant time acquiring and integrating El Camino in order to build the franchise, First Republic would pursue a more organic path toward growth moving forward, by adding new banking offices and professionals rather than acquiring full institutions.

DYANN TRESENFELD

Dyann Tresenfeld, Executive Managing Director, used a desk in a conference room as her first office at First Republic Bancorp when she joined in May 1986. When someone needed the conference room for a client meeting, she slipped her files into her briefcase and took her work to a nearby coffeehouse. She did not spend much time in the office, in any case. This was not much of a transition from her previous career as a real estate agent, where she spent much of her time in her car or meeting with clients and visiting properties.

Tresenfeld was most often out in the field working with the real estate agents she knew and telling the First Republic story: This little storefront thrift on Pine Street, committed to providing extraordinary levels of service, was making decisions on loan opportunities before many large banks had even returned a client's call.

"We'd take our notes, meet the customer, see the property, run back downtown, sketch out the information to Jim and Katherine, say this is what we want to do,

this is who the customer is," Tresenfeld said. If the loan met First Republic's stringent lending standards, Tresenfeld and other loan officers got their answer on the spot: Approved. "We just had the charge of offering the most incredible service, the fastest response anybody could possibly imagine. We just blew the socks off the real estate community because we got it done."[34] She quickly became, and remains, one of First Republic's biggest producers.

estate banker. "Everybody's producing and has their feet on the ground and their hands on whatever they need to do to take care of issues."[35]

Herbert and August-deWilde recruited professionals with a "can do" attitude, like David Lichtman and Margaret Mak, along with First Republic's first Relationship Managers, Dyann Tresenfeld and Carmen Castro-Franceschi. What these new hires had in common was a desire to work hard and learn, and the ability to be part of a team of fast-moving, ambitious entrepreneurs. That entrepreneurial spirit and agility in decision-making was already distinguishing First Republic in the marketplace from its larger, slower-moving rivals. And the tenure of these key hires helped sustain this spirit and assisted in shaping the growth to come at First Republic.

DAVID LICHTMAN

The development of First Republic's credit culture of personal responsibility and ownership in a collective success is due to a significant extent to its Chief Credit Officer, David Lichtman. Lichtman joined First Republic at age 22, in June 1986, when there were still fewer than 20 employees. He studied economics at Vassar College and was interested in business. A job right out of school with a large corporation, however, had not seemed right for him.

Lichtman learned about First Republic from his father, a lawyer, who was an associate of Roger Walther, and he was attracted to the start-up atmosphere. "You did everything that was asked of you, from answering the phones and delivering the mail to going to FedEx before there was FedEx pickup," he said. "I started learning and doing lots of different things on the lending side and grew from there." One of Lichtman's early assignments was as a loan processor for Dyann Tresenfeld. Balancing work and school, in 1990 he obtained an MBA from the University of California, Berkeley.[36] He became the Bank's Chief Credit Officer in 1995 at the age of 32, and remains in that position to this day.

MARGARET MAK

Margaret Mak, Executive Director of Preferred Banking, was glad she did not take her finance professor's advice regarding her first job after college. He told her to go with one of the Big Eight accounting firms, or with Citibank or Bank of America if she wanted a banking career. Definitely not First Republic. Too small, not enough opportunities to advance. Then she met Jim Herbert. "He told me, 'This is not a bank. This is a marketing organization that just happens to be a bank.' I trusted the guy, and I took the job," she said.[37]

Mak worked in the first-floor deposit-taking office at Pine Street, while the Relationship Managers worked upstairs on the second floor. They were often serving a separate clientele, but the success of one side of the business quite clearly benefited the other. "At that time, the savers and the borrowers were different. The savers were much older, the borrowers were much younger. We didn't merge the two until we started the Preferred Banking division," she noted.

Mak, who has focused on innovations to attract more deposits throughout her career at First Republic, feels as much of an entrepreneurial spark at First Republic today as the day she joined. The Bank and accounts may have expanded, but as far as Mak is concerned, "We are always in start-up mode. If you look at our history and you think about the growth, I don't think that's ever changed," she said. "You've got to make it on your own, entrepreneurially." [38]

CARMEN CASTRO-FRANCESCHI

Carmen Castro-Franceschi, Executive Managing Director, also joined First Republic in 1986, only a few months after Tresenfeld. Castro-Franceschi was an accomplished banker at San Francisco's Crocker National Bank, which had recently been acquired by Wells Fargo Bank. The difference between First Republic and the large banks where she worked previously was immediately apparent.

"There was this absolute spark. There was this energy level that you could never feel in another organization," Castro-Franceschi said. "I noticed one thing. Nobody was walking. Everybody was running. Everyone ran from one office to another. I thought it was unusual, but I liked it. I thought, 'Wow, this is amazing!'"[39]

Castro-Franceschi, whose background did not include mortgage lending, worked closely with Tresenfeld at the start in order to gain a better understanding of mortgages and the business of real estate. Then she was off on her own. "I got in my car and I basically drove to Silicon Valley five days a week. I never was in the office. If Jim Herbert saw me in the office, he actually wouldn't like it," she said. "He would get very upset. He would knock on my window. He said, 'What are you doing here? Why aren't you out in the street with clients?' I said, 'You're right. I'm on my way to Menlo Park and Palo Alto.'"

By the end of her first year at First Republic, Castro-Franceschi had made inroads into the Silicon Valley investment banking community. "I did all their loans. I drove the documents to their homes. I met their children, their spouses. I literally parked myself in Menlo Park," she said. Then she asked them to help her build her business. "I need to get this bank to become the best private bank in the industry. Will you help me?" she asked. "They would actually call and say, 'I've got two hours for you. I'll set you up in the conference room. Bring your business cards and your rate sheets and you will meet all my colleagues.' That's how it began."[40]

The First Initial Public Offering

With its business growing rapidly in 1986, and the U.S. economy rallying as well, the First Republic leadership team decided to explore taking the company public. Herbert and August-deWilde talked with a number of investment bankers in San Francisco. August-deWilde reconnected with Jim Marver, a longtime friend who was running the San Francisco office of New York investment bank L.F. Rothschild, Unterberg, Towbin, Inc. He was intrigued by the First Republic story and impressed with its leadership team. In fact, he became an early client of First Republic and served with Herbert for years on the Board of the San Francisco Ballet.[41]

Jim Marver, Co-founder of VantagePoint Venture Partners LP, was featured in a 2009 client testimonial. He became a client of First Republic after playing an integral role in its 1986 IPO.

Herbert and August-deWilde's grasp of the complexities of California thrift regulation impressed Marver. "What I saw were two really smart people who were dedicated to customer service, who really understood finance and were really good with people," Marver said. "Thrift and loans were not a type of institution that most of us were accustomed to thinking about or dealing with."

But it was First Republic's business strategy that made it stand out among the typical mortgage-industry players. "I liked what they were doing in terms of focusing on high-end mortgages, which at the time was a true niche," Marver said. "They were going to be so focused on understanding their customer that they were unlikely to have a lot of loan loss. That was going to make them pretty unique."[42]

First Republic moved quickly to capitalize on the favorable market conditions. The leadership team chose L.F. Rothschild as their lead underwriter and made the customary "road show" tour of U.S. financial centers. They also traveled to London to visit The English Trust Company Ltd., which acted as joint underwriter of the offering. In August 1986, First Republic sold 840,000 shares to the public at $10 a share, and the stock began trading on the NASDAQ electronic market under the symbol "FRBC," with an *initial total enterprise value of $23 million* – a considerable increase from the $8.8 million of total initial capital raised just one year prior.[43]

In August 1986, First Republic Bancorp completed its initial public offering and began trading on the NASDAQ market under the symbol "FRBC."

"WHAT ARE THESE THINGS?"

First Republic's initial public offering of stock occurred more than a decade before the dot-com boom of the mid- to late 1990s made IPOs and the young companies they were financing part of popular culture. As a result, even many well-educated employees were unfamiliar with the concept of receiving shares of stock from their employer. "I remember when I first came in and shortly afterwards we went public," said Margaret Mak. "I was very young, and Jim gave all of us, every single employee, stock certificates. And I didn't know what those were. I remember asking his assistant, Jeanne, 'What are these things?' And she said keep them, because she had bought her first home with stock certificates from Jim in his last bank. I had no idea."[44]

WILLIS NEWTON

Willis Newton saw commitment, vision and a sound business model in First Republic Bancorp and quickly agreed to join its leadership team as the Chief Financial Officer in August 1988.

By 1988, Herbert decided that going forward, both August-deWilde and Taubenheim would hold the title of Executive Vice President. August-deWilde also joined the First Republic Board, and the search for her replacement as Chief Financial Officer commenced.

One of the candidates on their short list for the position was Willis Newton, Controller of Homestead Financial Corp., who had received an MBA from Stanford University and served three years in the Army. Recommended by August-deWilde's husband, David deWilde, an expert in executive searches, Newton was brought in for an interview. After answering several questions about his experience, he then had a few questions of his own.

"The question was, 'What are you going to be doing in five years?'" Willis said. "They said, 'Well, we're going to be doing more of the same. We're going to do what we're good at. We're going to stick to it until our clients say they don't want us to do it anymore. Then we'll find out what they do want us to do.'"

That was what he wanted to hear. "I saw right away that there was a business model and a vision and a commitment. All of the values that we articulate in our publications and presentations today were there at the outset. And I said, 'Let's go. Giddy up!'" He joined as Chief Financial Officer, and among many other duties also handled shareholder communications.[48]

Strong Results

First Republic had recorded a slight decline in the dollar volume of mortgages originated in 1987, compared to 1986. The company cited increased competition as the reason for lower initial interest rates on adjustable mortgages, as well as thinner profit margins and reduced initial profitability on new loans. The company assured shareholders that it would adjust to the competitive environment in 1988. True to form, First Republic over-delivered.

First Republic nearly doubled the dollar volume of mortgages from $177 million in 1987 to $344 million in 1988.[49] Since its inception in mid-1985, the company had

STOCK EXCHANGE LISTING

First Republic's stock reached an important milestone on March 1st, 1988, when it began trading under the symbol "FRC" on both the Pacific Stock Exchange in San Francisco and the American Stock Exchange in New York City. The listings raised the company's profile with both California clients and investors, and enabled improved liquidity for shareholders.[50]

The Bank's leaders on the first day of First Republic Bancorp's listing on the Pacific Stock Exchange, under the symbol "FRC."

FIRST REPUBLIC
BANCORP INC.
FRC

The Pacific Stock Exchange (PSE) is pleased to announce the listing of the common shares of First Republic Bancorp Inc.

Headquartered in San Francisco, California, First Republic Bancorp Inc. has assets of $184 million and subordinated debt and shareholders equity of $36 million, as of December 31, 1987.

Operating as a mortage banker, it also provides a range of financial services through its two chartered thrift and loan subsidiaries, First Republic Thrift & Loan, with offices in San Francisco and Los Angeles, and El Camino Thrift & Loan in San Diego County.

First Republic reported net income of $671,000 on gross revenues of $21,123,000 and net interest income of $4,559,000 for the fiscal year ended December 31, 1987.

———————————————

By listing on the Pacific Stock Exchange—consistently a top participant in the Intermarket Trading System and the West Coast's only national exchange—First Republic Bancorp Inc. gains greater liquidity and visibility.

DAVID DEWILDE

David deWilde, a former lawyer, investment banker and financial services executive, was appointed President of the Government National Mortgage Association by President Ford, and also served as Deputy Commissioner of the Federal Housing Authority and Deputy Assistant Secretary of the Department of Housing and Urban Development. He later moved into the executive search field, founding the firm Chartwell Partners in 1989. Prior to his shift into recruiting, he served as Executive Vice President for Policy and Planning of Fannie Mae, which introduced him to Katherine August.

DeWilde first met August in 1982 in an attempt to recruit her as part of the team at Fannie Mae. After several failed attempts over the phone, deWilde thought he might have better luck persuading her in person. "I took her out to dinner and I gave her the best pitch I'd ever given," he recalled. "At the end of the dinner I was expecting a positive answer and I said, 'Are you ready to take the job?' She replied, 'Definitely not.'"

Despite his unsuccessful pitch, August agreed to another interview. "The next interviews turned into dates," said deWilde. "I couldn't hire her, but I was lucky enough to marry her." [51]

originated more than $750 million in loans with no losses incurred to date. On the strength of that performance, gross revenues were up 65 percent year-over-year and net income jumped 43 percent, further strengthening the Bank's capital position through retained earnings. And one of Herbert's favorite metrics for measuring efficiency – assets per employee – had soared from $974,000 in 1985 to $5,197,000 by 1988.[52]

Savings and Loan Crisis

Though First Republic Bancorp was establishing its footing and gaining momentum, and despite the fact it was not a savings and loan institution but rather a thrift holding company, there were signs that the industry as a whole was headed for trouble.

Until 1980, savings and loans were subject to state laws that imposed a maximum mortgage interest rate cap, or ceiling. If interest rates moved upward to very high levels, these entities, unlike commercial banks, were forced to comply with the interest rate cap, rendering their rates below market. At the same time, to remain competitive with the rest of the financial industry and fund their lending activities, they were forced to offer high-yield deposit products such as passbooks and certificates of deposit. As rates rose, the long-term loans with capped interest rates on their books were not able to support the costs of the interest rates they were offering depositors. The result was extreme "maturity mismatching," and an inability to manage interest rate risk, which came to a head in the mid-1980s.

Further complicating matters, restrictions on out-of-state expansion and operations, like Herbert had overcome with San Francisco Bancorp, meant savings and loans were prevented from geographically diversifying their credit risks. As a result, they were extremely vulnerable to regional economic downturns that compromised their real estate collateral. One by one, savings and loans in California and other parts of the country succumbed to this unsustainable "borrow short, lend long" model. The industry fell into a full tailspin in 1989, when the Federal Savings and Loan Insurance Corporation (FSLIC), the FDIC's sibling agency that insured saving and loan deposits, folded due to insolvency.[53]

By the end of 1988, First Republic Bancorp had originated more than $750 million in mortgages and had not incurred a single loss.

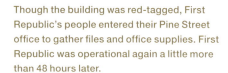

Though the building was red-tagged, First Republic's people entered their Pine Street office to gather files and office supplies. First Republic was operational again a little more than 48 hours later.

"I'll never forget when we were going back into the building to move things out. It was totally voluntary. I said to everybody, 'This is voluntary activity. We're not supposed to be in this building. It's been red-tagged. If there's a major aftershock, I don't know what's going to happen.' Everybody showed up and everybody moved their stuff out. There was just no question about it."[65]

For help, Herbert reached out to Doug Shorenstein, a fellow member of Young Presidents' Organization, a professional development group comprised of young Chief Executives. Shorenstein, a real estate developer, rented to First Republic on a month-to-month basis some excess office space at 425 Market as a temporary corporate headquarters. As for the banking office, Herbert found a desirable space at 101 Pine Street, only one block from the original location.

Tresenfeld, Castro-Franceschi, Mak and other producers spent the weeks immediately following the earthquake contacting all of First Republic's clients in the area to see how they were faring. They compiled a report on the condition of all the properties for which First Republic had provided mortgages. This included both those mortgages First

Republic kept on its books and those it sold to investors in the secondary market. Several investors and insurers would later tell management that it was the most comprehensive reporting on the earthquake they had seen from any financial institution.

First Republic's response to the earthquake had a lasting impact on clients across the region. Relationship banking was not just a marketing phrase at First Republic. "For the next couple of weeks, all we did was call clients. We said, 'Are you all right? Any loss? Are you okay? What can we do for you? We are here for you,'" recalled Castro-Franceschi.

The catastrophic event would move the team, as well. "We came together. I have never seen anything like that," Castro-Franceschi said. "We were reporting to Jim Herbert, who wanted to know about every single client. I was so impressed with management. They never left us. They were there with us every step of the way." [66]

"JUST SIGN THE LEASE"

Herbert went to negotiate lease terms at Wells Fargo, which owned the space at the corner of Front and Pine Streets that First Republic wanted to lease for its new flagship office. Tom Deuel, who had worked closely with Herbert during his Pop Shoppe days and joined him at San Francisco Bancorp and then First Republic, had been in charge of finding mobile phones for the leadership team – not an easy task, as the relatively newly invented devices were rare. Working with Newton, he was also tasked with packing the office and its mainframe computer, making sure everything made it onto their chartered moving truck, and then assembling furniture and equipment for the new office.

This semi-trailer was parked outside as Herbert did his best to negotiate terms with the Wells Fargo banker. The young banker, after noting that inhabitable San Francisco real estate was in short supply, said, "Mr. Herbert, it has come to our attention that the entire contents of your bank is sitting outside of our branch on the back of a truck. I think you ought to just sign the lease." Herbert, unable to refute this particular point, ended negotiations and signed. [67]

YOUNG PRESIDENTS' ORGANIZATION

Young Presidents' Organization (YPO) was founded in 1950 with the mission: "Better leaders through education and idea exchange." When Herbert joined in 1985, members had to be under the age of 45 and the head of a company that fulfilled minimum size requirements. World Presidents' Organization (WPO) now serves this same group as they become more experienced and cross the age of 50.

Among many other programs offered each year, members have the opportunity to participate in the Harvard Presidents' Program, a weeklong immersion seminar providing the opportunity to learn from the best of Harvard Business School's professors and from one another. A popular draw, it is the Business School's oldest outside program and well over-subscribed.[68]

Herbert, an active member of YPO, having served as former Chairman of the Golden Gate chapter, and also CEO/WPO, has been an avid participant in the Harvard Presidents' Program, attending over 20 of the weeklong sessions. Herbert brought this continuing executive education concept into First Republic, initiating in 2013 a broad program with the same goals, which would send over 65 First Republic senior management representatives to executive programs at Harvard Business School, Stanford Graduate School of Business, the Tuck School of Business at Dartmouth College and the Wharton School of the University of Pennsylvania.

Firm Footing

In its first four years, First Republic grew rapidly and withstood repeated and significant tests of its strategy, adaptability and leadership. It navigated the troublesome acquisition of El Camino Thrift & Loan, adopted a compensation strategy counter to the industry norm in order to protect its clients and investors, secured FDIC insurance for its depositors, and continued to grow and innovate through the savings and loan crisis. And it emerged from the damage of the 1989 San Francisco earthquake with a one-time loss of less than a half-million dollars, mostly from lost leasehold improvements, and damage-related loan write-downs estimated at less than $150,000.[69]

Despite the challenges, each episode was also an opportunity for the company to demonstrate its commitment to safe lending, along with its flexibility and nimbleness in responding to change and taking swift action. This time period further evidenced the powerful commitment to the client throughout the enterprise. These shared experiences in the early days of First Republic Bancorp shaped, solidified and still inform First Republic's culture today. As Herbert says:

> "Our job is to make it a good place to work – a safe, fair place to work – and to take care, very good care of our clients. If we do our job in making it a good place to work and get the right people, the clients will be taken care of well. When banks wake up in the morning and think that the corporate entity with the name on the door is the bank, they are dead. There isn't a bank here. There is a collection of individual relationships that's predicated on all of the people in the bank taking care of clients one at a time, every day."[70]

First Republic's first four years were a story of both success and survival. Not sitting still for long, the team looked forward to the future as First Republic Bancorp moved into the next decade. ❖

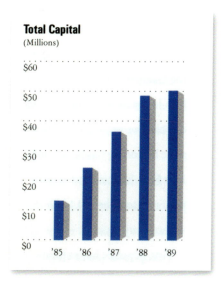

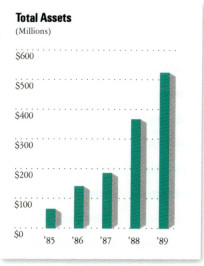

Despite the challenges of the late 1980s, First Republic, against substantial odds, was prepared to enter the next decade on a continued path of growth.
First Republic Bancorp 1989 Annual Report

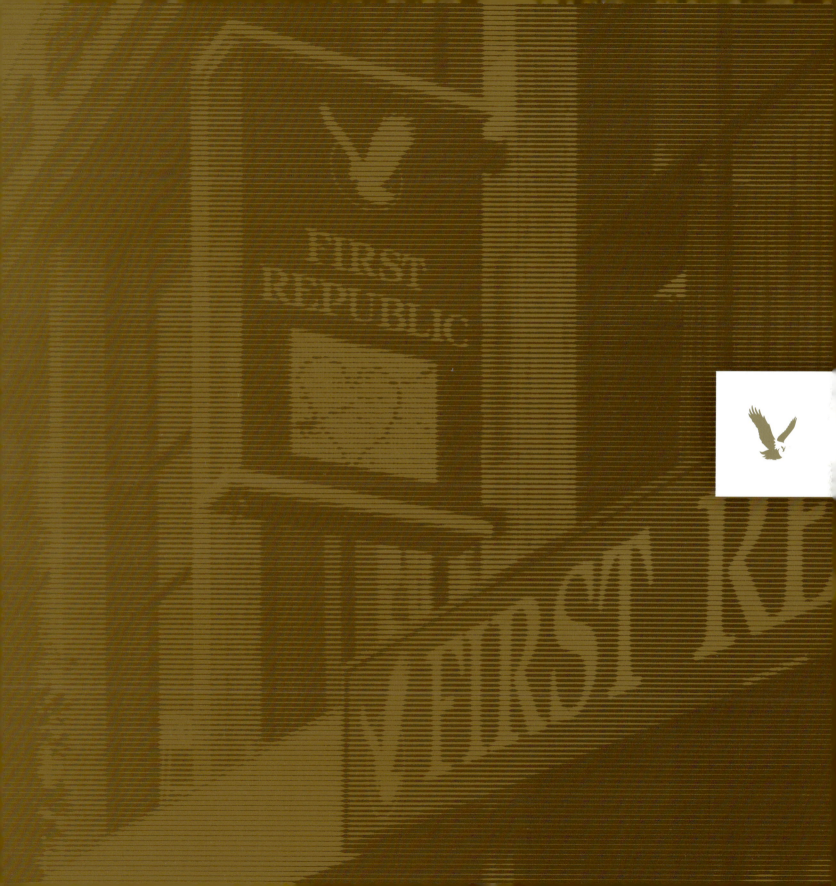

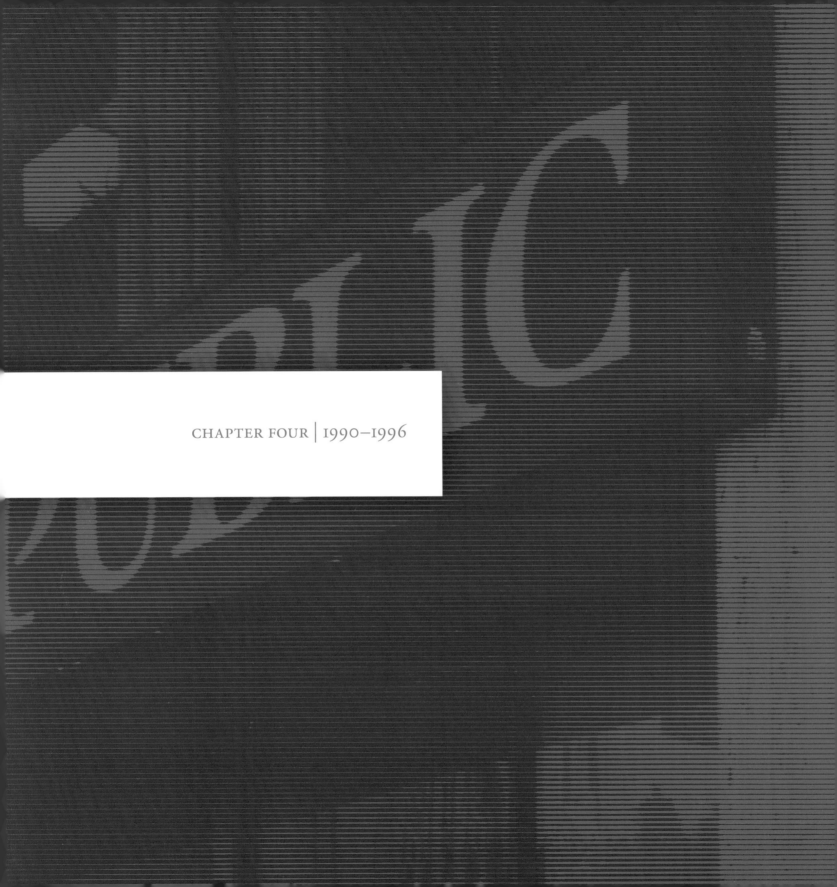

CHAPTER FOUR | 1990–1996

IT'S A PRIVILEGE TO

Serve You

FIRST REPUBLIC

1990

The San Francisco earthquake of 1989 was a harbinger of the multiple shocks California would suffer during the first half of the 1990s. A bursting real estate bubble triggered a severe recession across the state, with 600,000 jobs lost between mid-1990 and the end of 1993. Social unrest, fires, drought and another major earthquake followed. Commentators speculated that this could be the end of the California Dream that for a century and a half had attracted those seeking new opportunities and wealth.[1]

Many rivals pulled back in the face of such challenges, but First Republic Bancorp forged ahead. The organization took market share from banks and thrifts retreating from the jumbo mortgage market, while its strict credit standards and controls minimized losses. This early 1990s recession, coupled with the 1994 Northridge earthquake in Southern California, was an important influence as First Republic refined its strict credit standards and strategy, which remain distinguishing traits today. At the same time, First Republic, with a continued eye on growth opportunities and commitment to maintaining a strong capital position, repeatedly raised additional capital.

Despite this macroeconomic turmoil, First Republic Bancorp remained focused on the needs of its clients. As a thrift holding company, however, it was only able to provide limited products and services. On the liability side of the balance sheet, these included passbook savings and money market accounts but did not include the basic checking account. Amid growing demand for additional products and services, Jim Herbert decided that the company might better serve clients by operating as a bank rather than as a thrift holding company. And to reinforce the importance of keeping the client at the center of all its activities, First Republic adopted the motto that continues to underscore the Bank's commitment to clients today: "It's a privilege to serve you."

***

First Republic Bancorp's offices at
388 Market Street in San Francisco.

NYSE LISTING

California may have remained mired in recession, but First Republic's corporate profile rose a notch among investors and on Wall Street when its stock was listed on the New York Stock Exchange (NYSE) as "FRC" on July 28th, 1992. The company described the Big Board's imprimatur as "a significant step which recognizes First Republic's development, while enhancing stockholders' liquidity and improving access to the capital markets."[21]

Roger Walther and Jim Herbert, top, celebrated First Republic's listing on the New York Stock Exchange. Below, Dona Gibbs, Marty Gibbs and Jim Joy joined Herbert on the trading floor.

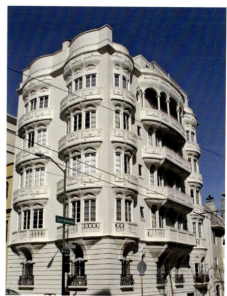

Apartment Building Loans

First Republic saw an opportunity to gain market share among buyers of small to medium-sized apartment buildings in the late 1980s and early 1990s. The highly competitive apartment building market required buyers to get fast responses from their mortgage lenders. And they had to be able to rely on their banker's word as they moved quickly to close on prime properties. Many big banks were too bureaucratic to respond promptly to the needs of what, for them, was a relatively small market.

Russ Flynn, an investor in San Francisco multi-family buildings, started working with San Francisco Bancorp in the early 1980s. By the early 1990s, First Republic was his go-to bank. "In my business, usually, I was not big enough to be with a Wells Fargo or a Bank of America or any of the major banks; they just forget you," Flynn said. "First Republic had the ability to take the medium-sized client, or even the smaller client, and make them feel like they were with the best bank in the city."

"The key in our business is if someone says, 'Okay, we can make that loan,' that you could rely on it," Flynn added. "At the larger banks, you can't do that because nobody really has the authority to say that. Somehow, First Republic figured out how to give their people authority, and then they backed them up." Within a few years of working with First Republic to finance his business, Flynn moved his personal banking to First Republic.[22]

In a competitive market, First Republic Bancorp developed a reputation for quick turnaround times, key for buyers of small to medium-sized apartment buildings.

Entrepreneur and First Republic client Russ Flynn began working first with San Francisco Bancorp in the early 1980s, and later First Republic Bancorp, as he invested in multi-family properties in the San Francisco area.

"It Helped Us Be a Part of Our Community"

First Republic persisted in its commitment to serve all members of the communities in which it was based. By the end of 1990, the company made more than $120 million in housing loans for properties defined as low income under the Financial Institutions Reform, Recovery, and Enforcement Act of 1989. The loans, made without government assistance, provided housing for thousands of lower-income families. More would follow.[23]

"We did have a little bit of a barbell business in that we did low- and moderate-income housing as well as jumbo mortgages," Chief Financial Officer Willis Newton said. "It helped us be a part of our community and to meet the needs that the community had."[24]

This commitment to the community positioned First Republic to take a leadership role among lenders in response to the 1992 Los Angeles riots. In April, a jury acquitted four police officers in connection with the beating of Rodney King. The assault, which was caught on video and broadcast around the world, inflamed racial tensions in the Los Angeles area. 53 people died and the city was convulsed by days of rioting, especially in the moderate- to lower-income neighborhoods of South Central Los Angeles.[25]

The rioting destroyed scores of lower-income housing units in predominately minority neighborhoods. Many businesses left the area, and some lenders were slow to respond to the need for funds to rebuild.[26] First Republic stepped in, working closely with government agencies to fill the void and help finance the recovery. It was the first and largest user of Federal Home Loan Bank Community Rebuilding Funds to reconstruct portions of South Central Los Angeles that had been hard hit by the riots.[27]

First Republic Bancorp provided construction loans for renovation of the historic Flood Building, a San Francisco landmark built in 1904.

Community Preservation and Revitalization

By the end of 1993, 63 percent of all residential units in buildings financed by First Republic Bancorp were in low- to moderate-income neighborhoods. The company worked closely with apartment owners to tailor loans to meet their needs and those of their communities.[28]

First Republic helped rebuild the urban communities in which it operated in other ways as well. The company supported seismic upgrades to several schools and helped preserve the character of these neighborhoods by financing conversions of industrial spaces into residential lofts and other uses. In 1993, it provided a construction loan to renovate the historic Flood Building on Market Street in downtown San Francisco. With First Republic's help, the landmark building was given a new lease on life and successfully converted into retail shops and office space.[29]

BRANCHING OUT

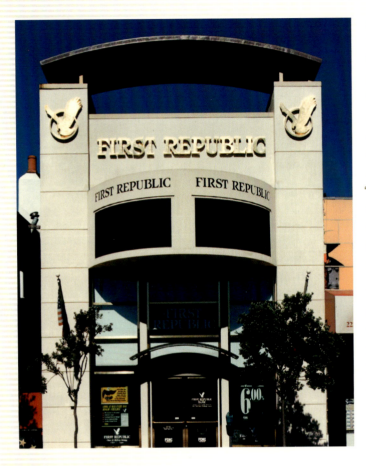

In 1993, First Republic Bancorp's first neighborhood deposit location opened on Geary Boulevard in San Francisco.

In addition to providing funds to clients and community members to improve their homes and workspaces, First Republic expanded its own office space. It moved its headquarters to 388 Market Street, a building owned by the Ho family from Hong Kong, in 1990. Initially, the Hos were concerned that all U.S. banks were going bankrupt, and therefore they were not sure First Republic was the ideal tenant. They agreed to lease the space but certainly were not going to invest in any tenant improvements. "Fine, we'll make our own improvements, in exchange for free rent," Herbert suggested. They settled on a 50-month rent-free period, and First Republic remains in this space currently, occupying multiple floors in the building.

In September 1993, it opened its first neighborhood deposit office on San Francisco's Geary Boulevard, and in January 1994, it opened another deposit office nearby in Chinatown.[30] Two more followed in 1995; one in San Francisco at 19th Avenue and Irving Street and one in San Rafael in Marin County.[31]

First Republic Bancorp opened its San Francisco office at 19th and Irving in 1995.

In early 1994, First Republic acquired Silver State Thrift and Loan, a very small Reno, Nevada company and converted it to First Republic Savings Bank.[32] First Republic Savings Bank was then moved to Las Vegas, giving First Republic a full deposit-taking presence in the area. In 1994, the company also introduced Saturday hours and began offering money market accounts on which clients could write checks.[33]

Welcoming Clients with Feng Shui Flow

Anna Hirano, Senior Vice President and Director of Deposits, joined First Republic in 1993.

Anna Hirano, Senior Vice President and Director of Deposits, joined First Republic in 1993 as the first Manager of its first neighborhood deposit office on Geary Boulevard, following 10 years in retail banking at Wells Fargo Bank. The basic layout of the retail space already had been determined by the time she arrived. Building upon the welcoming aspects of the Bank's original office, there would be bankers at desks with comfortable chairs for clients, instead of tellers behind windows, and carpeted floors throughout, giving the space a warm, living-room feel. What remained to be determined were other key details of the office's interior design, however.[34]

San Francisco Regional Savings Manager Margaret Mak, who is now Executive Director of Preferred Banking, worked closely with Hirano to outfit the branch. She advocated adapting the layout and look of the office – and the one soon to be opened nearby in Chinatown – in accordance with the ancient Chinese concept of feng shui. Feng shui focuses on the five elements of wood, fire, earth, metal and water, and the way in which they are thought to interact in productive and destructive cycles. Applied to interior design, it addresses the harmonious flow and balance of positive and negative energy through placement of furniture, as well as the use of natural light, plants and water features.[35] Herbert embraced the concept and said he wanted the Geary Street and corporate offices, along with all future offices, to incorporate feng shui elements. "My approach to it was, number one, I like the design ideas; number two, why not? What's the downside?" Herbert said.[36]

Feng shui consultant Pun Yin advised the Bank on the treatment of these, and other forthcoming offices. Mak helped choose phone numbers, which included the number 8 or numbers that added up to 8, which signifies success according to feng shui precepts. In the Geary office, the windows were framed in red, a positive color, and an octagonal-shaped clock was placed at the end of the entrance hall to help foster the positive flow of energy.[37]

玄機風水

GEOMANCY FENG SHUI CONSULTANT
12 CALLE AMIGO DR., FREMONT, CA 94539
510/818-0388   FAX: 510/818-0188

2001-3-21

FIRST REPUBLIC BANK 101, PINE ST. S.F. CA

ANNA HUI HIRANO

12-14- ▆ MASTER'S LIFE DIVINE:

- 12 ANIMALS OF CHINESE ZODIAC — 牛 OX
- EIGHT TRIGRAMS — THUNDER ☳ 震卦
- FIVE ELEMENTS — WOOD — 木
- LUCKY POSITION — ES • E • N
- AVOID POSITION — W • NW
- FORTUNAT COLOR — GREEN • BLACK
- AVOID COLOR — WHITE • SILVER
- LUCKY NUMBER — 3 • 4 • 1
- UNLUCKY NUMBER — 6 • 7

* 2009-1-28 → 2010-2-25

IN DAILY LIFE AND AT WORK IN
ORDER TO ACQUIRE GOOD HEALTH
AND FORTUNE, YOU MUST HAVE YOUR
BACK AGAINST THE NORTH WHILE
FACING SOUTH, REMEMBER THIS RULE.

A feng shui expert helped guide the design of First Republic Bank's 101 Pine Street Preferred Banking Office.

First Republic Bank offices have a variety of water features, including fish tanks and fountains. Water is an ancient symbol of wealth and prosperity, according to feng shui precepts.

Client comfort comes first. Wheeled chairs and carpeted floors help create a relaxed, welcoming feel.

TUESDAY ALCO MEETING

Similar to the Loan Meeting, held weekly and attended by all lending and lending support professionals, First Republic also holds weekly ALCO – or Asset/Liability Committee Officers – Meetings. It began with a smaller group initially, with the objective of sharing information on the different markets in order to inform deposit pricing decisions. The meeting evolved as the Bank grew, and now includes all deposit-gathering teams and Preferred Banking Office professionals across the company, along with management and department heads.

"In my experience, these meetings don't exist in other institutions. For me, when I joined, this was a 'wow' factor," recalled Anna Hirano, Senior Vice President and Director of Deposits. "To know that my suggestions and input could impact the Bank's actions was powerful. It cements the entrepreneurial mindset. My office, and the business we generate and ideas we have, are really a part of the success."

Though the Tuesday ALCO Meeting still holds the same objective of sharing information on the different markets, it also serves the very important mission of keeping the team connected to a collective and shared success. "When you are in an office 20 or 2,000 miles away," Hirano said, "and you can connect and make an impactful contribution, it is empowering."[38]

"When you first entered the front door, you saw the end of the hall, which was a 'dead' wall," Hirano said. "We put a clock there just to make sure the energy flowed in nicely."[39]

Feng shui concepts were applied to the designs of other offices according to their specific locations and layouts. When the Bank added an office on Park Avenue in New York later in 1999, it included its first lobby fountain as a feng shui element, which was designed by Herbert's younger daughter, Deirdre. Its purpose was to repel the harmful spirits that might be fleeing the historic St. Bartholomew's Episcopal Church on the opposite side of the street. A variety of water elements were later added to all Bank offices to enhance the flow of positive energy. [40]

Herbert felt the client experience in the office was a natural extension of providing extraordinary service. First Republic's offices continue to evolve in order to enhance the client experience. More recently, wheels were added to chairs to make it easier for clients of all ages to engage comfortably and efficiently with their bankers. For that same reason, reading glasses are available as well, along with doors that automatically open. The unique office atmosphere, whether at the corporate headquarters in San Francisco or any one of First Republic's Preferred Banking Office retail spaces, is centered on maximizing the client experience and is a reflection of the focus on detail, quality and service.[41]

Northridge Earthquake

In the predawn hours of January 17th, 1994, the Los Angeles area was rocked by an earthquake whose epicenter was near Northridge, CA, in the San Fernando Valley. The largest quake to hit Los Angeles in the 20th century caused more than two dozen deaths as buildings and freeways collapsed. On the heels of widespread brushfires followed by mudslides as rain soaked the denuded hills, the earthquake was widely viewed as the latest in a string of deadly blows to southern California. "Riots, wildfires, mudslides, now a deadly earthquake. How much bad luck can Los Angeles – and its battered economy – stand?" *The Wall Street Journal* asked.[42]

Herbert, August-deWilde and others scrambled the morning of the earthquake to make sure that First Republic's staff was unharmed. Communication was complicated by the fact that the quake had knocked out phone service to portions of Los Angeles. Mary Deckebach, who joined the Beverly Hills location in 1991 and now serves as Regional Managing Director for the area, discovered this when she tried to call August-deWilde before dawn on the 17th. She ended up using her home fax line to communicate with Bank officials in San Francisco that first morning.[43] Fortunately, First Republic team members in the area escaped serious injury.

A 6.8-magnitude earthquake rocked Los Angeles in the early morning of January 17th, 1994, damaging more than 110,000 residential and commercial buildings.

Brick Buildings

Even before Herbert and August-deWilde received firsthand reports on the damage in Los Angeles, they feared that the situation was not good. First Republic had been an active lender to many owners of older brick apartment buildings in the Los Angeles area, usually with no more than 30 to 40 units per building. Most of the loans had been made to fund seismic upgrades so these structures would conform to recent earthquake-related building codes.

The leadership team of First Republic Bancorp took swift action. Herbert gathered a team in Los Angeles and took charge of assessing First Republic's exposure to the disaster. August-deWilde stayed in San Francisco and spent most of her time directing the rest of the company's operations. Neither would have much down time for the next several months.[44]

"Good Bank, Bad Bank"

"We decided to do what we called a 'good bank, bad bank,'" Herbert said. "We had to isolate the problem in order to not damage the rest of the enterprise."[45] Herbert and his team grouped together the nonperforming loans into the theoretical "bad bank" and quarantined them from the other business lines that had not been affected by the earthquake. They quickly found that all of the potential losses were on loans secured by low- to moderate-income apartment buildings in Los Angeles County. Of those, about 70 percent involved masonry buildings that had already been seismically reinforced.[46] Fortunately, like First Republic team members in the area, these tenants escaped major injury. Unfortunately, however, the bad bank had more clients than they had originally anticipated.

The vast majority of the brick buildings securing First Republic's loans did not have significant damage. They were habitable, and the owners were anxious to get tenants back into the units. However, a key element of the federal earthquake relief response was the provision for up to six months of free rent to tenants who could

claim damage to their units. "So people took the free housing voucher and moved into a new apartment building, despite minimal damage in many cases," Herbert said. "That policy emptied about half of these brick buildings." These owners, their own financial foundations already undermined by four years of recession, turned the buildings over to First Republic.

Many other lenders in Los Angeles walked away from such properties. Not First Republic. "Our approach was that the building wasn't bad. It was the lack of financial strength of the borrower that got us into trouble," Herbert said. Unlike virtually every other lender, First Republic decided to finance new buyers of the buildings it had foreclosed on. "We were glad to help," Herbert said. "It worked out quite well, actually. We came out better than most, because with financing you can get a better price for the building from the new buyer." [47]

After the Northridge earthquake, First Republic Bancorp's offices in Los Angeles worked with a team that included Jim Herbert to understand the thrift and loan's losses.

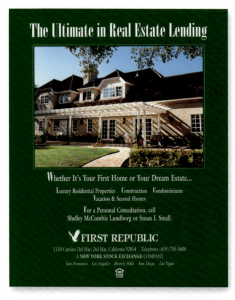

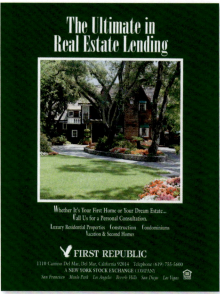

After the 1994 Northridge earthquake, First Republic Bancorp focused on single-family homes in all of its markets, not just in Los Angeles.

First Republic had set aside $7.8 million in reserves in 1994, and set aside more in 1995, to cover potential earthquake-related losses. Like most lenders, First Republic most likely over-reserved initially, relative to the problem loans on its books, Herbert said. Indeed, the company would eventually recover roughly 80 percent of the funds set aside in reserve.[48]

The lingering effects of the earthquake, and a sharp spike in interest rates that began in 1994 as the national economy bounced back, made 1995 a challenging year for First Republic. For the first and only time in its history, First Republic had a quarter in which it lost money – $3.1 million in the second quarter of 1995. But the company reported a profit for the full year of 1995, thus maintaining the leadership team's uninterrupted record of annual profitability, beginning with San Francisco Bancorp in 1980 and continuing with First Republic to this day.[49]

Lessons Learned

Applying the lessons learned from the Northridge earthquake, First Republic refused to lend against brick buildings in excess of the value of the land on which the building stood. In effect, that meant no longer allowing brick buildings as collateral. "As a bank headquartered in California with a lot of California real estate, we felt very strongly that we didn't want to take the risk on brick above land value," August-deWilde said.[50]

Another takeaway from the Northridge experience, according to General Counsel Ed Dobranski, was that "we needed a more robust credit administration function and a loan review program." Typical of an organization operating in an entrepreneurial mode, "we all wore a lot of different hats," Dobranski said. "We had people that had dual, maybe triple, types of functions. They would do some auditing or loan review and then something completely unrelated." The leadership team moved to carve out distinct credit administration and loan review roles and responsibilities in the wake of the Northridge earthquake.[51]

First Republic Bancorp moved forward, with a renewed focus on the single-family market, not just in Los Angeles but in all markets. With multi-family home markets in disarray across the region, single-family homes accounted for more than 85 percent of the Bank's loan growth in 1995, and more than 60 percent of its total loan portfolio by year-end.[52] Amid that growth, however, the company's commitment to low- and moderate-income multi-family housing in the communities it served continued.

A Turning Point

Herbert was in need of a sabbatical following the year-long, intensive, high-stakes effort to clean up the Los Angeles area portfolio in the wake of the earthquake. In the spring of 1995, he decided to take a few months off to recharge his batteries. While August-deWilde and the rest of the management team ran First Republic in Herbert's absence, he carefully considered what course adjustments should be made to First Republic's future strategic direction. This break led to one of the most important decisions and key inflection points in the history of the enterprise.

Full-Service Relationship Banking

Major banks in California and nationwide were consolidating at an accelerating clip as proposed changes to interstate banking restrictions appeared to inch closer to reality.[53] The merger of institutions, usually smaller into much larger enterprises, often resulted in a deterioration of service and subsequent client dissatisfaction. This flood of dissatisfied clients inspired a pivotal moment in First Republic's history. Herbert could not help noticing that existing clients were also disenchanted with their outside banking relationships; they craved a financial institution with better client service. *They wanted to do more with First Republic.* But as a thrift holding company, First Republic Bancorp did not offer the full range of products needed – including checking accounts, business banking and wealth management.

"The consolidation of banks really opened up our window of opportunity to take what we had, a lending client base, that very much liked us and had been asking to

"Giving helpful service and advice in an unhurried manner is as much a part of our job as providing competitive rates. Knowing our customers by name is a point of pride for us," said Susan Hart, Branch Manager, San Rafael.

A DEVELOPING PARTNERSHIP

In 1991, after five years of leadership, Gordon Taubenheim left First Republic to pursue other activities in the industry and Katherine August-deWilde stepped up to take on additional responsibilities. In 1996, Herbert named her Chief Operating Officer of First Republic Bancorp. The new title recognized the role she had grown into, particularly with her oversight of general operations, while Herbert tended to the recent challenges caused by the Northridge earthquake.

Having spent 10 years by the mid-1990s working together, Herbert and August-deWilde had developed a partnership that strengthened the enterprise through a "divide and conquer," team-based management approach. First seen in 1986, when Herbert tended to the acquisition of El Camino Thrift & Loan – actually moving to Southern California for a period of time – and August-deWilde minded the day-to-day operations in San Francisco, the duo's ability to manage as a united front had further matured. Again, when needed in 1995, Herbert was free to address the challenges brought by Northridge while August-deWilde continued to keep a steady state with the daily operations.

The duo's complementary talents and lockstep leadership during this period of turmoil within California and the banking industry in the early 1990s enabled stability within First Republic Bancorp and enhanced confidence in the enterprise with its professionals, clients and shareholders. Unbeknownst to them at the time, it also prepared them for what might be considered their greatest challenge yet to come, as they would tackle a management-led buyback in another 15 years, at which point the full leadership team would be considered one of the key value drivers at First Republic.

do more with us, and transform," recalled Scott Dufresne, who joined First Republic from The Boston Company in 1993, as a Relationship Manager in Los Angeles, and later moved to lead the Bank to Boston in the mid-2000s.[54]

"It became obvious to me that we had missed a turn," Herbert said. "And so I woke up and said, 'This is crazy. We have the wrong charter! We need to be doing full-service banking for our clients. They love us. They have a lot more to do, and we need to be able to serve them.'"[55] Though he knew this shift would require significant investment and time, the opportunity was too great to ignore. Herbert reached out to First Republic's Board of Directors to explore feasibility and next steps.

Nevada Bank Charter – Revisiting the Law

Where were they going to find a full-service banking charter? Converting its industrial thrift charter in California into a bank charter was not realistic; it would be too expensive and time-consuming. There had to be a better solution.

First Republic turned its attention to Nevada. Herbert had used a presence in Nevada to convert San Francisco Bancorp into a multi-state organization in the early 1980s. In 1996, his team set about leveraging First Republic's activities in Nevada to drive change. It would turn out to be a very good bet.

First Republic retained the Las Vegas law firm of Lionel, Sawyer and Collins, and its financial services team led by partner Dan Reaser, to help make its case. First Republic's goal was to convert the former Silver State Thrift it had purchased in Nevada into a state-chartered bank. Herbert worked on drafting the proposal and then lobbied the Nevada Bankers Association to support the proposed legislation, which would put state banks more on a par with national banks in terms of product offerings. The Bankers Association threw its weight behind the idea, saying it would even the playing field.[56] First Republic sponsored the effort by covering most associated costs, and Herbert testified before the Nevada Senate Banking Committee upon introduction. In July 1997, this banking reform bill passed and was enacted into law.[57]

First Republic had executed a reverse merger of its much larger California holding company into the Nevada bank in 1996. Once the new law took effect, the entire company could then operate under a Nevada state bank, rather than an industrial thrift, charter. The only thing that would change for First Republic's clients: a noticeable increase in the number and variety of banking products and services offered – indeed, as broad an offering as a national bank could provide – over time.

"Why Do We Have to Have a Holding Company?"

Ed Dobranski, General Counsel, had not only worked at Wells Fargo, he had also worked with a federal banking agency. When Herbert asked Dobranski to lead the group working to amend Nevada banking law and convert the entire company into a Nevada bank, he raised what for him was an obvious issue. "Well, okay, we're going to have to go to the Federal Reserve and have a holding company," Dobranski said.

Herbert, always trying to keep the company as focused and streamlined as possible in regard to its core businesses and clients, asked, "Why do we have to have a holding company?" A nonplussed Dobranski sputtered, "Well, everybody has a holding company." For every case Dobranski made in support of a holding company, such as the ability to efficiently raise capital, Herbert responded by pointing out that a bank could manage it just as well as, or even better than, a holding company.

Dobranski began to realize that maybe First Republic did not need one. He tested Herbert's logic with outside counsel to make sure he was not missing something. The outside lawyers could not make a convincing case for a holding company, either. So be it, he concluded. No holding company. "That was just Jim thinking outside the box and pushing everybody, saying, 'Okay, if we need to have it, fine, but convince me,'" Dobranski said.[58]

Evolution into a Full-Service Private Bank

By the end of 1996, the First Republic bank conversion team, led by Herbert, Dobranski and Jim Baumberger, President of the First Republic Las Vegas office, felt confident the plan would succeed. They had spent months working with the Nevada Bankers Association and state banking regulators to ensure that they had fully explained their goals and how their proposed legislation would bring more business to the state and increase banking options for Nevada consumers. And First Republic's thrift and loan subsidiaries had already been merged into its single Nevada banking subsidiary, First Republic Savings Bank.

First Republic Bancorp had introduced money market checking accounts in 1994 and granted worldwide ATM access. On the lending side, First Republic had recently rolled out home construction loans and loans collateralized with securities. A full array of banking products and services, including the essential checking account, was being readied in the wings, to launch following passage of the bill and completion of the charter conversion.[59]

JIM BAUMBERGER

Jim Baumberger's critical role in helping the Bank obtain its Nevada commercial bank charter in 1997 capped nearly 14 years of leadership in the Las Vegas banking market, most in partnership with Herbert. Herbert recruited Baumberger in 1983 to lead the Nevada First United Thrift & Loan subsidiary of San Francisco Bancorp when the unit had little more than $5 million in assets. When San Francisco Bancorp was sold to Atlantic Financial Savings Bank in 1984, Baumberger stayed with Atlantic Financial and helped build its presence in the Nevada market.[60]

In May 1990, Baumberger rejoined Herbert, at First Republic Mortgage, a new subsidiary of First Republic Thrift & Loan in Nevada. Following the purchase of Silver State Thrift in early 1994 and the move to Las Vegas, Baumberger became President of the division. By the mid-1990s, he and his team were able to offer a broader range of deposit-taking options and originate mortgage loans, as the subsidiaries merged to become First Republic Savings Bank.[61]

Baumberger also influenced the development of First Republic's credit culture. Only a few months after Baumberger joined First Republic Mortgage in 1990, a young David

Lichtman moved to Las Vegas to learn under Baumberger's tutelage. Spending close to two years there, Lichtman worked with Baumberger in evaluating and financing small apartment, commercial real estate and construction projects.

"We went out to 'kick the tires' on the projects," recalled Lichtman. "Not to just look at the finances of the deal, but to also get to know the borrower and see the project in person." Lessons learned during this time would carry through, as Lichtman's career progressed at First Republic and eventually led him to take on the role of Chief Credit Officer.[62]

Las Vegas has a reputation for attracting high rollers, but a substantial portion of the business Baumberger and his team developed in the early 1990s was for first-time home buyers and those of more modest means. In fact, First Republic financed the construction of over 13,000 housing units in the area, the majority of which were starter homes or low- to moderate-income multi-family properties. Baumberger's part in growing the business in Las Vegas turned out to be key in the conversion of First Republic to a full-service private banking institution.[63]

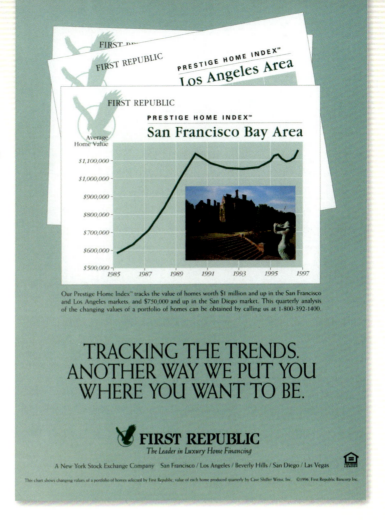

First Republic produced its Prestige Home Index from 1995 to 2014.

FIRST REPUBLIC PRESTIGE HOME INDEX

The enhanced focus on single-family homes in 1995 led Herbert to come up with a branding concept that helped define the high-end home market in California for almost 20 years. His goal was to communicate and share First Republic's expertise in the state's luxury home market. Why not create a First Republic-branded index covering this sector? "I have a lot of ideas, and some of them are good and some are terrible," Herbert said. "If they're any good, Katherine and others tend to execute."

August-deWilde thought the branded index was a great idea. She researched the subject and found Case-Shiller Weiss, Inc., a recognized corporate expert and early leader in the real estate index field. The company initially selected properties in the San Francisco and Los Angeles markets

worth at least $1 million, and in the San Diego area worth at least $750,000, for inclusion in the index.[64] A First Republic Relationship Manager visited each property to ensure it met company standards for quality and was properly representative of the area.

Updated quarterly, the First Republic Prestige Home Index became the first statistical model of its kind, customized to measure changes in home values in the luxury market. Drawing upon Case-Shiller

Weiss's economic database and years of experience in tracking single-family home values, combined with First Republic's extensive local market knowledge, the First Republic Prestige Home Index came to be viewed as a very reliable barometer of the changing values of high-end homes across the state. "It took a while to catch on," Herbert said, "but once it did, we discovered it had a deeper following than we initially thought it would."[65]

CLIENT TESTIMONIALS

As the 1990s progressed, First Republic increasingly incorporated Herbert's idea of client portraits and testimonials in its annual reports, in which these clients voluntarily and happily attested to the Bank's exceptional service. The reports also highlighted examples of First Republic's community engagement and philanthropic activities, such as its First Republic Scholars program. It featured builders of low- and moderate-income housing and community-oriented projects as well, including the redevelopment of San Francisco's Presidio military base, for which First Republic served as the first lender on the initiative.

In 1994, Herbert was looking for a new creative firm to produce the Bank's annual report. A few years prior, he had met Jill Howry, Creative Director for Howry Design, during a photo shoot for the American Institute of Foreign Studies (AIFS). Roger Walther, Co-Founder of AIFS, was serving as its Chairman of the Board of Directors at the time. Herbert was impressed with Howry's ideas and attention to detail, and he hired the firm to produce the Bank's annual report. This began a creative collaboration spanning over two decades.

Today, while the design has both remained consistent with the First Republic brand while evolving over time, the focus on the client experience still remains paramount. Inclusion in the First Republic annual report has grown into a coveted opportunity, with clients increasingly and eagerly volunteering each year. "We get literally hundreds of people saying 'I would love to be in your annual report. I'd love to give you a testimonial,'" notes Dianne Snedaker, Chief Marketing Officer. Year after year, the reports reflect the diversity of First Republic's clients and products and uniquely demonstrate how the Bank

has grown and evolved while remaining committed to providing extraordinary service. The client testimonials permeate the overall branding strategy, now appearing in a variety of manners and materials, as a cornerstone of First Republic's marketing efforts.[66]

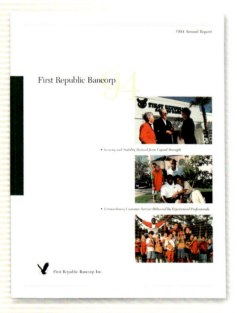

"They feel more like a friend than a business. As our lives become more complicated, they consistently find new ways to help."

Brigette Lau and Chamath Palihapitiya, Peninsula/Silicon Valley

"First Republic understands how a law firm operates. They have an instinctive sense of what we need and how fast we need it."

Vincenti & Vincenti, P.C., New York

"The financial health of our school has been improved by our relationship with First Republic."

The Hamlin School, San Francisco

"I've been banking with First Republic for several years now and they keep getting better."

Stephen Ross, New York

It's a Privilege to Serve You™

As First Republic prepared for the transition from a thrift and loan to a full-service private bank, "we thought we needed to improve the breadth and depth of our image relative to service," Herbert said. The company brought in brand consulting firm Landor Associates to facilitate the process. The consultants tweaked the First Republic logo and color palette, with the support of Bill Tracy, First Republic's longtime graphic arts designer. "Things were a little more high-end. The company was going in that direction," Tracy said. Herbert, Tracy said, knew what he wanted the brand to evoke as the Bank evolved. "He specifically wanted this green for First Republic from Day One. He wanted a good, deep green."[67]

Landor also honed First Republic's brand messaging. In one of many discussion groups held to generate ideas, a Landor employee tossed out the phrase "It's a privilege to serve you." Herbert was sold immediately. "That's what we're about," he said. "It came from them, and we liked it a lot." "It's a privilege to serve you" quickly became First Republic's tagline. "It's actually one of the better things we've ever done, in terms of communicating our identity," Herbert said.[68] The tagline has remained in place ever since and is a core descriptor of the company's service-focused culture. As Paul Gardner, who later joined to build the business banking division, explains: "The privilege part is very different than saying, 'It's a pleasure to serve you.' It's truly a privilege to do business with you because we're lucky that we can come together and create this partnership."[69]

It's a privilege to serve you℠

FIRST REPUBLIC
BANCORP

1996 Annual Report

First Republic Bank's "It's a privilege to serve you™" tagline made its first appearance on the cover of First Republic Bancorp's 1996 annual report.

A Pivotal Moment

First Republic Bancorp had survived its most challenging period to date. It came of age in the early to mid-1990s as a multibillion-dollar financial institution that was recognized as a leader in the California jumbo mortgage market.[70] And with its plan in place to convert from a thrift and loan holding company to a full-service private bank, First Republic had reached a pivotal moment and was poised to further grow by better serving its clients through offering a full range of financial products and services. ❖

CHAPTER FIVE | 1997–2001

BECOMING A FULL-SERVICE

Private Bank

Jim Herbert and Katherine August-deWilde recognized that First Republic's commitment to extraordinary service and its relationship banking model resonated in the marketplace. As clients' financial needs expanded, they turned to First Republic to meet those needs. In keeping with its focus on client service and responsible growth, First Republic responded to the demand for broader offerings.

First Republic Bancorp completed its conversion from a thrift and loan holding company to a full-service private bank in September 1997. It grew its range of lending and deposit products and services, introduced online banking and private wealth management, and expanded eastward to the New York metropolitan region. "Truly, we expanded because of the request from clients," said Dyann Tresenfeld. "Jim and Katherine set up the model in the other departments to have the same responsiveness, to work very quickly, to not be bureaucratic, and they took that overlay of the culture into the other areas." [1]

This was one of the most important inflection points for the enterprise to date. "Our strategic approach has always been one that considers our constituent groups – our colleagues, clients and shareholders – inseparable," Herbert said. "Taking care of our team members, and empowering and trusting them to make good decisions, is what best serves our clients. These clients then do more with us, and they take First Republic to their friends and associates, allowing us to grow, gain market share and return value to our shareholders. Tending to all three, with their interrelated nature in mind, is key to our strategy." Because First Republic was a publicly traded institution, this transformation into a full-service private bank, which was more highly valued from a price-to-earnings perspective in the marketplace, was done in partnership with the Bank's long-term shareholders. [2]

Despite the shift that would take place over the next few years, the more things changed, the more they stayed the same. Continuing to foster an entrepreneurial culture that empowered its people to make the best decisions for clients – a stark contrast to the declining quality of service available elsewhere as consolidation in the financial services industry continued to prevail – the Bank's competitive edge in attracting high-quality professionals and clients was more apparent than ever.

***

Margaret Mak helped First Republic Bank
launch its Preferred Banking services in 1997.
"My goal is to make banking as easy as possible
for my clients," Mak said. "These are busy people
who want a single point of contact and a single
decision-maker that doesn't change each month
or year at their bank. This is precisely what my
colleagues and I at First Republic provide –
stability and service."

Preferred Banking

As part of the transformation to full-service banking, First Republic Bank integrated
its lending and deposit-gathering sides. Herbert was not sure how it should work,
but he knew he wanted his top deposit-gathering banker leading the effort. "I asked
Margaret Mak if she would start Preferred Banking," Herbert recalled. Mak asked
him what that was. "I don't know," he said. "That's why I want you to start it, and
let's figure it out."

Mak moved to an office on the second floor of First Republic Bank's headquarters at
388 Market Street in San Francisco, where the Preferred Banking group took shape.
Several colleagues helped assemble the new team structure, including Crocker Bank
alum turned First Republic Relationship Manager Carmen Castro-Franceschi. The
mortgage teams already consisted of a Relationship Manager and a Loan Processor.
To work with existing mortgage clients to transfer their deposit relationships to First
Republic, and to attract new clients, the Bank added a new position, the Preferred
Banker. Modeled after Mak, who set the tone for the role and designed many of the
services, Preferred Bankers joined the existing mortgage teams and added an additional
level of deposit focus and expertise in serving the client's full banking needs.[3]

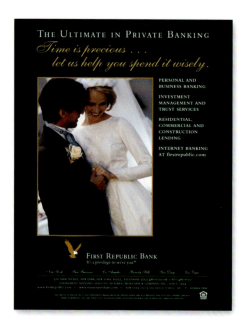

THE ULTIMATE IN PRIVATE BANKING

Time is precious . . .
let us help you spend it wisely.

PERSONAL AND
BUSINESS BANKING

INVESTMENT
MANAGEMENT AND
TRUST SERVICES

RESIDENTIAL,
COMMERCIAL AND
CONSTRUCTION
LENDING

INTERNET BANKING
AT firstrepublic.com

FIRST REPUBLIC BANK
It's a privilege to serve you™

Preferred Banking offered individualized care and attention to those who found the service lacking at large commercial banks.

"In Preferred Banking," the Bank explained to shareholders when the service was introduced in 1997, "each customer has a personal banker who is available to handle all the details of their banking requirements. Our bankers' goal is to make doing business with us as easy as possible and to build long-term relationships based on service, discretion and trust."[4]

Mak and other First Republic Bank professionals listened closely to clients while developing the Preferred Banking service and role. They paid especially close attention to the concerns of clients from other institutions about declining service quality as smaller banks continued to be acquired by megabanks. The ultra-wealthy still received excellent personal service from their bankers, Mak realized. But that left many other very successful clients who felt neglected and undervalued, and who were amenable to changing banks. "We were very thoughtful on how to get them. And we did, one client at a time," Mak said.[5] The potential for growth was staggering. The Bank calculated that as early as 1998, its then-modest in size, existing client base had more than $8 billion of personal liquid assets that were not with First Republic Bank.[6]

INVESTMENT-GRADE STRENGTH

First Republic Bank took several steps in 1997 to further strengthen its already strong capital position. The Bank raised $70 million in the largest capital market transaction in its history by issuing 15-year subordinated, fixed-rate debentures. It also called an earlier issue of convertible subordinated debentures and converted them to common stock, adding another $30 million to shareholder equity.

Rating agencies took notice, granting an investment-grade rating on the $70 million in debentures, as well as on First Republic's deposits and other senior debt obligations. On the equities side, FRC was included in the Russell 2000 Stock Index. The ratings upgrades and inclusion in the Russell index were yet another signal that First Republic Bank's accomplishments were beginning to be acknowledged by the industry and market.[7]

Silicon Valley Expansion

In addition to growth through referrals from existing clients and the focus on client acquisition by the sales force, First Republic also grew throughout the 1990s by opening new deposit-gathering, or Preferred Banking, offices. And in February 1997, with the dot-com boom in full flower, First Republic returned to Walther and Herbert's Westcoast Thrift & Loan roots by expanding down the Peninsula with a full-service office in San Mateo, CA. Mary Kasaris, who joined First Republic in 1996 after 16 years with Bank of America, led First Republic's further expansion into the Peninsula as its Regional Managing Director for the area. In June 1998, First Republic Bank opened its next Silicon Valley office, in Menlo Park, with Palo Alto to follow.[8]

First Republic further expanded into Silicon Valley with an office in San Mateo, CA, and growth into Menlo Park, Burlingame and Palo Alto.

Mary Kasaris led First Republic Bank's further expansion into Silicon Valley. "The essence of banking at First Republic is relationships," Kasaris said. "I work with my clients over a period of years, not just days or months, to earn their trust, their respect and their ongoing business by delivering outstanding service time and time again."

First Republic Bank's website in 1997 included online banking services through its NetBank program.

Internet Banking

As a young banker at nearby Silicon Valley Bank, Jason Bender had the opportunity to partner with Kasaris on a handful of projects in 1997. At that time, Silicon Valley Bank and First Republic were not considered competitors, as each had a very different product and service offering. Bender was impressed with First Republic's culture. After receiving his Stanford MBA in 1999, Bender interviewed with Herbert and the team in San Francisco and was hired.

Bender's first assignment in 1999 was to develop and implement an Internet banking service for First Republic Bank clients. The Bank had offered a basic website for a few years, but First Republic's online platform needed upgrading to increase user-friendliness and the services offered. At the time, the trend among financial institutions was to launch Internet-only products. The Internet was seen as a low-cost delivery channel for lower-margin products and services, such as no-frills checking and savings accounts. First Republic Bank took a different approach, offering online banking as one of several ways to interact with the Bank.

Jason Bender, Chief Administrative Officer, joined First Republic Bank in 1999 and immediately began developing its Internet banking service.

"It was important for us to not dictate to our clients how they should do business with us," Bender said. "On Monday, they might feel like banking with somebody in the office, and on Tuesday they might want to do it online, and on Wednesday they may want to do it through the call center. That should be the client's decision … I think that's part and parcel of our client-centric approach to things."[9]

By the year 2000, more than 30 percent of First Republic Bank's clients with personal checking accounts had signed up to use NetBank, as the new online banking service initially was called, and 11 percent, including many larger clients, were active users. The popularity of the service was growing by the day.[10]

The Beginning of Wealth Management

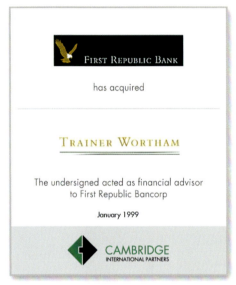

First Republic's 19.9 percent purchase of Trainer, Wortham served as its entry into private wealth management and the East Coast in 1997. In 1999, First Republic fully acquired the firm.

"We don't know anything about wealth management," Herbert told a First Republic Bank shareholder over breakfast in the spring of 1997. While Herbert and others certainly understood wealth management from a client's perspective, the enterprise had yet to expand operationally into that arena. So when his breakfast companion, Charles Moore, head of the New York investment advisory firm Trainer, Wortham & Company, said he and his three partners were interested in selling the firm, Herbert saw an opportunity that was too good to pass up.

Understanding already that clients, under First Republic's relationship banking model, wanted an institution that could service all of their financial needs, Herbert felt the demand for wealth management already existed. In the continued spirit of trying new things very carefully, and despite the fact this was not at the top of his to-do list, Herbert was not going to let the chance slip away.

"Why sell it? Why don't you come with us?" Herbert asked. "Why don't we invest in you and give you access to our client base?"[11]

First Republic agreed in late June 1997 to buy 19.9 percent of Trainer, Wortham for $7 million and retained an option to buy the entire firm, which it later exercised in 1999.[12] One of the nation's oldest investment advisory firms, Trainer, Wortham was formed in 1924 and managed more than $2 billion for wealthy individuals, foundations and endowments, with much of its funds invested in growth stocks.[13] Many of its individual existing clients, though primarily domiciled on the East Coast, already resembled the profile of First Republic Bank's typical jumbo mortgage client. Trainer, Wortham began providing wealth management services to First Republic Bank clients from its office at Third Avenue and 51st Street in Manhattan. To better serve West Coast clients who were rarely in New York, the firm also took space in First Republic's San Francisco headquarters.

"We had been a part of another bank prior," recalled Henry "Bill" Ghriskey Jr., Senior Managing Director at First Republic Investment Management, "but this was different. My father and I joined Trainer, Wortham together in 1978. He worked well into his

90s and was always welcomed by the team at Rockefeller Center. Because at First Republic, it was always all about the people. Even from the start, it was never 'this is what you have to do.' We were always made to feel a part of the team."[14]

Expansion into New York

Through its investment in Trainer, Wortham, First Republic both took its initial step toward wealth management and established a presence in New York City. Herbert felt that the banking opportunities on the East Coast were very attractive. He and August-deWilde had proposed just such a move to the First Republic Board of Directors a few years earlier. Each had lived in and around Manhattan and felt that the urban, coastal, vertical nature of Manhattan – which they considered key to the success of First Republic's brand recognition and growth on the West Coast – fit the definition of their ideal landscape. First Republic had also increasingly utilized its teleconference capabilities – installed just a few years earlier, in 1995 – to further the scalability of its model on the West Coast. The Board, however, felt the team already had its hands full managing the rapidly growing business on the West Coast and postponed any such move.

One day, Moore called Herbert with an opportunity: Through an acquaintance, he had learned that Fidelity Investments had what was, in effect, a spare trust company licensed in New York that it might be willing to sell. The trust company's only asset was $1.5 million in cash and could be purchased for a few hundred thousand dollars more, Moore estimated.

Herbert contacted Board member Marty Gibbs and asked his law firm to quickly research whether the Bank could use a trust company license to open a Preferred Banking Office in New York. One of Gibbs' fellow attorneys, who had worked for the State of New York's banking department, concluded that the trust company plan, although very unusual, would work. In the meantime, a ZIP code analysis of First Republic Bank's existing clients revealed that more of them had residences or did business in New York than Herbert and August-deWilde had realized. With the Board's change of heart and blessing, they seized the opportunity and bought the New York trust company from Fidelity.[15]

First Republic Bank expands east into New York City.

"A Fishbowl on Park Avenue!"

In expanding to New York, Herbert initially tried to lease space for First Republic in the Waldorf-Astoria Hotel on Park Avenue. In terms of a prestigious address, it was hard to beat. But Herbert was glad to have lost the space to a financial services rival when he learned that it was blocked as many as 50 days a year to accommodate special events and VIP visitors at the hotel.

Herbert's second choice, on the opposite side of Park Avenue at 51st Street, turned out to be an ideal location. BMW had maintained a showroom at that corner for years that was considered a local landmark. With a tremendous amount of foot and vehicle traffic passing by, the ground-level space was perfect for introducing First Republic to the New York market.

Bill Dessoffy was not so sure. An industry veteran with private banking and investment experience at Chemical Bank and Chase Manhattan Bank in New York, Dessoffy had been recruited by Herbert and August-deWilde in mid-1999 to lead the First Republic Bank move into New York. He walked over to the Park Avenue address one day that summer and could see that the space was under construction. He presumed his office would be in the same building, but on a floor higher than the ground-level retail space. When Dessoffy called Herbert in San Francisco to inquire, he was told he would sit right there on the floor of the ground-level Preferred Banking Office. The blunt, fast-talking New Yorker responded, "I don't want to work in a fishbowl on Park Avenue!"[16]

Herbert explained that First Republic Bank did not deliver private banking services from behind mahogany doors in high-rise offices, a standard practice among Manhattan's private banks. Dessoffy trusted that Herbert and August-deWilde's vision for private banking, which was such a success on the West Coast, would work in New York as well. He moved into the office as the Regional Managing Director for the New York metropolitan area with a staff of 7, all from the East Coast, and a mandate to hire the right entrepreneurial-minded bankers to help First Republic Bank grow. One of his first hires, from among the best bankers he knew at Chase, Ruth Aronowitz, continues to be one of First Republic's most successful Relationship Managers in New York.[17]

First Republic Trust Company

By the late 1990s, First Republic Bank clients were expressing interest in trust services for estate-planning, fiduciary and other custodial functions. Many of the entrepreneurs and professionals who became clients in the early days of First Republic – which also happened to be the early days of their careers – had become quite successful over time. First Republic did not have a trust department and worried that it would take too long for a start-up trust business to turn a profit. It did, however, recognize the opportunity to continue to grow alongside its clients by evolving to serve their needs. So when San

Bill Dessoffy and Jim Herbert at a Bank holiday party, singing Frank Sinatra's classic "New York, New York."

The "fishbowl on Park Avenue" was an ideal location for the Bank's first New York Preferred Banking Office. Every day, thousands of people and cars pass by this First Republic location at 51st Street and Park Avenue.

First Republic's leadership would later thank Bruce Anderson (seated center) with a dinner in his honor.

Francisco-based Pacific Bank, which had a highly regarded trust operation, approached First Republic in 1998 to gauge its interest in a possible acquisition, First Republic was interested. The potential deal never materialized, though, as Pacific Bank eventually sold to a third party.

Shortly after the Pacific Bank sale to another party was announced, Herbert and August-deWilde met with Bruce Anderson, who headed the Pacific Bank trust operation. They probed him on the details of building and operating a trust company. The following Monday morning, Anderson called August-deWilde and said, "You don't really want to know what I think about starting a trust company. You want me to come do that for you, don't you?" August-deWilde did not hesitate. "Absolutely, you're right," she said. "We do want you to come do it for us."[18]

Anderson joined First Republic as the Senior Vice President of First Republic Trust Company. He and a group of senior trust officers he brought with him collectively had 115 years of experience in the trust and investment business. The group gave First Republic instant credibility in the trust field.[19]

Roger Walther, who, along with Herbert, had been involved in talks about acquiring Pacific Bank, chuckled at the thought that First Republic got the core trust business it wanted all along without having to acquire another entity. Anderson and the other trust officers were not allowed to bring former clients with them. But First Republic got exactly what it was looking for, regardless: the leadership team that could establish, build and grow its trust business.[20]

First Republic Securities Company

The same clients who asked First Republic Bank to provide trust services often were interested in brokerage services as well. August-deWilde will never forget the time an entrepreneur who sold his business for a substantial sum was looking to park the proceeds in short-term Treasury securities while he contemplated his future. "We didn't have an outlet to do that. Someone else did," she said. "Guess who got to manage the money?"[21]

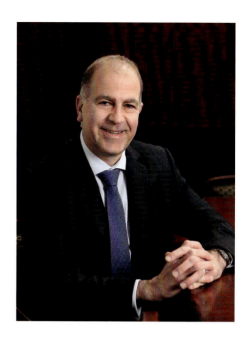

First Republic's reputation for extraordinary service convinced David Tateosian to join the Bank's young brokerage division in 2003.

So, in 1999, First Republic launched a brokerage division of its own, First Republic Securities Company. First Republic's securities staff worked with clients who were primarily interested in directing their own investments, and they offered expertise in agency securities, municipal and corporate bonds, and equities. By the end of the year, First Republic had about six brokerage and securities desks, with one in New York and the others located in its largest West Coast locations.[22]

David Tateosian, President of First Republic Securities Company, remembers his decision to join the newly opened division in its earlier years. "I asked my friends and colleagues about First Republic while I was interviewing," recalled Tateosian, "and they all said the same thing – it's a different place, all about the people and the service. I remember going to a party at the time and speaking with the host, who also happened to be a client. At his own two-hour party, he raved for about 30 minutes about how great First Republic was." The service proposition at First Republic resonated with its banking clients and would extend into its wealth management platform.[23]

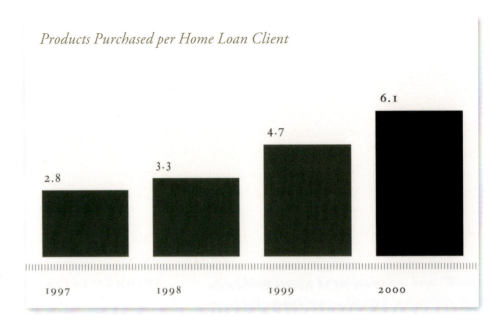

Products Purchased per Home Loan Client

6.1

4.7

3.3

2.8

1997   1998   1999   2000

Cross-Selling Success

As First Republic expanded into new products, services and locations, its ability to market each successive new product or service gained momentum year over year. This cross-sell success affirmed Herbert's instinct and strategic decision to shift to a full-service private bank, by reflecting clients' desire to do more with First Republic. It also reflected the sales teams' increasing ability to deliver a wide array of offerings, spanning lending, deposit, business banking and private wealth management.

Key to this successful transition was First Republic's core client base, which had been loyal to the enterprise dating back to its earlier incarnations, Westcoast Thrift & Loan and San Francisco Bancorp. This expansion of products and services aligned First Republic more closely with the needs of its successful clients, who had grown in both size and complexity alongside the institution.

It also enabled First Republic to attract a wider array of new clients. In all, the Bank added more than 7,000 new clients in 1998, with many utilizing these additional offerings, including free worldwide access to ATMs. That same year, each new mortgage transaction resulted in a client relationship that averaged 3.3 products, up from 1.1 products in 1996.[24] By 1999, the average number of products utilized by each new mortgage client jumped again to 4.7, and in 2000, to 6.1.[25]

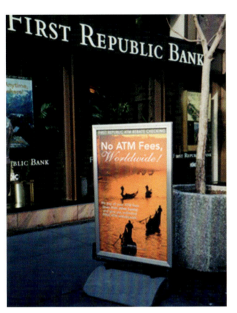

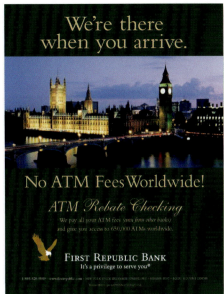

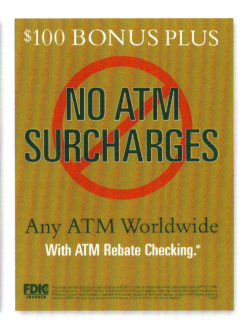

The shift in charter to become a full-service private bank represented a turning point, while the increase in products per client from 3.3 in 1998 to 6.1 in 2000 provided evidence that the transition had positioned the enterprise to fully capitalize on the relationship banking opportunity. Clients wanted to do still more with First Republic Bank, and the more they interacted, the more the extraordinary service proposition resonated, resulting in increased products as well as referrals of new clients.

"A Balancing Act"

Within a few years, First Republic had evolved from a thrift and loan holding company focused almost exclusively on jumbo mortgages, certificates of deposit and passbook savings accounts to a full-service private bank. This required First Republic to substantively revamp the way it compensated and trained its teams, in order to ensure the full company was aligned with this shared vision of the future.

There was a broad, team-based, multiyear effort to implement the full-service private banking model that the Board had agreed upon during its Annual Planning Session. This included, importantly, adjusting the compensation structure. "In the '90s, as we added products, we had to change our compensation plan," August-deWilde said.

"We had 10 ATM machines," said Willis Newton, First Republic's Chief Financial Officer. "We were never going to be as convenient to our clients."[26] First Republic's solution was relatively simple: The Bank offered free access to any ATM worldwide with its innovative ATM Rebate Checking product, starting in 1998.

Carmen Castro-Franceschi (second from right), one of the bank's most successful Relationship Managers, with First Republic's leaders – Katherine August-deWilde, Roger Walther and Jim Herbert – at a Relationship Manager awards luncheon.

It was not always a smooth transition. The Bank introduced the concept to some of the Bank's long-term Relationship Managers, who traditionally came from strictly lending backgrounds, saying, "We're going to begin to pay you 20 percent of your compensation for deposits." They responded, "You're going to do what? We don't know about deposits, we don't like deposits, we don't care about deposits. We're lenders."[27]

The Bank gradually instituted a plan that increased compensation for newer products more quickly than it reduced it for the lending products. "It's a balancing act," August-deWilde said. Initially, many were less adept at selling new products. "So first, you say we're going to take down the lending compensation a little bit, but we'll raise the deposit compensation quite a lot, because it will take you time to learn how to do it. And we did workshops and we did training, and they had to use the products themselves to get comfortable."[28] This was the internal version of "do anything to get trial."

SINGLE POINT OF CONTACT

First Republic's role of Relationship Manager grew from the traditional mortgage industry role of loan officer. More than a matter of nomenclature, the use of the Relationship Manager title reflects the Bank's emphasis on the client experience and a model centered on providing customized advice and solutions, not selling products.

With formal training and meaningful experience in credit, Relationship Managers' expertise in lending, along with the credit clawback provision, is key to the safety and stability of the enterprise. Rather than pigeonhole these lenders into one limited function, the open architecture of the enterprise encourages an entrepreneurial spirit of personal initiative and creative strategizing in serving the client. Utilizing a team-based approach, Relationship Managers are given the ability to deliver the full bank, providing their clients a single point of contact. Each professional is trusted to choose how to best serve the client – drawing on the expertise of colleagues in Preferred Banking, Wealth Management and Business Banking as appropriate to determine which products and services might work best – and then empowered to deliver as part of a team rather than passing off clients to another department.

"At First Republic, there's a respect for how everybody who works here is going to have a little bit different source and avenue for how they're going to obtain and how they're going to do their business," said Dyann Tresenfeld, one of the Bank's pioneering Relationship Managers, who joined in 1986 and now serves as an Executive Managing Director. "It works well for people from a sales or an entrepreneurial background."[29]

Giving the client a single point of contact – a contact who, thanks to the very low turnover within the First Republic team, remains constant – is the essence of relationship banking, allowing the banker and client to grow together. "People call us for all sorts of things," said Mary Deckebach, Regional Managing Director in Los Angeles and one of the Bank's early hires. "They call, 'Can you guys do this?' And I'll say, 'Well, sure we can do that – if I don't have the expertise, I know my colleagues will.'"[30]

Carmen Castro-Franceschi, also a veteran Relationship Manager who joined First Republic in 1986 and serves currently as an Executive Managing Director,[31] captures the role's essence and First Republic's overarching relationship-banking philosophy: "This is how we started this: One client at a time. My goal was to sell my service, to sell me. Like Jim said, 'Don't sell the product, sell you.' Clients want to be understood. They want performance. They want you to execute."[32]

Mary Deckebach, Regional Managing Director

Committed to New York

First Republic Bank's New York headquarters remain in Rockefeller Center, at the corner of 48th Street and Sixth Avenue.

Herbert was staying in his apartment in the Flatiron district of Manhattan the night before the terrorist attack on the World Trade Center in 2001. He was in town in part to finish negotiating space for a second Preferred Banking Office and a New York headquarters location on Sixth Avenue in Rockefeller Center. The transaction was quite far along, but was put on hold the morning of September 11th.

Herbert, in New York, and August-deWilde, in San Francisco, along with many other Bank leaders, moved quickly to make sure none of First Republic's professionals or their family members had been harmed in the attacks. The team had experienced other tragic and unexpected events in the past, including two earthquakes, so they were ready and quick to respond to the crisis. They checked on clients and canceled a Bank board meeting scheduled for later in the week in Washington, D.C.

With many close ties to the city, Herbert focused his energy on First Republic's newest region. The Bank, having many clients who, like Herbert, called both California and New York home, was committed to New York and a continued expansion into the community. First Republic proceeded with the Rockefeller Center lease, and the space at Sixth Avenue and 48th Street, which still serves as the Bank's New York headquarters, opened in 2002.[42]

With Chief Executive Officer Jim Herbert, Chairman Roger Walther and Chief Operating Officer Katherine August-deWilde at the helm (pictured here in the new Rockefeller Center office), and a variety of new products and services, First Republic entered the new millennium with confidence it would expand its client base on both the East and West Coasts.

Positioned for Continued Growth

First Republic Bank had grown significantly since becoming a full-service private bank in 1997, and by the end of 2001 it ranked among the nation's 80 largest banks.[43] This five-year period marked a transformational period in the Bank's evolution. It substantially added products and services to meet clients' needs and expanded into the East Coast through its New York presence. The ability to offer a full range of deposit and lending products, serve businesses through the burgeoning business banking division, and care for clients' investment management needs afforded First Republic even greater opportunity for growth. The more robust offerings attracted new clients while also allowing First Republic's bankers to deepen existing relationships. The demand for the Bank to serve all facets of financial needs, and the commitment to service embraced by the team, was evidenced in the more than doubling of products per client from 1997 to 2000.

First Republic had vaulted to the top ranks of its private bank peer group as well, developing a reputation on both coasts for unparalleled personal service. And with its founding leadership team still in place, the enterprise continued to cultivate an entrepreneurial spirit, empowering all employees to act quickly and decisively, in a manner that was unique in the financial services industry. All of these factors prepared the Bank for the era of continued growth and expansion that lay ahead. ❖

CHAPTER SIX | 2001–2006

ONE RELATIONSHIP

at a Time

First Republic Bank began 2001 having passed an important inflection point. In just over 15 years since the founding of First Republic Bancorp in 1985, the enterprise had grown from a thrift and loan mortgage lender, which was not federally insured and was entirely West Coast-focused, to a full-service private banking institution with a bicoastal presence and FDIC coverage.

First Republic prepared for the next phase of its evolution in the early 2000s, as it continued to build out a full platform of private banking and wealth management products and services. At the same time, the leadership team continued to focus on ensuring that growth would not come at the expense of the culture and values that made First Republic Bank so uniquely attractive to clients, employees and shareholders. It highlighted a "back-to-basics" emphasis on the Bank's key lead product on which to build a full banking relationship – the home mortgage. And it recommitted to acquiring new clients just as First Republic had done since the day it opened its first branch: one relationship at a time.[1]

"It is not just about how you add assets, how you become a bigger company and a more profitable company," said Chief Administrative Officer Jason Bender, who in 2001 was named Head of Finance for the Bank. "It is how you preserve and evolve appropriately and safely the things that allow your company to work the way that it does and retain the competitive edge that it has."[2]

* * *

Values and Culture

Chief Marketing Officer Dianne Snedaker played an important role in formally articulating the Bank's culture and values as it entered into the early 2000s. But her initial reaction to being asked by Jim Herbert to join First Republic Bank was less than enthusiastic: "I couldn't say no fast enough! The whole idea of working for a bank gave me the jitters."

A prominent member of the San Francisco advertising community, Snedaker met Herbert through the Young Presidents' Organization in the early 1990s. The former President of Ketchum Advertising had worked with financial services firms but had never been employed by a bank. In her experience, banks had not always been the most engaging of clients.

But Herbert convinced her to work with his team as a consultant beginning in the summer of 2000. "He didn't give me a really tight definition of what he wanted me to do. He just basically said, 'Why don't you look at the company and tell us where you think we might need some course correction?'" The Bank had about 400 employees and was poised to continue growing. "He was concerned that getting bigger might challenge the internal environment a bit," Snedaker said.[3]

The thought of working at a bank seemed foreign to Dianne Snedaker, who had worked as an advertising executive prior to joining as a consultant for First Republic – until she started talking to the Bank's employees and clients.

"This Enormous Pride"

Snedaker teamed with Jason Bender, another newcomer to First Republic, who was handling a number of marketing projects during the summer of 2000 prior to moving into his finance department role, to take the collective cultural pulse of the Bank's professionals. She was surprised to feel genuinely welcomed. In her experience, that was not the reception given to consultants at most companies.

"The next thing I felt was this enormous passion within the company. This enormous pride. This enormous sense of wanting to be so helpful to clients. And all of that was pretty apparent pretty quickly here," she said.

"Things were not defined in specific language. This is just the way it was. This is just the way people behaved," Snedaker said. "It struck me, without wanting to compress it in any way, that some – not exactly definition, but some codification would help."

She and Bender went on a road trip to First Republic Bank offices across its footprint to meet with members of the team. The similarities in what they heard across the board were striking. "It wasn't rehearsed. It wasn't practiced. At that time, it wasn't really written down in a great way. They just shared the vision," she said. "The vision was what Jim said from the beginning: 'Serve our clients. Serve them in an extraordinary way. Give them things they need. Don't give them things they don't want. Make sure you always keep their interests at the forefront.'"[4]

Snedaker took the lead in committing First Republic Bank's values to paper based on what she and Bender had gathered during their time on the road visiting with employees. Her hesitation dissipated, she joined the Bank full-time as Chief Marketing Officer in 2001. "That's why our values work here and that's why they're real, because they weren't written in a room and then foisted upon an organization," Bender said. "They were just a distillation of practices and feelings and passions that we already had. It was a matter of teasing it out."[5]

First Republic Values

Do the Right Thing
Provide Extraordinary Service
Respect the Team
Take Responsibility
Think Positively
Move Forward, Move Fast
Grow
Have Fun

First Republic Bank already had a strong culture of putting the client first. Dianne Snedaker simply helped to put practice to paper.

"Our values are all linked together, under the spirit of how we operate," shared Iggie Alferos, Senior Vice President and Controller at First Republic Bank, who joined the enterprise in 1987. "While they are on paper today, it is truly a reflection of what we do. We live our values."

FIRST REPUBLIC VALUES

Do the Right Thing

We strive to do things right at First Republic. We also recognize that we're a business of humans; mistakes will happen. Therefore, our mandate is to do the right thing: act with integrity, own your actions, correct mistakes, learn from experience.

Provide Extraordinary Service

We always aim to exceed expectations and serve our clients in unexpected ways. We'll take on only what we can do right. Our business may be about wealth management and banking, but our success is all about service – exceptional customer service.

Respect the Team

Everyone at First Republic makes a difference and everyone at First Republic deserves to feel that his or her contribution is valued. We place high value on collaboration because we know that the power of many is greater than the power of one.

Take Responsibility

At First Republic, it's not enough to do our own jobs well. Making sure our clients are satisfied is everyone's job. So if something needs fixing, we step up to the plate, "own" the problem and make things right.

Think Positively

We operate in an environment of trust and encourage openness and flexibility. We hire positive people who act positively. Our goal is to "manage toward yes."

Move Forward, Move Fast

There are two types of organizations – organizations that spend time checking and organizations that spend time doing. We're doers. We value action and decisiveness and recognize that the best opportunities come to those who act quickly.

Grow

We've evolved greatly since our inception, expanding ourselves and our business purpose. At First Republic, we embrace change and every person has the opportunity to grow and contribute. We want our people to soar.

Have Fun

We know that if everyone enjoys their work they'll do a better job – and our clients will feel the difference. It's really that simple.

"The Very Foundation of Our First Republic Brand"

In addition to capturing the values at the core of the First Republic culture, Herbert did not want to lose the focus on service that made First Republic unique and, in many ways, defined the Bank in the marketplace. "Exceptional, differentiated client service remains the very foundation of our First Republic Bank brand," he said. "It has become a competitive advantage in the marketplace. It originates from empowered, talented professionals, at all levels, who genuinely care about our clients."[6]

Soon after Snedaker, Dan Ben-Ora, Chief People Officer, joined First Republic Bank in 2002 to run the newly created human resources department. Familiar with the Bank because of his years consulting for First Republic, Ben-Ora immediately immersed himself in deepening his understanding of this client-focused service culture. Being on the "inside" strengthened his appreciation for how simple and powerful the First Republic Bank culture was. He saw first-hand how the leadership walked the walk rather than just talking the talk.

Chief People Officer Dan Ben-Ora joined First Republic Bank in 2002 to head the Bank's human resources department.

"Every meeting I went to, I heard Jim Herbert talking about culture and client service, and I realized that every meeting that is all he talked about," Ben-Ora said. "When management makes people think about 20 or 30 things, they don't get very focused. Here we have leadership with a very strong passion for serving clients. And the statement that Jim would make is that everything else is a by-product of that – the success, profitability, growth – all of that is just about serving clients, one at a time."[7]

This commitment to providing extraordinary client service and embracing the First Republic values in an actionable way was paramount to the Bank's philosophy on hiring. "When we hire here, we hire people that have a great attitude, that are nice to be around, that you know will be helpful to our clients," Snedaker said. "We don't try to make superstars here for the purpose of them being superstars. We want people to be superstars in performance. It is rewarding. It's just plain rewarding."[8]

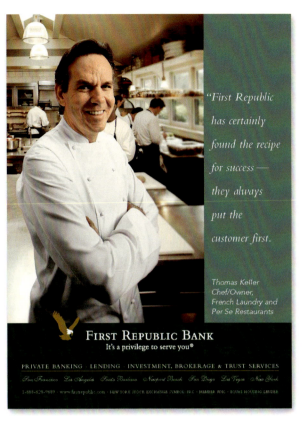

"First Republic has certainly found the recipe for success — they always put the customer first.

Thomas Keller
Chef/Owner,
French Laundry and
Per Se Restaurants

Chief Marketing Officer Dianne Snedaker standardized the Bank's marketing campaigns, using its long-standing client testimonials from its annual reports in a broader fashion.

"The Power of Clients Talking About Us"

Snedaker resisted the temptation to put her marketing stamp on the organization as quickly as possible after joining the Bank. Instead, she wanted to build on the strong expressions of the Bank's values that she witnessed with almost every interaction she had at First Republic. Her first task was to make the Bank's marketing materials as consistent in tone and message as the collective voice of its employees.[9]

"When Dianne joined us," Katherine August-deWilde recalled, "she said, 'Your annual report is fantastic and the testimonials are fantastic, but your marketing is all over the place. Why don't you use these fantastic testimonials as marketing?' She insisted on that."[10]

Snedaker took the lead in making the long-standing client testimonials not just the focus of the annual reports but also the focus of all of First Republic Bank's marketing efforts. While prominently featured in the annual reports already, the messaging clearly spoke to a key driver in First Republic Bank's ability to acquire new clients – the positive, organic word-of-mouth recommendations from existing clients that reinforced and spread First Republic Bank's brand recognition as a high-touch, service-focused enterprise.

Magazine ads and window displays in the offices began to uniformly display these testimonials, which included clients sharing, in their own words, their experiences with First Republic's client-centric service approach. Snedaker was able to convey this concept successfully via radio ads, overcoming Herbert's initial skepticism.

"Dianne really tuned the testimonial advertising campaign, took it into newspapers, took it into radio," Herbert said. "I told her she was crazy with radio. She was brilliant. It is very targeted media, works perfectly, and she can turn out ads very quickly. We basically got anecdotal stories, and she got actors to do the verbal, but they're all true."[11]

From Snedaker's point of view, client testimonials are the Bank's not-so-secret weapon. "The power of clients talking about us is far greater than the power of anything we can say ourselves," she said. "We are lucky to have these fabulous clients, we really are."[12]

The Ongoing Investment in Safe Growth

Fresh from working with Snedaker on the articulation of First Republic Bank's values, Bender took on another assignment from Herbert. "I remember specifically an analysis that Jim asked me to do at one point, which we called the headwinds analysis," Bender said. "It was an effort to try to articulate just how much our different initiatives were costing the Bank and when we thought we might get past it."

In the few years prior to 2001, First Republic had undertaken a deliberate, strategic expansion in products, services and locations. It had allocated significant resources both to this build-out and the corresponding marketing efforts for these new offerings. But the slumping stock market following the dot-com bust in 2000, coupled with the concurrent recession and continued economic impact of the terror attacks on September 11th, made for a challenging time to reinvest profits back into the company's growth.

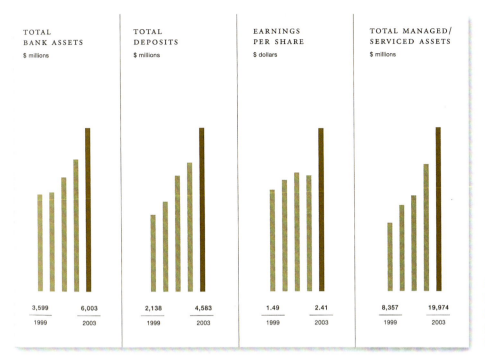

TOTAL
BANK ASSETS

$ millions

3,599	6,003
1999	2003

TOTAL
DEPOSITS

$ millions

2,138	4,583
1999	2003

EARNINGS
PER SHARE

$ dollars

1.49	2.41
1999	2003

TOTAL MANAGED/
SERVICED ASSETS

$ millions

8,357	19,974
1999	2003

First Republic took strategic steps to expand its locations, products and services in the early 2000s, investing heavily in the Bank's future growth and success.
First Republic Bank 2003 Annual Report

The Bank was committed to its strategic plan for building out a robust platform of private banking products and services, but at the same time wanted to be sure its shareholders and other stakeholders understood the cost of this growth. "The expenses did build during that time period because we were doing a lot of different things all at the same time," Bender said. "We had invested very heavily in the company. We were transparent about that. We were telling the Street and others that we're investing in the franchise, this is our strategic vision, we're executing on it, but there are going to be headwinds."[13] As a growth company, management understood that this investment in expansion was key to building future shareholder value. Using Bender's study, the build-out continued methodically while growing earnings per share 14 percent per annum during the time period, from 2001 to 2005.[14]

Having now spent a number of years both developing an expanded platform of products and services and focusing the sales teams on learning and delivering this fuller menu, at the same time First Republic recognized a need to return to its core growth driver – acquiring new clients through the home mortgage.

In 2002, First Republic Bank recommitted the team to its key lead-in product in client acquisition – the jumbo home mortgage.

"Back to Basics"

"We decided that we had gotten a little too fancy too fast for our own good, in some of the product offerings we were doing, and with cross-sell and so on, and we decided to go back to banking," Herbert said. "We decided we had to get back to home lending and pull more clients in. So we started to do that in a very successful way over the next couple years." As the leadership team told shareholders in its review of 2002, "We adopted a 'back-to-basics' plan, restricting nonessential bank activities and placing priority on the activities always important to our success – unrelenting client service, the development of new client relationships and the thoughtful introduction of new products."[15]

Mortgage Boom

Herbert and August-deWilde played to First Republic Bank's strengths by refocusing on its carefully underwritten, fully documented jumbo home mortgage lending in the early 2000s. Unbeknownst to them, they were also positioning First Republic to benefit significantly from the Federal Reserve Board's stimulative economic policies that were beginning to take hold and would result in a boom in mortgage lending.

FIRST REPUBLIC ICONS – COOKIES AND UMBRELLAS

In addition to its signature client testimonial marketing campaigns, First Republic Bank is also well known for the smell of freshly baked cookies that greets clients as they enter each office. The idea originated in one of the Bank offices and was quickly adopted system-wide, August-deWilde said. "They're wonderful. We've seen some of our competitors try to copy us. They copy us by going to Safeway and buying store-bought cookies that are still in their box. We make the cookies in every office, and people love it."[16]

Another icon of First Republic's branding is the umbrella. "On a rainy day – the more people we have who have opened that green umbrella, the happier we're going to be," August-deWilde said. "It makes the client happy, it makes the prospect happy, it's wonderful marketing."[17]

First Republic Bank offers clients a superior experience both inside and outside of the Bank, with freshly baked cookies and First Republic umbrellas available each and every day.

With funds readily available for lending, the U.S. economy entered a multi-year phase of growth with relatively low inflation and stable employment that economists, including then-Governor and future Chairman of the Federal Reserve Board Ben Bernanke, referred to as the "Great Moderation." In retrospect, the period of prosperity, which lulled many into underestimating the growing risks in the financial system, would prove too good to last. Fiscal stimulation and monetary policy would contribute to a spike in subprime lending that played a central role in the global financial crisis of 2008.[18] But in the early 2000s, and particularly in First Republic's urban, coastal markets, the housing markets and real estate industry were booming.

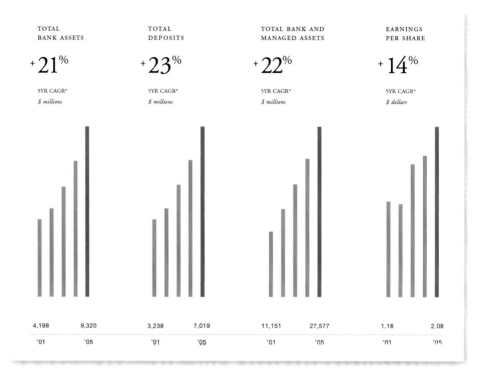

TOTAL BANK ASSETS		TOTAL DEPOSITS		TOTAL BANK AND MANAGED ASSETS		EARNINGS PER SHARE	
+21%		+23%		+22%		+14%	
5YR CAGR*		5YR CAGR*		5YR CAGR*		5YR CAGR*	
$ millions		$ millions		$ millions		$ dollars	
4,198	9,320	3,238	7,019	11,151	27,577	1.16	2.08
'01	'05	'01	'05	'01	'05	'01	'05

As other banks lowered their lending standards, First Republic Bank refused to compromise, and the Bank continued to grow without altering its strict lending criteria or accepting a lower standard of credit quality.
First Republic Bank 2005 Annual Report

Never Compromise Quality Standards to Compete

First Republic Bank posted successive record results during this bull market in loan growth, growing total loans from $3.4 billion in 2001 to $6.7 billion in 2005. However, unlike many financial services companies in the United States and abroad, it was never tempted to loosen its stringent credit standards and quality controls. At the same time, the Bank took advantage of the rebounding demand for bank stocks in the equities market to raise capital and enhance its capital base. In the third quarter of 2005, it issued 660,000 shares of common stock. It was the Bank's fifth such transaction; over the course of two years, these transactions raised a total of $165 million in tier 1 capital, supporting the balance sheet growth.[19]

At a time when other banks and the government agencies Fannie Mae and Freddie Mac were routinely lending 90 to 95 percent of the value of a property, First Republic Bank posted average loan-to-value ratios for single-family homes at the time of origination of just 56 percent. Home equity loans – used by consumers across the country during this period as a way to tap their rising home values for instant cash – were subjected to the same tight standards at First Republic.[20]

As other banks nationwide were lowering credit criteria as a way to profit on the housing bonanza, First Republic Bank refused to budge. "We will never and have never compromised our underwriting standards to compete in our markets," August-deWilde told investors and securities analysts in the fall of 2005.[21]

August-deWilde also noted that the Bank underwrote all adjustable-rate mortgages for income debt service coverage qualification using interest rates that were substantially above the starter rates, adding a significant margin of safety in the event of a rising rate environment. As of October 2005, the Bank was underwriting adjustable rate mortgages at 8 percent, 3 percentage points higher than the actual starting rate at the time. That dedication to underwriting discipline was evident in the very low 1.5 basis points of cumulative loan loss on home loans, including home equity lines, that the Bank experienced in the 20 years from its founding in 1985.[22]

Preferred Banking Deposit Growth

The Bank's deposit growth was strong as well by mid-decade. Though the Preferred Banking division was not fully developed until the late 1990s, by 2005 Preferred Banking deposits totaled $3.6 billion, or 52 percent of all deposits, representing 22 percent growth over the previous year.[23]

The growth in deposits generated by both the Preferred Banking division and the Preferred Banking Office network came as no surprise to First Republic Bank's leadership. "Satisfied clients are the best generators of new clients and additional new deposits," Herbert said.[24] "We live and have lived for years on word-of-mouth marketing. It is the single most potent force to build an enterprise. Clients have been bringing their friends to us with increasing regularity and often take great pleasure in sharing this secret with their friends."[25]

Our goal is to change the way you feel about banking.

FIRST REPUBLIC BANK
It's a privilege to serve you®

PRIVATE BANKING · LENDING
INVESTMENT, BROKERAGE & TRUST SERVICES

FOR THE LOCATION NEAREST YOU,
CALL 415-392-1400

First Republic Bank clients, pleased with the extraordinary customer service provided, regularly refer their friends and colleagues to the Bank.

"First Republic is very savvy about schools. They know nonprofit businesses inside out," noted Arlene Hogan, founding Head of School of The Archer School for Girls (left).

First Republic Bank follows its clients' passions and hearts, serving educational nonprofits, charities and the arts. "For us, banking is all about relationships," said W. Brewster Ely IV, Headmaster of Town School for Boys (center). "First Republic goes out of its way to satisfy us."

"First Republic not only cares about their communities, they care about the future of the kids in those communities," adds James Steyer, Founder and Chief Executive Officer of Common Sense Media (right).

Banking Clients' Passions

The business banking team realized another opportunity in serving their existing clients, not only where they worked but also where they served on boards of nonprofit schools and organizations. First Republic set out to become a recognized expert in nonprofit lending, deposit and wealth management needs, and found that it further deepened the client relationship when the Bank was able to serve personal, business and passion projects. As Herbert likes to say, "We follow our clients to their businesses and their hearts."

Clients welcomed the support and were more than willing to provide the Bank with further business opportunities. "We will make a loan or do a bond offering for a nonprofit," Gardner said. "But then we say, 'We'd like you as a client, we want to be your bank, and we would like to help you say thanks to your donors and to your directors.'" The ability to build additional relationships from within the organization was a focus of the business banking team at the onset.[28]

Sales Teamwork

By the mid-2000s, as business banking grew and the investment advisory business recovered from the market downturn at the start of the decade, management continued to adjust the Bank's compensation program. The sales and referral process was constantly being tweaked in order to better align it with the offerings of a full-service bank. The management team was convinced that the entire sales effort had to be more seamless.

BALLET BOARD TO BANK BOARD —
THE SAN FRANCISCO BALLET

The San Francisco Ballet is one of Jim and Cecilia Herbert's nonprofit passions, as well as a favorite of many Bank clients in the Bay Area. As a corporate supporter of this venerable company – the oldest ballet company in the country – and to reach like-minded potential clients, First Republic Bank would often run ads in the programs for specific performances.

Herbert's longtime involvement with the Ballet included acting as Chair of the Board of Directors for several years. It also introduced him to fellow Ballet Association Board member Pamela Joyner, with whom he co-chaired the Ballet Board for several additional years. Herbert was impressed with Joyner's intellect, range of professional and personal contacts in the Bay Area, and broad experience in asset management that would add an important point of view to Board discussions. He invited her to join First Republic Bank's Board of Directors in 2004, and she accepted.

Joyner had friends who were devoted First Republic Bank clients, but she was not a client and had not met Herbert until their paths crossed at the Ballet. Accepting Herbert's offer to join the Bank Board was

an easy decision. "What's very compelling about being civically engaged and working in a hands-on way for arts organizations that you love is you sit with people who don't naturally necessarily come into your professional sphere or even social sphere, but you get this diverse group of people working on a common cause," Joyner said. "That is where I got to know Jim, and in that environment I think he works and operates exactly like he does professionally: with a great deal of enthusiasm, with an eye for detail, with a great deal of integrity and in a genuine way. That, I think, epitomizes the basis of the culture of First Republic Bank, which is maybe the secret sauce and formula for its very long-term success." [29]

Helgi Tomasson, Artistic Director of the San Francisco Ballet, pictured with his wife, Marlene, would share a 30th anniversary with First Republic, having joined the company at the same time as the Bank's founding – July 1985.

Pamela Joyner has served on the First Republic Bank Board of Directors since 2004. Herbert and Joyner met while serving on the Board of the San Francisco Ballet, where First Republic Bank client Yuan Yuan Tan is a Principal Dancer.

First Republic Bank began its expansion into the Portland area by focusing on wealth management.

motivated by recent job restructurings and the changing compensation plans at U.S. Trust, which had been acquired by the Charles Schwab Corporation in 2000.[47] The leader of the team, Tige Harris, reached out to Herbert, and the Bank decided to form a Portland office with these professionals as the foundation of its first presence in the state. "Portland was opened starting with investment management, and we built banking around it," August-deWilde said.[48]

"Not Following the Herd over the Cliff"

Meanwhile, as First Republic Bank continued its product, service and footprint expansion, the management team continued to focus on the macroeconomic operating environment. The discussions at the Monday Loan and Tuesday Asset/Liability (ALCO) meetings held company-wide since 1986 to discuss both the company's business and the overall landscape were not unlike those held earlier in the decade: Business was booming across every division, and the only constraints to growth seemed to be a lack of enough hours in the day.

"Real estate markets were going up and everybody was entering the markets," Jason Bender said. "There was just a lot of talk – Are you originating fast enough? Are you securitizing effectively?"

During one particular Monday Loan Meeting at the end of 2005, however, Herbert sat at the table looking increasingly concerned as he listened to his team. The room fell silent. "I hear all of this," he said. "And what this says to me is this is exactly the time for us to tighten our credit underwriting standards." His message did not sink in at first, Bender recalled.

"Everybody kind of said, 'Huh, well, but we're moving up, we're moving up.'"

"Well, things don't go up forever, so now is the time for us to get a bit more conservative," Herbert said matter-of-factly. The Bank tightened its already stringent credit criteria and slowed down a bit, starting at the end of 2005 and continuing into the beginning of 2006. It was a watershed moment for the Bank's leadership team, even if they could not appreciate it fully at the time. Herbert was already preparing them for the downturn that would inevitably follow. He had no way of knowing the severity of the financial crisis to come, but his experience piloting both Westcoast Thrift & Loan and First Republic through good times and bad prepared them for the worst. His instinct for sensing when trouble might be at hand would be highly beneficial – as it was when he led First Republic Bancorp in the late 1980s and secured FDIC deposit insurance before the thrift industry's systemic problems cratered it.

"We were probably a year or so ahead of the curve," Bender said. "I just thought that that was a very interesting example of leading by intuition, but also paying attention and not following the herd over the cliff." [49]

Engine Built and Ready to Run

Following the inflection point of the late 1990s, when First Republic transitioned into a full-service private bank, the first half of the following decade had seen significant strategic and creative expansion – into new geographic markets, and new products and services. At the same time, First Republic continued to produce stable returns for its shareholders, provide exceptional service to its clients, and foster a team of entrepreneurial professionals that were best in class. By 2006, the First Republic engine – its newly expanded platform along with First Republic's client-focused service culture – was finally built out and ready to really run. [50]

The outstanding success, meanwhile, of the Bank and its insightful, experienced leadership team did not go unnoticed. The enterprise had continually attracted inquiries from institutions with an appetite for possible mergers in the past, all of which Herbert and the Board had passed on. And in late 2006, First Republic again caught the independent attention of several leading financial institutions. Among them was one whose accomplished army of financial consultants had earned it the nickname the "thundering herd": Merrill Lynch. ❖

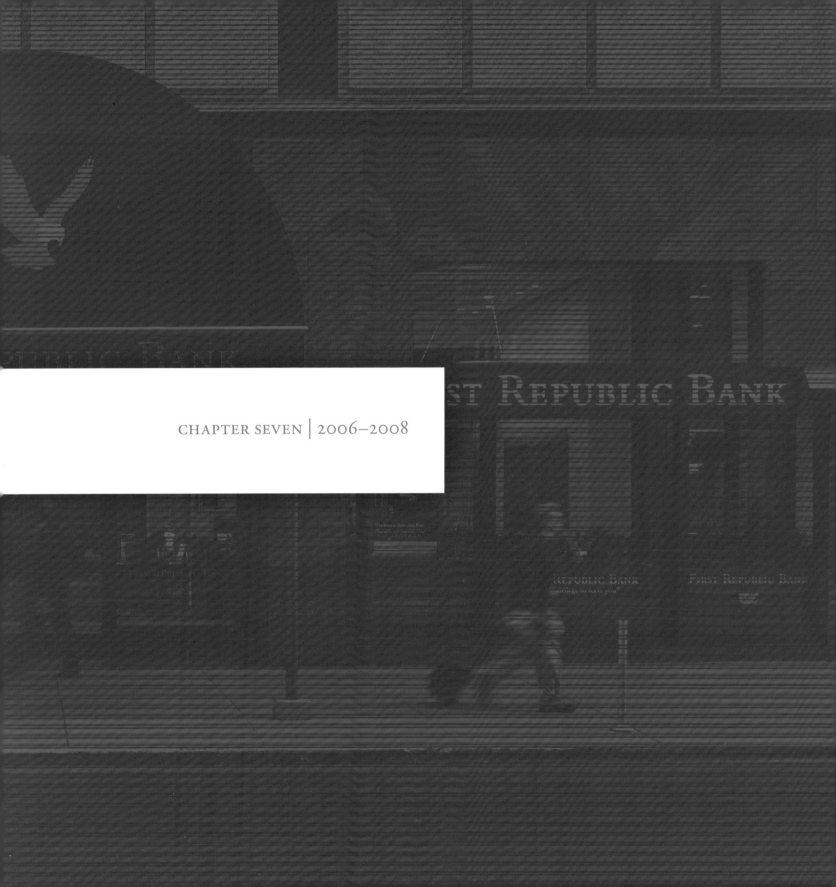

CHAPTER SEVEN | 2006–2008

WALL STREET

Comes Calling

First Republic Bank was on track by the fall of 2006 to post the most profitable year in the Bank's history, with record growth in deposits and loan volume.[1] The Bank's stock, NYSE: FRC, had also risen to an all-time high of $45.96 that summer. Many of its clients also toasted their own success as the securities and real estate markets roared ahead. As First Republic's San Francisco headquarters bustled with the team hard at work, Jim Herbert ducked into his office to take a call one morning.

Merrill Lynch wanted to speak with Herbert. In fact, the financial services giant might be interested in buying First Republic Bank. Herbert's response was immediate and visceral: "That's a crazy idea!" he recalled thinking at the time. "They were so big. Great firm, but so big!"[2] That phone call launched a chain of unforeseen events that unfolded over the next few years, challenging yet ultimately reinforcing First Republic Bank's identity and culture.

* * *

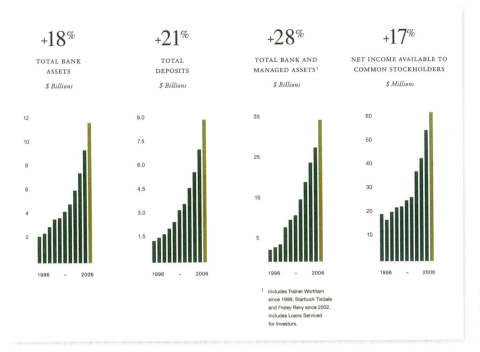

+18%
TOTAL BANK
ASSETS
$ Billions

+21%
TOTAL
DEPOSITS
$ Billions

+28%
TOTAL BANK AND
MANAGED ASSETS[1]
$ Billions

+17%
NET INCOME AVAILABLE TO
COMMON STOCKHOLDERS
$ Millions

[1] Includes Trainer Wortham
since 1999; Starbuck Tisdale
and Froley Revy since 2002.
Includes Loans Serviced
for Investors.

First Republic Bank was experiencing
record results when it was first approached
by Merrill Lynch.
First Republic Bank 2006 Annual Report

In early October 2006, Herbert took a call from Terry Laughlin, Merrill Lynch Senior Vice President and Head of Strategic Growth Opportunities. Herbert agreed to meet Laughlin on October 13th at First Republic Bank's regional headquarters in Manhattan's Rockefeller Center.[3] In order to maintain confidentiality, however, meeting details were not included on Herbert's calendar.

Unexpectedly, Laughlin was accompanied by H. McIntyre "Mac" Gardner, Merrill Lynch's Senior Vice President – Head of Global Private Client Americas Region and Global Bank of Merrill Lynch. Laughlin did most of the talking while Herbert answered his numerous questions and described the Bank's business model – a standard presentation for an audience of investors and Wall Street analysts. It was a cordial meeting, with no specific discussion of Merrill Lynch's interest in the Bank and no plans for a follow-up session.[4] Herbert assumed it was a stand-alone, dead-end meeting. The assumption proved very wrong.

Merrill Lynch's interest persisted and was echoed by others in the industry. Within about two weeks, First Republic Bank was approached by two other potential suitors completely independent of one another. Merger and acquisition activity was on the rise within the financial services industry as a whole. Perhaps, despite having bypassed numerous lesser opportunities in the past, this could be the right time for First Republic to seriously consider such action.

Herbert and his team had not been looking for a buyer or strategic partner. On the contrary, Herbert and Willis Newton, Chief Financial Officer, were laying the groundwork for the Bank to raise additional capital through another preferred stock offering in January to support, in advance, their continued growth. "We weren't looking to sell," Newton said. "In fact, Jim and I, we spotted the opportunities that were going to arise going forward. And we already had a shelf registration to raise the next round of perpetual preferred capital. We were ready to face that next hurdle … We were ready to go."[5]

"It Was a Good Time to Listen"

The unanticipated interest of multiple major financial firms in First Republic Bank, including Merrill Lynch, altered the status quo. "All of a sudden, we had interest from Merrill Lynch and two other well-known firms in a couple of weeks, without solicitation," Herbert said. "So I'm thinking to myself, hmm, I like all the firms. They're great names, but how are we going to merge with any of these folks?"

Herbert and the Board of Directors chose to think through the situation on their own for a bit. During this period of reflection, and with the fiduciary responsibility to shareholders at the forefront, it became clear that economic conditions in general, and specifically conditions in the banking business and in bank stock valuations, were very strong. It was certainly an unusual moment in time. They concluded that it was a very good time to listen carefully, and very possibly take action.

From November through year-end, a small group of senior Bank leaders and their support teams, including Herbert, Newton, Katherine August-deWilde and Jason Bender, played an active role in considering their options, while Herbert confidentially met with the Chief Executive Officer of each Wall Street suitor. He wanted to determine whether there was genuine interest along with a compelling opportunity for the Bank to operate within one of these larger organizations.

Merrill Lynch proposed that First Republic become the bank to complement their highest net worth Private Banking and Investment Group offices.

Following Herbert's lead, the team maintained a strict veil of secrecy over the corporate courtship ritual to ensure that no inkling of a deal might unnaturally inflate the Bank's stock price or otherwise tip off Wall Street that a potential deal was afoot. The confidentiality even extended to spouses, as Crystal Bryant, Herbert's assistant, learned. Bryant reported to Mollie Richardson, Herbert's primary Executive Assistant, and had just joined the Bank that September. "I remember Jim told me it was very confidential and not to tell anyone, including my husband of six months," Bryant said. "So I didn't. I was working weekends, working until midnight, and he would ask, 'Well, what are you working on?' I said, 'I can't tell you.'"[6]

A Partnership Outlined

Despite the fact that Herbert favored continued independence, Laughlin said he wanted to arrange a meeting between Herbert and E. Stanley "Stan" O'Neal, Chairman and Chief Executive Officer of Merrill Lynch.[7]

When O'Neal and Herbert met on December 11th, the Merrill Lynch executive arrived holding a single sheet of paper. As Herbert recalled, Merrill Lynch was interested in First Republic to serve as its "Tiffany's" bank, focused on Merrill's highest net worth clients. Herbert was intrigued but not convinced it would work. He pointed out that Merrill Lynch had nearly 16,000 Financial Advisors,[8] far too many to pair with First Republic Bank's 150 or so Relationship Managers.

The piece of paper O'Neal was holding was a presentation outlining Merrill Lynch's highest net worth Private Banking and Investment Group offices in the United States. They were concentrated in only seven cities, including four of the cities where First Republic already had offices, and they contained only approximately 600 Financial Advisors. The idea was that First Republic would work exclusively with this ultra high-net-worth group. The transaction would be structured to maintain First Republic Bank's brand identity and operations separate from Merrill Lynch and keep First Republic's management team in place.[9]

O'Neal's approach appeared to address many of First Republic's concerns about disappearing into a big institution. But it was not enough to sway Herbert on the spot. "Well, it's interesting," Herbert said. "But this would be a very unusual transaction for us." The meeting ended cordially, with Herbert agreeing to speak further with Robert "Bob" McCann, Merrill Lynch Vice Chairman and President of its Global Private Client Group.[10]

Valued Constituents

As the First Republic Bank team prepared for its next meeting with Merrill Lynch, it was also in discussions with the other two suitors, who appeared equally serious about acquiring the Bank. Herbert attended several private meals and meetings with each, including the Chief Executive Officer of each interested party. The timing seemed like it could be right to pursue such an opportunity, and the offers appeared intriguing and genuine. It did not hurt, Herbert felt, that there could be a bit of a competitive environment in bidding, should it come to that. But Herbert had three important constituent groups to consider: First Republic Bank's shareholders, of course, but also, very importantly, its clients and team members.

He took his fiduciary responsibility to shareholders very seriously, and he realized that these discussions might turn into a tangible opportunity that could create handsome returns. But he also knew that the value of First Republic Bank – and what these suitors most wanted to buy – was in its culture, its best-in-class professionals and ultimately, its clients. Any opportunity would have to take very good care of all of these in order to preserve and maximize buyer value.

"Do We Want the Train to Leave the Station?"

With talks with the various firms progressing – though without any discussion of price with anyone – Herbert decided it was time to raise the corporate courting process to a more serious level. He was spending the first week of January at a health retreat in Florida, with his youngest daughter, Deirdre, which provided a perfect cover for continued talks.

On January 9th and 10th, 2007, in a New York hotel, he, August-deWilde and Bender met with senior leaders of each of these firms, all of whom signed non-disclosure agreements, to discuss additional information in order to better understand how First Republic Bank might fit with each entity.[11] They also met with the Bank's investment banker, Kirk Wilson, who was Vice Chairman of Investment Banking at Morgan Stanley. Wilson had been involved in general discussions with management in early 2006 about strategic alternatives that might include financial partners for the Bank, but the team had only recently sought his advice regarding the current opportunities.[12]

During a special First Republic Board of Directors meeting via telephone on January 11th, 2007,[13] the discussions were reviewed in detail. When talks turned to engaging an investment banker, Herbert replied: "The train leaves the station when you engage a banker. Do we want the train to leave the station or not?" The Board's response, given the high quality of the potential buyers and their apparent seriousness, was yes. Several highly reputable firms were interested in the Bank.[14] And the stocks of First Republic Bank, Merrill Lynch and most other publicly traded financial service companies were trading near record levels, thanks to the 2006 global bull market. The timing looked unusually good.

An Offer on the Table

By mid-January 2007, with the release of its record 2006 financial results only a couple of weeks away, First Republic Bank realized that it could not keep a lid on merger discussions much longer. It still had not discussed price with any suitors. Herbert was concerned that the talks had progressed far enough that some disclosure might soon be required, or that information regarding a potential deal would leak.

First Republic Bank's Board of Directors considered the offer from Merrill Lynch and voted unanimously to proceed with negotiations.

The leadership team was determined to see if it could get any firm offers out of the suitors, or even sign a deal, by the time the Bank was ready to announce its annual earnings. They continued to share financial information with each of the potential buyers and met again with Wilson and his team of investment bankers at Morgan Stanley to discuss strategy.

Following a series of meetings between officials at the Bank and Merrill Lynch on January 16th, Herbert and McCann had lunch alone on January 17th at Merrill Lynch's Lower Manhattan headquarters. As they were wrapping up, Herbert put forth that Merrill Lynch would have to make a very attractive offer. "Well, quite frankly, you have to do something very peremptory," he said. He pointed out that Bank of America had recently agreed to pay around four times tangible book value to the Charles Schwab Corporation for the venerable private bank, U.S. Trust.[15]

Laughlin of Merrill Lynch called Herbert the next morning and asked if they could arrange a meeting that day. They were ready to present their vision for a First Republic-Merrill Lynch partnership. Herbert contacted August-deWilde, who was on the West Coast, and arranged for her to participate in the New York-based meeting via teleconference.[16]

McCann and Gardner arrived at Herbert's Rockefeller Center office and got right to the point. They offered to pay $55 a share for the Bank, with First Republic Bank shareholders able to choose payment for their shares in cash or stock. That equaled $1.8 billion – nearly 3.6 times the Bank's tangible book value and more than a 40 percent premium to the current trading price. Within about 20 minutes, the two Merrill Lynch bankers left.[17]

The First Republic Bank management team met with the Bank's Board of Directors on January 21st to brief them on the offer. They noted that Merrill Lynch wanted Herbert and August-deWilde to sign three-year employment contracts with Merrill Lynch as part of the deal, and that Merrill Lynch wanted the Bank to operate effectively as a stand-alone entity within the proposed parent company. Herbert also voiced that Merrill Lynch was the best fit among the three suitors, feeling that the proposed structure would care best for the Bank's clients, professionals and culture.[18]

The Merrill Lynch offer was a game-changer, as far as the Board was concerned. "We thought that there comes a time, and this may be the time for us, to really take the next substantial step," said Chairman Roger Walther.[19] Longtime Director Marty Gibbs was more emphatic. Accepting the offer was the right thing to do, he said. "It was an offer too good to refuse."[20]

Tom Barrack, Founder, Chairman and Chief Executive Officer of the private equity firm Colony Capital, had served on the First Republic Bank Board since 2001. He had made a career of judging when to buy and sell companies, and he also agreed that the offer was too good to pass up. "The offer from Merrill Lynch was so attractive for shareholder value at the time, that we all looked and said, 'This is a great opportunity,'" Barrack recalled. "An opportunity where a great conglomerate like Merrill could pay an extraordinary price, which would allow this culture to then have a much greater platform to harvest. So it was a win-win for everybody."[21]

The Board voted unanimously to authorize Herbert and his team to continue negotiations with Merrill Lynch. Talks with the other parties continued for a few days but did not proceed.[22] Herbert phoned McCann at Merrill Lynch with the news. In addition, he said that First Republic Bank was going to announce its 2006 year-end earnings in just a few days, on Tuesday, January 30th, 2007, and that it needed to have a signed contract with Merrill Lynch by that date. McCann checked with his management team, called Herbert back and reported that Merrill Lynch was committed to getting a definitive agreement signed in time.[23]

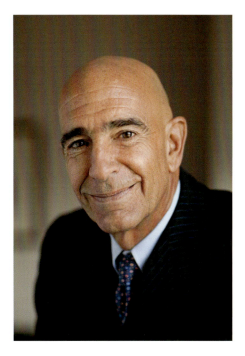

Tom Barrack, who first joined the First Republic Bank Board of Directors in 2001, called the opportunity to sell the Bank to Merrill Lynch a "win-win for everybody."

Maintaining the Culture

Contract negotiations continued throughout the last full week of January 2007. First Republic would relinquish its charter, and Merrill Lynch would operate the Bank as a distinct division within Merrill Lynch Bank & Trust Co., a federal savings bank.

The First Republic Bank brand would remain separate and its management team intact, with substantial autonomy to make strategic and operational decisions. First Republic would not be required to close any branches or divest any deposits. Also, Herbert insisted that members of the First Republic Bank Board of Directors have the option to serve on a non-governance Advisory Board of the First Republic Bank Division for at least one year. The function of this Board was to advise Bank management "with respect to employee matters and strategic business decisions and to assist with the continuity of First Republic client relationships." This very unusual move to retain the Advisory Board would turn out to be extremely valuable.[24]

As the week wound down, the outstanding issues dwindled. Herbert realized, however, that "nowhere in the contract had we laid out clearly the delicacy or importance of the First Republic culture." Herbert very carefully drafted three key paragraphs on the Saturday evening before signing. It was too late to insert them into the merger contract, but they could still include them in Herbert's and August-deWilde's employment contracts. The inclusion of this "culture" section clearly conveyed gravity. This proved essential later, when cited by Herbert in various meetings. "I pulled out the contract and showed them that, and I always said, 'This is the basis upon which we made the deal and it's the basis upon which we'll have a problem should the culture of the enterprise be disrupted.'"[25]

CULTURE IN A CONTRACT

Jim Herbert's insistence that the unique First Republic Bank culture be addressed in his and August-deWilde's employment contracts demonstrated his depth of conviction that the culture of the Bank is its biggest asset. The contract language described First Republic as "a carefully and highly developed culture based upon a fundamental belief that extraordinary client service is a brand differentiator." It characterized its "choice of employees, their ongoing education/training, a complex, highly evolved performance incentive system, and extraordinary fair and respectful treatment" as the key to the success of the enterprise.

Herbert and August-deWilde's contracts also addressed First Republic's ability to deliver extraordinary service through its signature relationship-based model, which is reliant on the empowerment of each individual to best serve his or her client: "each employee's empowerment to individually act to deliver the company's services for the benefit of its clients is essential to continued success. A high level of respect, trust and appropriately delegated authority throughout the organization is the cornerstone of this culture." The contract highlighted the importance of First Republic's ability to remain nimble and continue to evolve within a parent company. It concluded that "both parties agree that changes to such culture, both form and substance, are best undertaken with great care."[26]

A Deal Announced

By the afternoon of Sunday, January 28th, 2007, the final version of the merger contract was ready for a vote by the Boards of First Republic Bank and Merrill Lynch, and it won unanimous approval from both. Early on the morning of Monday, January 29th, 2007, the companies issued a joint press release announcing the transaction.[27]

Herbert's focus on confidentiality throughout the merger process paid off. The $55-a-share price represented a 44 percent premium to the Bank's share price of $38.30 the day prior to the announcement. The lack of movement in the stock prior to the

**MERRILL LYNCH TO ACQUIRE FIRST REPUBLIC BANK
FOR $1.8 BILLION**

*Bi-Coastal Private Banking Presence and Complementary Business
Model to Enhance Merrill Lynch's Private Client Capabilities*

*First Republic to Retain Name, Management, Advisory Board and Strategic Focus as
Separate Division of Merrill Lynch Bank & Trust Co., FSB*

NEW YORK, Jan. 29, 2007 – Merrill Lynch **(NYSE: MER)** and First Republic Bank **(NYSE: FRC)** today announced that they have entered into a definitive agreement for Merrill Lynch to acquire all of the outstanding common shares of First Republic in exchange for cash and stock valued at a fixed price of $55.00 per First Republic share, subject to shareholder elections, for a total transaction value of $1.8 billion. The transaction is expected to be completed in the third quarter of 2007, pending necessary regulatory approvals and approval by First Republic shareholders.

A press release issued January 29th, 2007 outlined details of the Merrill Lynch-First Republic Bank merger.

announcement, despite a flurry of merger-related activity during the preceding few weeks in the market, was a testament to the Bank's success in keeping the deal under wraps.[28]

A shareholder who purchased FRC at the initial public offering in August 1986, and held through the sale to Merrill Lynch in September 2007, experienced a compounded annual growth rate of 23 percent over the 21-year period – more than double the S&P 500, which returned 11 percent over the same period of time.[29]

"A Lot of Trust in the Leadership"

Due in part to the extended regulatory review required, the merger of First Republic Bank into Merrill Lynch did not take effect until September 21st, 2007. Herbert and August-deWilde spent much of the time between the announcement on January 29th and the deal closure on September 21st assuring colleagues and clients that the merger would not in any way diminish the Bank's culture or its commitment

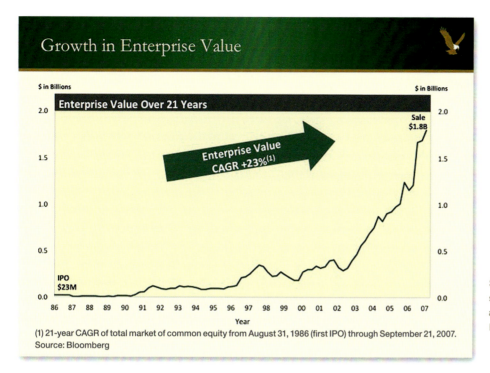

Growth in Enterprise Value

$ in Billions

$ in Billions

Enterprise Value Over 21 Years

2.0

2.0

Enterprise Value CAGR +23%[1]

Sale $1.8B

1.5

1.5

1.0

1.0

0.5

0.5

IPO $23M

0.0

0.0

86 87 88 89 90 91 92 93 94 95 96 97 98 99 00 01 02 03 04 05 06 07

Year

(1) 21-year CAGR of total market of common equity from August 31, 1986 (first IPO) through September 21, 2007.
Source: Bloomberg

Shares of First Republic Bank experienced steady growth since its 1986 IPO, attracting the attention of Merrill Lynch, which purchased the Bank for $55 per share in 2007.

to unparalleled levels of client service. And in some ways, they noted, the deal was likely to boost the Bank's capabilities by providing access to additional capital to fund growth and a wide range of wealth management capabilities.[30]

The trust that Herbert and August-deWilde had developed with the professionals throughout the Bank played a vital role in easing the ownership transition. "They had taken this company through a lot of different cycles and a lot of different chapters," Bender said. "I think a lot of people viewed this as the next chapter. It was a little agonizing, but I think people really trusted Jim and Katherine to lead through this phase just as they had trusted them in the past. I think there was a lot of equity built up and a lot of trust in the leadership of the organization."[31]

Colleagues pulled together in support of the move. Carmen Castro-Franceschi, Executive Managing Director, was on vacation with her husband in Mexico when Herbert reached her by phone to tell her about the deal. She caught the next plane back to San Francisco and headed straight to the office to help with contacting clients.

Castro-Franceschi said that as much as she valued the Bank's independence – which she had experienced over most of the life of the Bank, having joined as one of its first Relationship Managers in 1986 – she had hoped the Bank would make this type of move. In order to continue on its growth trajectory and maintain its superb relationships, especially with its largest clients, this next step would be very beneficial, she felt. "It was at a perfect moment in time in our life as a bank," she said. "We had reached the point with our clients where we were starting to tap out. Our clients were starting to perceive that we weren't large enough for them, and that's a problem. Our clients were growing so fast we had to keep up. We needed more capital. Merrill Lynch allowed us the opportunity to grow with our clients. Clients were very happy; I did not lose one client."[32]

"We Are a Separate Group within Merrill Lynch"

Dyann Tresenfeld, Executive Managing Director and also one of First Republic's first Relationship Managers hired in 1986, felt a similar sense of enthusiasm following the announcement. "It was exciting; it was entering the unknown," she said. And, at least initially, being a part of Merrill Lynch provided a source of new business. "After they purchased us, they did refer some clients. We would receive calls from the 'mother ship' and receive clients for banking and for mortgages," she said. "That actually worked quite well."[33]

First Republic Bank also added clients from among the ranks of Merrill Lynch itself. "I was in charge of helping the traders transition their accounts to First Republic," Margaret Mak said. "Many of them are still my friends."[34]

Bill Dessoffy and his team in the New York region faced a slightly different set of challenges. They were operating in the same market as Merrill Lynch's headquarters. "Clients wanted to know if we were going to be integrated into the Merrill Lynch culture, because they didn't come to us for that," he said. "They were questioning about the ultimate game plan. Were they going to get their information shared with Merrill Lynch, or were they going to have products pushed at them?" He explained, as did so many other First Republic Bank officials during this period, "We are a separate group within Merrill Lynch … that's not our style." [35]

Bob Thornton, President of Private Wealth Management at First Republic, also faced a unique situation. He spent much of the time between the acquisition announcement and its closing assuring his team that they would continue to operate as is. But that was not without its challenges. "What Merrill didn't quite understand was we had worked over the years to build relationships with our clients to meld the wealth management and the banking piece together. It was more of a relationship sale, not a product sale," Thornton said. [36]

Within this atmosphere of combined excitement and apprehension, one thing was clear – the First Republic Bank team banded together across the board to be sure that the clients knew that they would be well taken care of. And confidence in the leadership team was unwavering.

First Republic Bank's clients continued to experience the Bank's same exceptional service before, during and after the sale to Merrill Lynch.

Michael Mondavi, Founder and Coach, Folio Wine Company

Jeff Atkinson, President, Concar Enterprises, Inc.

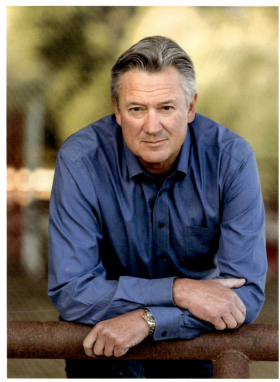

John O'Hurley, Actor, Television Host, Singer/ Pianist/Composer, Author, and Lisa O'Hurley, Wife, Marketing Executive, Mom

"I Don't Think I Noticed Any Interruption"

The Bank worked hard to ensure that the client experience post-merger remained the same as it had always been. "Importantly, the client-facing systems never changed," August-deWilde said. "We were very focused on making sure that client-facing people had all the tools they needed to talk with their clients, and that the people who supported the client – IT, loan servicing, deposit services – that they were able to keep their eye on the client as well. The management of the Bank – the finance function, and to some degree, the IT function – had a lot of interactions with our parent company, but we worked very hard to keep it away from the people who were doing the day-to-day work of meeting with and supporting clients." [37]

Clients were initially anxious about the service implications of the Merrill Lynch partnership. But as their Relationship Managers and Preferred Bankers explained the deliberate structure of the deal, designed with the client experience in mind, their concerns were quelled. "I anticipated a tremendous difference," said First Republic client Russ Flynn, Founder of Flynn Investments, a San Francisco-based real estate company. "I felt, unfortunately, that once Merrill Lynch took over, somebody would start making rules in New York that really didn't apply to San Francisco, because it's a different market from most of the rest of the country."

"I remember having a meeting with Jim and some people from Merrill Lynch and raising those questions. They assured me that the decision-making wasn't going to change. It was going to stay right here in San Francisco," Flynn said. "That proved to be true. I don't think I noticed any interruption, not a ripple." [38]

Mortgage Losses Rock Merrill Lynch

The acquisition was finalized on September 21st, 2007. In announcing the closing, Herbert said he looked forward to providing his clients with access to Merrill Lynch's renowned expertise and broad range of financial services. McCann added that the Bank would accelerate Merrill Lynch's objective of growing its high-net-worth private banking business.

"We have watched and admired this Bank for some time now. Merrill Lynch very much wants First Republic to continue operating as it has. We have no intention of changing this successful formula, rather expanding it," said Merrill Lynch's Bob McCann of the merger.[39]

Unfortunately, however, the excitement over the tremendous opportunity was short-lived. Behind the scenes, and unbeknownst to the management team at First Republic Bank, Merrill Lynch's financial condition had begun to rapidly deteriorate. Fortunately, nearly 70 percent of First Republic Bank shareholders elected to receive cash instead of Merrill Lynch stock, which was trading at $75 at the time of closing, for their shares.[40] Importantly, early on Herbert had made it clear that the deal was to be a final dollar value price, not a final number of shares deal. The drop in Merrill Lynch's stock price, up to closing, therefore, did not have impact. With the exception of Herbert and August-deWilde, those who took shares were not subject to a lockup period and could choose to freely sell them immediately upon close of the deal.[41]

In early October, just a few weeks after the sale closed, Merrill Lynch stunned the team members of its newly acquired private bank, and the rest of the financial world, by predicting a third-quarter loss of $4.5 billion stemming from its exposure to mortgage-backed collateralized obligations. While First Republic Bank executives were still grappling with that news, the real shocker came a few weeks later, on October 24th, when Merrill Lynch disclosed that the actual loss was $7.9 billion, with much of it tied to Merrill Lynch's holdings in subprime mortgages. That left the firm with its largest quarterly loss ever. Its share price plunged to $54 a share by early November and continued to head south over the coming year.[42]

One month later, in November, Chairman and Chief Executive Officer O'Neal was replaced by John Thain, a former Goldman Sachs executive who was Head of the New York Stock Exchange.[43] Other Merrill Lynch executives would follow O'Neal in departing as well over the following months.[44]

"How Do We Keep This Intact?"

As bad as the news was for Merrill Lynch, First Republic's leadership stayed focused on taking care of its clients and colleagues, and on meeting or exceeding its performance projections during this time of crisis.

The Merrill Lynch losses "were clearly a shock to us," said Chief Credit Officer David Lichtman. "We realized that this was not what we had envisioned. We talked about it a lot internally. How do we stay focused on what we do and how we do it and at the same time figure out what to do from a pure corporate perspective? How do we keep this intact?"[45] The answer was to stick to the transition model they had in place for much of 2007, Lichtman said. "Jim and Katherine were exceedingly smart and wise to say 'Focus on doing business, focus on the customers, and let a small handful of people internally have the interface with Merrill.' And I think that worked quite well."[46]

"AT MY DESK, WE WERE OPERATING THE SAME AS ALWAYS"

Dyann Tresenfeld's role after the merger was the same as before, and the same as it had been since she joined First Republic in 1986: to provide outstanding client service and grow the business. As Executive Managing Director, Relationship Management, she closely monitored the First Republic Bank client relationship business and was extremely pleased with what she saw.

"At my desk, we were operating the same as always. The customer had the same experience as always. The customer always asked what was going on because they didn't want to have somebody else's culture," she said. "They wanted First Republic. But their experience was 'Hey, everything's the same. I walk into the branch. The same people are there.'

The way we are operating is exactly the same. We still have money to lend. The programs are the same. The Loan Committee is the same. On the customer service side, for the people on the ground, like me, we were operating as though nothing had happened, honestly."[47]

Under-Promise and Over-Deliver

The Bank determined that on the financial front, the best defense was a good offense. First, it scrutinized its budgets. It exceeded the goals it set for itself by a significant margin. "If we had not been performing well as a management team, then there would have been more pressure to do things differently," said Newton.[48]

The parent company was, for the most part, cheering them on. "Merrill Lynch wanted us to grow," Bender said. "They had a lot of assets that were going south. And they still had capital to spare at that point."[49] In fact, First Republic Bank's total assets grew by $4.2 billion in 2007, up 36 percent from $11.6 billion the year prior, to $15.8 billion. Total assets grew again in 2008, just shy of $4 billion to $19.7 billion, a 25 percent increase.[50]

"Our instructions were, 'You go do what you're best at, grow relationships, and for the time being we're not going to sell any of your loans,'" Bender said. "'We want to keep those, and we want to build up the balance sheet, and we want to build up that base of earning assets.' So for the most part, we just put our heads down and went to work."[51]

During 2008, First Republic put the capital of its parent company to work by continuing to lend within its never-wavering, conservative credit underwriting parameters. The management team decided to raise the Bank's loan rates a bit less than others. As other institutions grappled with their own mounting losses, they retreated from lending activities, particularly jumbo home mortgage lending. Many clients were left looking for alternatives, and First Republic proved to be a good option. Attractive pricing and the reduced competitive activity, coupled with First Republic's growing brand recognition for extraordinary service, resulted in 2008 as the Bank's best year to date, with record loan volumes and profits, along with continued clean credit, despite the turmoil in the markets and economy.[52]

Success at a Price

Herbert, August-deWilde and a handful of other leaders successfully shielded the rest of the Bank from the turmoil within Merrill Lynch. But this success came at a price. "The bottom line was going well, but the interface was not going well," Herbert said. "It was wearing us down tremendously." [53]

One of the most important ways Herbert and August-deWilde kept the small leadership team tasked with interfacing with Merrill Lynch together and focused was to meet regularly for lunch at Schroeder's, an old-fashioned German restaurant near the Bank's San Francisco headquarters. They joked that it was the closest thing First Republic had to an executive dining room. "We had to have a team of six or eight key people thinking exactly the same all the time," Herbert said. "My approach to that has always been just get together. Just have lunch and talk, and then leave. And everybody's on the same page." [54]

Schroeder's in San Francisco served as an informal "executive dining room," where Bank leaders would discuss the state of the Bank and Merrill Lynch, build consensus of perspective and strategy, and honor their cultural commitment to the team.

Developed initially with Babson College, the Culture Carrier Roundtable evolved over time and later included Boris Groysberg, professor of business administration in the Organizational Behavior unit at the Harvard Business School. Groysberg would join the First Republic Board of Directors in 2015 and bring his extensive expertise as a professor, researcher and author on how firms develop, hire, retain and utilize talent to the enterprise.

The First Republic Culture Council

By the spring of 2008, Herbert was concerned that despite its best efforts to keep the Bank insulated from the internal turmoil with Merrill Lynch, both the internal and external economic environment were wearing on all. At risk was a dilution of the unique culture First Republic had established and nurtured with such devotion. "We realized that Merrill Lynch was a different type of culture. Not better or worse, but different," said Dessoffy. "We, at that point, decided that we needed to keep our culture intact. We wanted to make sure that the entrepreneurial culture didn't get lost now that we were within a bigger organization." [55]

Herbert took the lead in establishing a group of Culture Carriers, originally referred to as the Culture Maintenance Council. The small group consisted of representatives across the company who were leaders in the preservation, evolution and communication of the unique First Republic "way." Richardson, Herbert's former Executive Assistant, who acted as Integration Liaison with Merrill Lynch, was charged with developing and leading this group. Its goal: "to guard and preserve for Merrill the core First Republic brand, operating principles and cultural values that have contributed to our historical success." Beginning in July 2008, weekly Thursday meetings were scheduled, during which the Culture Council gathered to discuss what actionable steps were underway to achieve the goal.[56]

Another example of the importance and emphasis placed on First Republic's people and culture, this initiative has since evolved. Today, the Culture Carrier Roundtable is a two-day offsite event, held twice a year, that includes roughly 65 participants, many of whom are new to the enterprise. The group represents all departments and regions, as well as a wide range of career tenures and experience. With discussions centered on the importance of First Republic's culture and how to ensure that it continues to thrive and grow, the diversity of the attendees is intended to stimulate and encourage a team atmosphere across departments and an open environment for discussion, regardless of title or tenure. The one inclusion criterion is that each department-nominated and chosen participant is recognized as a "cultural leader": one who embodies First Republic's values in an actionable way, irrespective of their seniority.

Mollie Richardson sometimes worked from Merrill Lynch's headquarters at Four World Financial Center, to streamline communication during the transition.

"Culture, to me, really means a shared belief system," Richardson said. "These shared values guide you when you don't have a manual, or a set of instructions, or a manager available for a particular opportunity or challenge. And it's important that everyone in the enterprise has an understanding of these values and our culture, in order to ensure that it continues to provide a solid and constant foundation for our interactions with one another and with our clients, as we grow and evolve into the future."[57]

Integration Liaison

Richardson had taken a leave of absence from First Republic Bank in early 2008, using the time to travel and consider her future path. She had served as Herbert's Executive Assistant for several years, including the very intense merger and closing period. Herbert reached out in the spring of that year to persuade her to return to the Bank in the new position of Integration Liaison. Her job was to coordinate communications between the Bank and its new corporate parent. "The role was developed to channel and funnel all of those requests that were causing a strain on the organization … to help minimize that and try to navigate the Merrill requests," she said.[58]

Herbert, August-deWilde and the rest of the leadership team were feeling the wear of juggling the challenges facing Merrill Lynch while also trying to facilitate the logistics of the merger. Herbert felt it necessary to establish a direct line of communication with the parent company. Richardson established an office on the 42nd floor at Merrill Lynch headquarters in Lower Manhattan, next to Gene McQuade, who, as Vice Chairman and President of Merrill Lynch Banks (U.S.), was the executive Herbert reported to at the time. Her job was to improve the Bank's understanding of the Merrill Lynch culture, model and structure; build relationships with their executive team; and assist in the smooth integration of First Republic Bank into the larger institution.

"They would talk to her about us," Herbert said. "And they'd begin to ask her how to get us to do things. And that was the flow of information that we needed. That's how we understood their culture. That was invaluable."[59]

Global Tremors

First Republic Bank's strong performance throughout 2007 and into 2008 was remarkable considering the rapidly deteriorating mortgage markets, primarily in the subprime sector. While a few critics had warned that the huge buildup of the global subprime mortgage market was unsustainable, the lucrative fees derived from packaging and selling subprime mortgages proved irresistible to Wall Street leaders Merrill Lynch, Bear Stearns, Lehman Brothers and others. Even as it was negotiating to buy First Republic Bank in December 2006, Merrill Lynch paid $1.3 billion to acquire First Franklin, which specialized in subprime mortgages.[60]

Within a few months, the global subprime mortgage business started to crumble. In June 2007, hedge fund units within Bear Stearns with such mortgage instruments collapsed, triggering a dramatic rise in interest rates on subprime mortgages. Reverberations from this seismic event in the subprime market played a direct role in the unprecedented losses Merrill Lynch would be forced to take on the market value of its mortgage holdings that fall.[61]

The subprime mortgage crisis brought down financial industry giant Bear Stearns, which would be purchased by JPMorgan Chase in 2008.

Bear Stearns never recovered from the mid-2007 hit to its subprime mortgage business. As the months passed, its financial condition went from bad to worse, and by early 2008 the brokerage firm faced a liquidity crisis. JPMorgan Chase, with financing aided by the Federal Reserve, stepped in to buy Bear Stearns in March 2008. Regulators believed that averted what could become a global financial crisis.[62] But within a matter of months, regulators and financial industry leaders realized that by finding a buyer for Bear Stearns, the global crisis had merely been postponed, not prevented.

Summer of Discontent

By the summer of 2008, "it became clear that the financial world was collapsing and Merrill was going to have to do something," Herbert said. Both Merrill Lynch and Lehman Brothers appeared to be seriously wounded by the mortgage crisis. Determining the depth of the crisis at each company proved difficult for insiders and outsiders alike, especially as the mortgage markets grew increasingly illiquid and the value of each company's mortgage securities portfolio continued to plummet.

Whatever future vision First Republic Bank had for Merrill Lynch as a parent company and partner was fading. The giant financial services firm was more than faltering. Herbert, August-deWilde and the leadership team came to a relatively quick decision. First Republic Bank was a valuable asset. Merrill Lynch needed capital. Herbert and the team decided to propose buying the Bank back from Merrill Lynch.

But even amidst the current turmoil, they could not anticipate the financial calamity that was about to ensue.[63] ❖

"First Republic's level of
service makes banking a
wonderful experience."

PAUL TAYLOR'S AMERICAN MODERN DANCE
Paul Taylor, Choreographer

FIRST REPUBLIC BANK

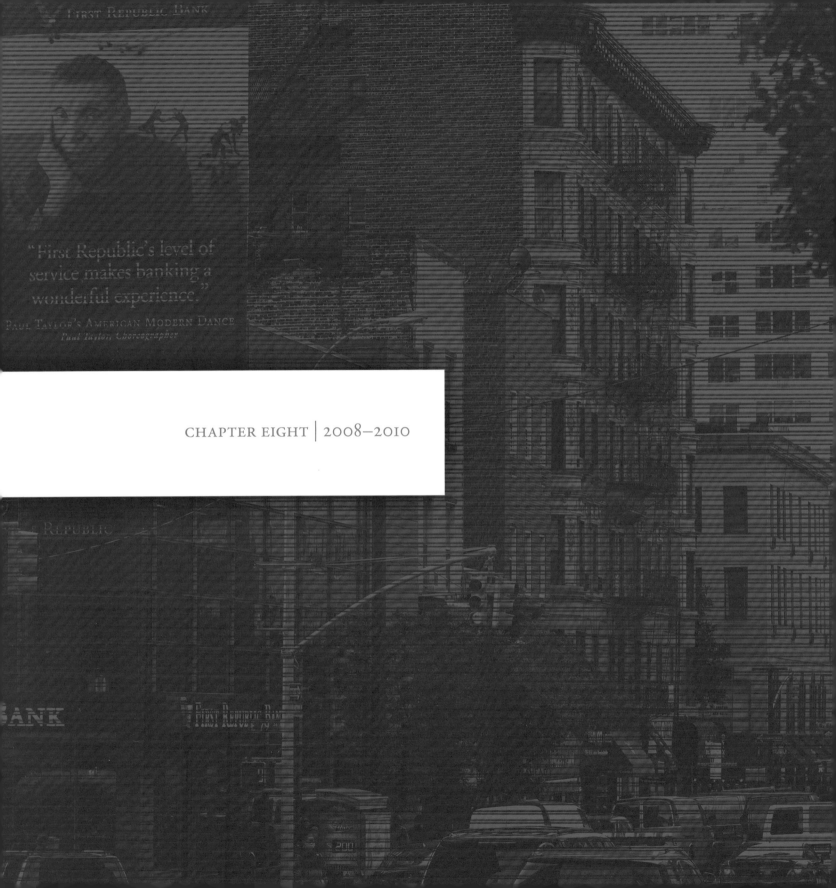

CHAPTER EIGHT | 2008–2010

"First Republic's level of service makes banking a wonderful experience."

PAUL TAYLOR's AMERICAN MODERN DANCE
Paul Taylor, Choreographer

Independent

AGAIN

"One of the Most Dramatic Days in Wall Street's History"

The systemic troubles afflicting the financial industry continued to build over the summer of 2008. JPMorgan Chase's acquisition of Bear Stearns following Bear Stearns' fatal exposure to subprime mortgages turned out not to be an anomaly, but rather just one of the first dominoes to fall. As Jim Herbert and the team recognized Merrill Lynch's precarious position due to the same exposure, they worked around the clock to find an alternative arrangement for First Republic Bank. While contemplating strategies in late August and early September, no one anticipated the events soon to come.

In what the *New York Times* described as "one of the most dramatic days in Wall Street's history," on Sunday, September 14th, 2008, a prominent and storied investment firm, Lehman Brothers, filed for bankruptcy protection, and Merrill Lynch – in the same 48-hour period – agreed to sell itself to Bank of America.[1]

***

The troubled financial services industry experienced another blow when Lehman Brothers filed for bankruptcy in September 2008.

John Thain, Chief Executive Officer of Merrill Lynch, and Ken Lewis, Chief Exective Officer of Bank of America, celebrate the merger of their two companies.

From: Bryant, Crystal **On Behalf Of** Herbert, Jim
Sent: Monday, September 15, 2008 6:35 AM
To: All Company
Subject: Our continued commitment to service

Last evening, Merrill Lynch agreed to be acquired by Bank of America for about $29 a share.

We have limited information about this acquisition. We expect to know more as the day progresses and will share information as it becomes available.

What we do know is this: First Republic Bank is a unique model in banking. We have built this model on a base of individual professional excellence and an extraordinary commitment to client service. We are not wavering from that commitment. And we ask each of you to do your best to continue the success of First Republic. Our clients deserve nothing less.

Jim and Katherine

FIRST REPUBLIC BANK
It's a privilege to serve you®

Bank of America Purchases Merrill Lynch

Bank of America Chief Executive Officer Ken Lewis agreed to acquire Merrill Lynch for roughly $50 billion, or about $29 a share.[2] The Board of Directors of each company approved the sale, which would close the first week of January 2009. The plan for First Republic to act as the private bank for Merrill Lynch's high-net-worth clients might have worked, had macroeconomic turmoil and financial deterioration not occurred. But it was challenging for management to now see how First Republic might fit within Bank of America, which had already acquired U.S. Trust to serve as its private banking enterprise.[3] A sale of First Republic could certainly be beneficial to Bank of America as well, eliminating the redundancy of holding two private banks – First Republic and U.S. Trust – and providing a much-needed infusion of capital.

The First Republic management team went into action. Herbert sent a letter to John Thain, the new Chairman and Chief Executive Officer of Merrill Lynch following Stan O'Neal's departure, proposing the buyback and requesting a meeting. Orchestrating a buyback would be an enormous undertaking and an unlikely feat to complete before the purchase by Bank of America closed in January, but Herbert was undeterred.[4] He, along with many, assumed that Thain would continue on as the head of Merrill Lynch post-merger. Unfortunately, that was not the case.

Bank of America completed its purchase of Merrill Lynch on January 1st, 2009.

 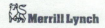

MERGER PROPOSED — YOUR VOTE IS VERY IMPORTANT

Dear Stockholder:

On September 15, 2008, Merrill Lynch & Co., Inc. and Bank of America Corporation announced a strategic business combination in which a subsidiary of Bank of America will merge with and into Merrill Lynch. If the merger is completed, holders of Merrill Lynch common stock will have a right to receive 0.8595 of a share of Bank of America common stock for each share of Merrill Lynch common stock held immediately prior to the merger. In connection with the merger, Bank of America expects to issue approximately 1.710 billion shares of common stock and 359,100 shares of preferred stock (the terms of which are described starting on page 93).

The market value of the merger consideration will fluctuate with the market price of Bank of America common stock. The following table shows the closing sale prices of Bank of America common stock and Merrill Lynch common stock as reported on the New York Stock Exchange on September 12, 2008, the last trading day before public announcement of the merger, and on October 30, 2008, the last practicable trading day before the distribution of this document. This table also shows the implied value of the merger consideration proposed for each share of Merrill Lynch common stock, which we calculated by multiplying the closing price of Bank of America common stock on those dates by 0.8595, the exchange ratio.

	Bank of America Common Stock	Merrill Lynch Common Stock	Implied Value of One Share of Merrill Lynch Common Stock
At September 12, 2008	$33.74	$17.05	$29.00
At October 30, 2008	$22.78	$17.78	$19.58

The merger is intended to qualify as a "reorganization" within the meaning of Section 368(a) of the Internal Revenue Code of 1986, as amended, and holders of Merrill Lynch common stock are not expected to recognize any gain or loss for United States federal income tax purposes on the exchange of shares of Merrill Lynch common stock for shares of Bank of America common stock in the merger, except with respect to any cash received instead of fractional shares of Bank of America common stock. However, under some circumstances described in this document, the merger will not qualify as a reorganization, and each of us has agreed that in such circumstances we would complete the merger on a taxable basis.

The market prices of both Bank of America common stock and Merrill Lynch common stock will fluctuate before the merger. You should obtain current stock price quotations for Bank of America common stock and Merrill Lynch common stock. Bank of America common stock is quoted on the NYSE under the symbol "BAC." Merrill Lynch common stock is quoted on the NYSE under the symbol "MER."

At a special meeting of Bank of America stockholders, Bank of America stockholders will be asked to vote on the issuance of Bank of America common stock in the merger and certain other matters. The stock issuance proposal requires the votes cast in favor of such proposal to exceed the votes cast against such proposal at the special meeting by holders of Bank of America common stock and 7% Cumulative Redeemable Preferred Stock, Series B, which we refer to as Series B Preferred Stock, voting together without regard to class.

At a special meeting of Merrill Lynch stockholders, Merrill Lynch stockholders will be asked to vote on the adoption of the merger agreement and certain other matters. To adopt the merger agreement and to approve the related certificate amendment requires the affirmative vote of the holders of a majority of the outstanding shares of Merrill Lynch common stock entitled to vote.

Holders of Merrill Lynch preferred stock and holders of depositary shares representing Merrill Lynch preferred stock are not entitled to and are not being requested to vote at the Merrill Lynch special meeting.

The Bank of America board of directors unanimously recommends that Bank of America stockholders vote FOR the proposal to issue shares of Bank of America common stock in the merger and FOR the other related proposals.

The Merrill Lynch board of directors unanimously recommends that Merrill Lynch stockholders vote FOR adoption of the merger agreement and FOR the other related proposals.

This document describes the special meetings, the merger, the documents related to the merger and other related matters. Please carefully read this entire document, including "Risk Factors" beginning on page 23 for a discussion of the risks relating to the proposed merger. You also can obtain information about our companies from documents that each of us has filed with the Securities and Exchange Commission.

KENNETH D. LEWIS
Chairman, Chief Executive Officer and
President Bank of America Corporation

JOHN A. THAIN
Chairman and Chief Executive Officer
Merrill Lynch & Co., Inc.

Neither the Securities and Exchange Commission nor any state securities commission has approved or disapproved the Bank of America common stock or preferred stock to be issued under this document or determined if this document is accurate or adequate. Any representation to the contrary is a criminal offense.

The date of this document is October 31, 2008, and it is first being mailed or otherwise delivered to Bank of America and Merrill Lynch stockholders on or about November 3, 2008.

A Bank within a Bank

Bank of America managed First Republic with a light touch, initially. "They were bankers. They knew we were bankers," Ed Dobranski said. "They knew what we were doing, and I think they said, 'These guys know what they're doing. We don't really have to have a lot of oversight with them.'" [5]

The First Republic management team worked nonstop during the fall of 2008, dealing with both the merger of Merrill Lynch with Bank of America and the building macroeconomic crisis. The team also quietly prepared to seize any chance to become independent again, should an opportunity become more concrete.

As challenging as it was for the team to see how First Republic might fit within Bank of America, it was equally as daunting for its team members and clients. A venerable financial institution, Bank of America was a much larger enterprise with a different approach to banking, compared to the boutique, high-touch banking experience afforded by First Republic. As Scott Dufresne, Regional Managing Director of First Republic Bank in Boston, recalled, "I think Bank of America woke up and said, 'What's this First Republic?' I don't think they realized when they bought Merrill Lynch that they also had this little tagalong called First Republic." [6]

While Herbert and the First Republic management team worked tirelessly on all fronts, Herbert also recognized that communication was more important than ever. Having always maintained a very transparent approach to management, the team spent time reassuring their First Republic colleagues of the importance of staying focused on taking care of their clients. "Jim and Katherine and Willis and Ed and David – the Bank's communication was amazing," remembered Mary Deckebach, Regional Managing Director of First Republic Bank in Los Angeles. "Their ability to buffer us from the problems that were going on was remarkable." [7]

Despite the substantial tumult in the financial services industry, First Republic continued to focus on providing extraordinary service.

Equally as important was communication to First Republic's clients. Emphasizing the continued stability and autonomy of First Republic, despite the storm surrounding it, Herbert, Katherine August-deWilde and the leadership team did not retreat to their offices but rather spent hours each week reassuring clients and the team, maintaining their visibility and open lines of communication.

Shelter from the Storm

While the disruption due to the Bank of America-Merrill Lynch merger was significant, it paled in comparison to the turbulence resulting from the United States' deteriorating economic condition. Scott Dufresne did not initially understand why, in the early stage of the economic crisis, so many of his peers at other financial institutions were calling to ask, "Are you okay?" From his point of view, it was business as usual. "Then, all of a sudden, the light went on and I realized that as much as it was business as usual for us, it was not for many other banks."[8]

As a result of First Republic Bank's tight and unwavering credit standards, it had very few loan delinquency problems. "We weren't in the subprime business," recalled Bill Dessoffy, Regional Managing Director of First Republic Bank in New York. "Quite frankly, we were maybe ignorant to it, that we never did that type of business. When we found out what banks were doing, we were astonished that so many were

putting money to work in that kind of space."[9] While media coverage circled around the growing number of financial institutions announcing losses, First Republic continued to lend as it always had – while reporting low delinquencies and record profits. "It was almost surreal going through the recent financial crisis," said Dyann Tresenfeld. "We operated like usual. Our underwriting standards didn't change. We asked for the same pieces of paper that we did when the Bank was started in the 1980s."

Though the crisis certainly presented significant challenges, it also afforded First Republic's relationship banking model an opportunity to further distinguish the Bank from its competitors. First Republic's bankers approach client relationships with the intention of serving as trusted advisors over a lifetime, rather than just engaging in transactions. This long-term, relationship-based banking, and the ability to stay focused on client service without being distracted by troubled assets, allowed First Republic Bank to continue to grow. While other banks froze their lending activity altogether in order to engage in damage control, "during the difficult times, we actually gained a lot of market share," said Tresenfeld. "People were grateful. Our current clients learned how fortunate they were that they had chosen an institution that happened to keep on trucking, keep lending during the very difficult time that was occurring in the entire country."[10]

First Republic stayed committed to and focused on providing extraordinary client service, despite the troubling times.

"You've Got Two Weeks"

Though First Republic thought it might not change hands for the moment, its future was still very uncertain. The First Republic Bank management team tried to ascertain Bank of America's intentions. In early September, out of frustration, Herbert flew to New York with no agenda except to try to engage the decision-makers at Bank of America.

When he could get no one to respond, he called Dick Barrett, Vice Chair of Merrill Lynch and a longtime investment banking acquaintance. Barrett agreed to have a cup of coffee that afternoon. Herbert explained that he had assembled a bidding group that included Colony Capital, General Atlantic and the First Republic management team. "We can go really fast, trust me," Herbert assured him. He outlined, in about four sentences, the proposed deal. "We played fairly. You've got to give us a chance." [16]

Barrett left the room, for what was seemingly forever to Herbert, to consult his colleagues. Upon return, Barrett stunned Herbert with the news: "Okay, you've got two weeks." [17]

Move Forward, Move Fast

If ever First Republic Bank had to embrace one of its core values – Move Forward, Move Fast – it was now. Herbert's first and second calls were to Barrack and Ford: "We've got it if we can move fast enough." Boarding a plane back to San Francisco, Herbert mobilized the teams into action. The Bank now needed to negotiate a letter of intent with Bank of America, get indications of regulatory approvals, and raise about $2 billion in equity in firm commitments – all in two weeks.

The first order of business was to take the verbal commitment and turn it into a firm letter of intent. Herbert believed that the Bank of America team did not just arbitrarily choose this two-week time period – he felt the full integration of First Republic into Bank of America's subsidiary U.S. Trust might be about to begin in the next few weeks.

In a conference room at Bank of America's partially open new headquarters at One Bryant Park, Jim Herbert received the news: First Republic Bank's management team had two weeks to pull together its management-led buyback of the Bank.

In order to negotiate a letter of intent, Herbert asked Barrack to take the lead as a "new face," working directly with Michael Rubinoff, Head of Bank of America-Merrill Lynch Global Financial Institutions Corporate & Investment Banking. Ford, in full support, also pledged his continued and critical backing to the management team. Barrack, in constant communication with Herbert, negotiated with Rubinoff extensively, skillfully, and quickly to hammer out a deal. A letter of intent was agreed upon that weekend.

Before becoming effective and being announced, however, absolutely firm commitments of funding had to be confirmed and likely regulatory approval determined. The two lead private equity firms, Colony Capital and General Atlantic, each independently committed approximately $400 million toward the $2 billion needed. The objective was to raise the purchase price, plus enough additional capital to provide the new First Republic with roughly 8 percent tangible equity capital post-deal, allowing plenty of room for development.

This left a remaining $1.2 billion still needed. The proposed buyback would have to be a "club" deal, as regulators would not approve a deal in which any one investor, or coordinated investors, owned more than 24.9 percent.[18]

"We thought it was a brilliant thing to do," Barrack said, "because we knew the team and we knew the culture. Jim really believed in it. It was absolutely the right bet for us at the time." Barrack, along with Nanula, who led Colony's team, was working once again with the First Republic Management team.[19]

"We felt that we were true partners with management and could help them accomplish their goal of buying the Bank back," Ford said about General Atlantic's involvement.[20] Marc McMorris, a Partner at General Atlantic, also served as a key leader of the General Atlantic team.

As part of the equity-raising process, Herbert and the management team reached out to other investors. "Jim went back to the old gang. He went around the table, and

First Republic Bank's reputation helped foster productive talks with federal regulators at the Federal Deposit Insurance Corporation in Washington, D.C.

we all put up money," said Roger Walther. Walther, who founded First Republic alongside Herbert, had stepped off the Board of Directors when the Bank was acquired by Merrill Lynch because he was a longtime member of the Charles Schwab Board of Directors.[21] He would return to First Republic Bank as Chairman Emeritus.

Herbert, August-deWilde and Dobranski, as well as Barrack and Ford, traveled overnight to Washington, D.C., for meetings with banking regulators at the Federal Reserve and the FDIC. The regulators were very busy dealing with troubled banks, so the request to form a new, known as "de novo," non-distressed, stand-alone bank of First Republic's size – with approximately $18 billion in assets – was unique. The team also met with the California state banking regulators to discuss obtaining a new charter. "They had not granted any de novo charters for about two years for a bank of any size, never mind ours," Dobranski said. "It was all troubled banks they were dealing with at the time."[22]

First Republic Bank's reputation and clean, profitable operating history, along with the help of its deal counsel, H. Rodgin Cohen of Sullivan & Cromwell, likely eased federal and state regulators' concerns. They could feel a certain confidence that this was not another troubled bank in the making. Also reassuring was the management team's arms-length relationship with the investors, as well as the fact that Colony Capital and General Atlantic had never worked together and had only recently been introduced to each other by Herbert and August-deWilde.

David Lichtman, Chief Credit Officer, and teams from credit approval, credit administration and loan servicing were also working around the clock, assisting potential investors in reviewing the loan portfolio. As part of the buyback agreement, First Republic could leave up to $2.5 billion in assets of its choosing with Bank of America. The credit team painstakingly reviewed each deal to determine what would stay behind. "We had to go find another approximately $2 billion of perfectly performing loans to leave behind," Lichtman said.[23] Only about $500 million identified were even classified.[24]

Bank of America selling First Republic Bank

Private-equity firms reportedly buying private bank for more than $1 billion

 Associated Press

updated 10/21/2009 2:20:53 PM ET

CHARLOTTE, N.C. — Bank of America Corp. said Wednesday it has agreed to sell First Republic Bank, a private bank it inherited from Merrill Lynch & Co., to a group of investors.

The buying group is led by private-equity firms General Atlantic LLC and Colony Capital. As part of the deal, the bank's top management, including founder and chairman James Herbert II, will stay on board.

Finish Line

After just over two weeks of around-the-clock work, the team made their deadline. On October 21st, 2009, a binding contract was signed with Bank of America to purchase the assets and liabilities of First Republic Bank.[25]

Merrill Lynch purchased First Republic Bank for $1.8 billion in September 2007. By October 2009, at the time of the contract with Bank of America, First Republic had nearly doubled its assets and tripled its profits since the purchase in 2007. Essentially, the institution that sold for $1.8 billion was repurchased, larger and more profitable, two years later for less – a true sign of the times.[26]

In spite of the dramatic downturn in the economy, First Republic Bank grew significantly during the time it was a part of Merrill Lynch, then Bank of America, recording a more than fivefold increase in profitability from $62 million in 2006 to $347 million in 2009.[27]
First Republic Bank 2009 Annual Report

STRENGTH, STABILITY AND GROWTH

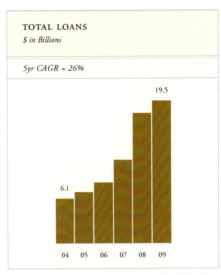

TOTAL LOANS
$ in Billions

5yr CAGR = 26%

6.1 ... 19.5

04 05 06 07 08 09

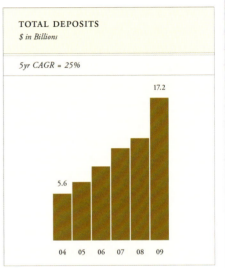

TOTAL DEPOSITS
$ in Billions

5yr CAGR = 25%

5.6 ... 17.2

04 05 06 07 08 09

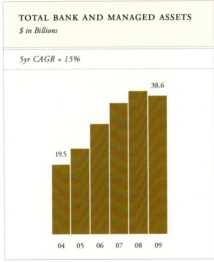

TOTAL BANK AND MANAGED ASSETS
$ in Billions

5yr CAGR = 15%

19.5 ... 38.6

04 05 06 07 08 09

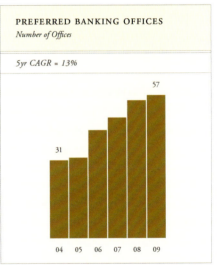

PREFERRED BANKING OFFICES
Number of Offices

5yr CAGR = 13%

31 ... 57

04 05 06 07 08 09

The transaction could not close until the Bank had all the necessary final regulatory approvals. That nine-month-long undertaking involved repeated meetings with regulators both in Washington, D.C. and San Francisco. Mollie Richardson took the lead in managing the complex divestiture process of separating First Republic from Bank of America. At the height of this effort, Richardson, along with Nancy Segreto, Senior Vice President of Lending Services, and Jared Souter, Vice President and Chief Data Officer, and their colleagues at Bank of America, was managing close to 40 work streams, as virtually every aspect of the way in which First Republic Bank interfaced with Bank of America had to be reviewed and, in effect, unwound. Several internal teams across First Republic worked diligently as people rallied around the effort to complete the transaction and cross the finish line. Luckily, First Republic's systems had remained independent, making this process, while extensive, more manageable.

Independent Future

At the close of business on June 30th, 2010, it was time to celebrate. The deal closed and First Republic Bank was a stand-alone entity once again.[28] Parties were held across First Republic's footprint, as employees toasted the achievement of regained independence.

One celebration in particular captured the enduring strength of the First Republic Bank culture. After First Republic Bank had been sold to Merrill Lynch in the fall of 2007, a dinner was held in California for nearly 40 senior officers of the Bank. Virtually the exact same group convened in the summer of 2010 to toast the success of buying the Bank back from Bank of America.

"That showed you that we stuck together as a team," said Bill Dessoffy, who gladly traveled from New York for both events. "We didn't have employees running for the door, and we didn't have clients running for the door," he said. "That's communication, that's working together as a team. We had 1,200 employees at the time, and we were able to keep the whole thing together through the midst of the storm. When you look back on it, it's truly amazing."[29]

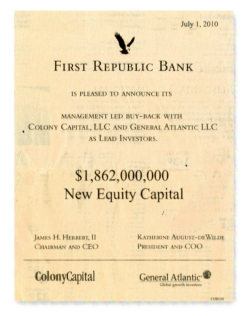

First Republic Bank announced the completion of its management-led buyback on July 1st, 2010.

After receiving First Republic Bank's new charter on June 30th, 2010, Jim Herbert and Katherine August-deWilde celebrated the Bank's independence with San Francisco colleagues, in the office and at Schroeder's, a local, favorite pub of the team.

Throughout the Merrill Lynch and Bank of America experience, one crucial element prevailed – the spirit of First Republic Bank's people and culture. The esprit de corps among employees was deepened by the experience of persevering and growing through multiple ownership changes and an economic crisis. The values articulated years earlier, emphasizing camaraderie and excellence in client service, guided the Bank through the internal and external turbulence. First Republic emerged from the onslaught of challenges strong, stable, autonomous, and well-positioned to capitalize on changing market conditions and competitive opportunities. Additionally, the Bank could now focus on nurturing the next generation of leaders to assume greater responsibility as it moved forward into the future. ❖

In December 2012, the First Republic Bank leadership team returned once again to Schroeder's to recount the days leading up to the buyback of the Bank. The site of many such gatherings, Schroeder's served as a "home base" for the team throughout the turbulent years prior.

"We're poised for
continued growth with an

extra

ordinary

base of clients."

CHAPTER NINE | 2011–2014

LOOKING BACK,

Moving Forward

Jim Herbert, Katherine August-deWilde and the management team paused to savor the moment as they took the helm of the newly independent First Republic Bank on July 1st, 2010. As fate would have it, First Republic Bancorp opened its doors 25 years earlier, almost to the date. "There is nothing that cements a culture more than a successful challenge that the team overcomes as a group," Herbert said. "When we came out, we had – and still have – a great deal of energy, a sense of group accomplishment and success in terms of having stayed our way through the storm."[1]

The team did not pause for long, however; they needed to make up for lost time. The Bank had roughly doubled in size since the sale to Merrill Lynch in 2007 from approximately $10 billion to $20 billion in total assets. While other financial service institutions were distracted by their own mounting problems due to subprime lending activity and investments, First Republic, as both a part of Merrill Lynch and later Bank of America, was able to focus on taking care of its clients and acquiring new ones. But limits on hiring while part of Bank of America left First Republic understaffed in some areas, as the team had not been able to engage in sustained succession planning. While the Bank had maintained its own systems and procedures, they were in need of some investment as well. And importantly, management needed to provide an exit strategy for their private equity investors, who owned approximately 73 percent of the private company's shares and would look to liquidate their investment in due course.[2]

"The fundamental tenet of the business plan," Herbert said, "was to re-establish the enterprise at all levels from a depth of leadership and management point of view, from a systems and procedures point of view, and of course from a capital point of view."[3] Having bought back the assets of First Republic at a discount – for approximately 96 cents on the dollar – the leadership team planned to use this income gained from the purchase discounts to fund the further strengthening and expansion of the enterprise.

* * *

Growing the Team

The need for greater depth and breadth of staff was company-wide. Beginning in 1997 and during the decade leading up to the sale to Merrill Lynch, First Republic had undergone a strategic shift into a full-service private banking institution. It then added investment management and business banking products and services, as well as expanded to New York and Boston. Though the expanded platform structure was completed, it was not fully developed or staffed prior to the Bank's sale in 2007.

Merrill Lynch and Bank of America could not justify adding significant numbers of employees at First Republic Bank as they slashed headcounts in other divisions during the financial crisis, irrespective of how well First Republic was performing. "They wouldn't let us hire any people, and I don't just mean at the top. I mean throughout the company," Herbert said. "We had been constrained considerably, so we launched a meaningful increase in hiring for the first 12 months or so."[4]

Within a matter of weeks of re-emerging as an independent bank, First Republic was adding people across departments. From Wealth Advisors and Relationship Managers in New York to Preferred Banking staff in San Francisco, First Republic was in the market for professionals who wanted to work in a safe environment where the client came first. By December 31st, 2013, First Republic Bank had 2,388 full-time equivalent employees, representing a close to 60 percent increase in headcount from year-end 2010.[5]

First Republic Bank has always looked for professionals who want to prove they can excel at client service using a range of skills. "We're looking for someone who does more than one thing," August-deWilde said. "We are looking for the person who, if they're a lender, has good credit skills, as well as skills in sales, service and advice. If they're an investment management professional, it's sales, investment management expertise and advice."[6]

Regional Managing Directors Barbara Palmer (top), James Meany (center) and Shiva Sattar (bottom) joined First Republic following divestiture to lead the Portland, OR, Palm Beach, FL and South Coastal California regions, respectively.

A Second Initial Public Offering

The process of adding new professionals was just getting under way during the fall of 2010 when Herbert and the Board of Directors perceived and seized an opportunity in the marketplace. Herbert and August-deWilde defined as their top priority exceeding the operating objectives in the business plan as they worked with their private equity partners. Going public once again, to raise capital and provide liquidity opportunities for the private equity groups, was a bit further down on their agenda.

Then, the investing climate shifted. In the fall of 2010, investors, who had shunned bank stocks since the early days of the financial crisis, suddenly had an appetite for them again. Broad stock indices in the United States had rallied dramatically from their early 2009 lows. Many investors appeared to believe that the bad news was mostly in the rear-view mirror as the economy slowly gathered momentum.[7]

BEST PRIVATE BANK IN NORTH AMERICA

First Republic Bank may have needed to get more hands in many of its offices when it emerged as an independent bank, but it clearly had not lost a step when it came to providing exemplary client service. That was the verdict from *Private Asset Management* magazine, which, in February 2011, named First Republic Bank the Best Private Bank in North America. The Bank also won top honors in the category of Best Private Client Service. It would continue to earn top honors in 2012, 2013 and 2014, as well. "This honor reflects First Republic's focus on exceptional client service and stellar credit quality," Herbert said.[8]

The leadership team of First Republic Bank celebrated an eventful year at the end of 2010. It had completed its management-led buyback from Bank of America and had already gone public once again.

The Board of Directors for the newly-independent First Republic Bank included new leaders along with those who were on the Board prior to the sale to Merrill Lynch.

Sandra Hernández, President and Chief Executive Officer of the California HealthCare Foundation, joined the Bank's Board of Directors in 2010. Prior to the California HealthCare Foundation, Hernández was the Chief Executive Officer of The San Francisco Foundation for 16 years, bringing a deep knowledge of the enterprise's home market to the Board.

Herbert, having sought input from many sources, met with the Bank's Board of Directors to discuss a quick "second" initial public offering, to take advantage of the strong market conditions. He wanted to leverage the interest in and demand for bank stocks to boost the Bank's capital levels and begin to create liquidity for the private equity investors. The Bank already more than met regulatory capital requirements, but a smaller offering – which would provide a modest amount of capital for the Bank along with initial proceeds to the private equity investors – seemed within the realm of possibility. The Board agreed. "The capital markets don't wait on anybody, so when you can go public, you go public," Herbert said.[9]

On December 8th, 2010, less than six months after the management-led buyback, First Republic Bank priced its offering, led by Bank of America Merrill Lynch Securities, and became a public company once again. The deal, with 12.6 million shares at $25.50 a share, represented a total enterprise value of $3.2 billion. Reinitiating access to capital markets was an important step to expanding the Bank's investor base. The deal raised $109.8 million for the Bank after expenses and provided handsome returns to the rest of the initial investor group.[10]

The offering served the important purpose of setting a share price of $25.50 for the Bank's stock, which was once again trading on the New York Stock Exchange under the symbol FRC. The private equity investors and the management group had paid $15 per share to buy the company only six months earlier. This significant increase of 70

First Republic Bank shares increased from $15 per share at the time of the sale from Bank of America to $25.50 as its initial public offering price, less than six months later.

percent in share value in less than six months was viewed by the market as evidence of a successful buyout and management partnership with private equity investors.[11]

Following the December 2010 offering, Herbert knew his next shareholder responsibility was "to create a deep public marketplace for our initial backers."[12] Private equity investors in general seek to liquidate investments at a profit over a relatively short time frame. The Bank's private equity investors, while strongly supportive of the management team, were no exception.

Investor Outreach

Herbert and Mollie Richardson, who headed Investor Relations for the Bank, along with Willis Newton, Chief Financial Officer, and Mike Roffler, Deputy Chief Financial Officer, led the effort to create a liquid market for FRC. They traveled on a series of non-deal road shows and participated in numerous other meetings and events in order to increase investor interest in First Republic Bank's stock. They also worked diligently to build research coverage, spending time with Wall Street securities analysts. Many investors and analysts alike found the story of First Republic Bank an interesting opportunity for investment or coverage. By the end of 2012, close to 20 investment firms had launched research coverage of First Republic.[13]

Jody Lindell first joined the Bank's Board of Directors in 2003. President and Chief Executive Officer of S.G. Management Inc., Lindell's experience leading the asset management firm and her background as a partner with KPMG provide valuable leadership perspectives for First Republic.

An expanded leadership team extended beyond management to the Board of Directors, with additional seats approved to address the needs of the growing enterprise. With experience as the former Chief Executive Officer of the New York Stock Exchange and as a prior partner at The Goldman Sachs Group, Inc., along with varied philanthropic ventures, Duncan Niederauer joined the First Republic Bank Board of Directors in 2015.

At the time of the buyback from Bank of America in July 2010, Colony Capital and General Atlantic owned 21.8 percent each of the company's shares, with the remaining private equity investors holding 29.1 percent in total. Through a secondary offering and a series of block trades, these firms liquidated their positions in the few years following. By April 2012, Colony Capital and General Atlantic had each reduced their holdings by about half.[14] By April of the next year, their stakes dropped by half again, each holding only approximately 5 percent of outstanding shares.[15]

By late July 2013, just over three years after the Bank regained its independence, none of the initial private equity funds had ownership stakes remaining in First Republic. From January 1st, 2012, through July 22nd, 2013, roughly 68 million First Republic Bank shares, or 52 percent of the total shares outstanding, were absorbed into the public market.[16] Despite the steady flow of shares into the market as the private equity firms liquidated their investment, FRC still appreciated 38 percent during this same time period, outpacing banking industry as well as broad stock market indices.[17] By June 2014, the Bank had also bolstered its capital by raising approximately $900 million through five non-cumulative, perpetual preferred stock offerings, as well as successfully ventured into the debt market, issuing $400 million in five-year unsecured senior notes.[18]

Succession Planning

As the Bank aggressively hired new professionals, it also embarked on a concerted effort to develop and define its leadership strength. "The number one thing we did was to go about putting a deputy leader virtually everywhere in the organization," Herbert said. "All of our Regional Managers now have deputies. We basically went about backing up everybody."[19] First Republic Bank had always fostered an entrepreneurial environment, where people were encouraged and empowered to grow. "I want to get the next generation on board or promoted up. And a lot of them were promotions, not outside hires," Herbert added. "I wanted to establish with great clarity that we had the power to double the Bank again based on the strength of capital and people."[20]

INSTITUTIONAL INVESTOR MAGAZINE'S ALL-AMERICA TEAM

In 2014, Jim Herbert, Willis Newton, Mollie Richardson and the teams supporting the Bank's Investor Relations initiatives were awarded for their efforts by *Institutional Investor* magazine. Reflecting the polling of more than 1,400 buy-side analysts and 1,200 sell-side analysts, companies are ranked for their corporate leadership and investor relations expertise, as "industry benchmarks by which performance and excellence are measured."

Recognized as part of *Institutional Investor*'s All-America Executive Team, Jim Herbert was awarded Best CEO by both buy-side and sell-side analysts in the mid-cap bank sector, and Newton was awarded Best CFO by the sell-side. First Republic also received the honor of Best Investor Relations Company in its sector, a tribute to Mollie Richardson's efforts.[21]

When meeting with investors and analysts, Herbert and August-deWilde were invariably asked the same question: What about succession planning? It took them by surprise, initially. They felt reinvigorated by the process of buying back the Bank, and they had recommitted to making First Republic Bank a platform for continued robust growth across its private banking business lines.[22] They were not thinking about retirement.

After careful thought and extensive discussions, mostly in closed sessions, Herbert put forth to the Bank's independent Directors in early 2012 a carefully crafted and detailed plan for succession. "It's an obligation to the employees and to our client base, as well as to the shareholders, to make sure that the Bank has a smooth leadership transition when it needs it," Herbert said. "I'd like to put this to bed once and for all."[23] The Board agreed with the plan.

In order to signal the planned succession and communicate continued stability, the Board extended Herbert's employment contract as Chairman and Chief Executive Officer until June 30th, 2017, at which point he would remain Chairman through 2020 subject to shareholder re-election. August-deWilde extended her contract

PARTNERSHIP DEFINED

Herbert and August-deWilde's partnership had developed over almost 30 years of leadership. Their "divide and conquer" approach had been refined over many challenges and opportunities – in 1986, when Herbert tended to the acquisition of El Camino Thrift & Loan in Southern California while August-deWilde managed the home base in San Francisco; again in 1994, when addressing the challenges brought about by the Northridge earthquake; and most recently, and certainly most acutely, when mounting the effort to buy back First Republic. While Herbert weaved through the intricacies of executing the deal, August-deWilde ensured the day-to-day operations continued seamlessly. Their fusion of Herbert setting strategy through focused vision and August-deWilde executing with unequalled precision was key to guiding the enterprise through the turmoil of the most recent recession. The task ahead – find the right leadership and ready this next generation to take the helm.

as President and Chief Operating Officer through 2013, at which point she would continue as President through 2015 and then act as Vice Chair and Senior Advisor through 2017.[24]

With the tenure of its top two leaders clearly defined, but also finite, First Republic Bank launched a search in early 2012 for a very senior candidate to add to the executive management team. With the aid of an executive search firm, the Bank looked for a seasoned executive it could bring in as Senior Executive Vice President – one who would be a good cultural fit for the Bank. After reviewing numerous highly qualified candidates, Herbert offered the position to Mike Selfridge, a rising star at Silicon Valley Bank.[25]

Selfridge learned retail banking as well as credit analysis at Wells Fargo and corporate banking at HSBC Holdings before joining Silicon Valley Bank in 1994.

MIKE SELFRIDGE

When Mike Selfridge landed his first banking job in 1987 as a Wells Fargo Bank teller, First Republic Bank was only two years old. Though still an undergraduate at California Polytechnic State University – San Luis Obispo, Selfridge already had a grasp of one key element of First Republic – relationship banking. "What I loved the most about that was meeting the people, meeting the clients and developing relationships," Selfridge said.[26]

Selfridge gained experience originating single-family mortgages at Wells Fargo before moving to Wells Fargo's corporate headquarters in San Francisco as a Corporate Banking Loan Examiner. Once there, he learned another key banking lesson, when he saw the impact of less-than-stringent lending standards as the bank worked its way through relatively risky real estate loans during the recession of the late 1980s and early 1990s. But he missed working with clients.

From mid-1991 through mid-1994, he worked primarily with mid-sized corporate clients in Northern California for HSBC Holdings. His client roster included the then-relatively unknown Cisco Systems. Watching innovative companies such as

Cisco grow revenues by more than 100 percent a year made him realize that Silicon Valley was as much a gold mine for banking as it was for technology. But HSBC, known for its international banking expertise, did not provide the best way to tap these riches close to home, he realized.

So Selfridge joined Silicon Valley Bank in 1994 to get "closer to the action." He held a series of progressively senior posts on both the East and West coasts and helped lead expansion into the U.K. and Israel. Selfridge assumed leadership of Silicon Valley Bank's flagship Northern California region in 2008 and later, in 2011, responsibility for commercial banking in 29 regions across the United States.

Though his career trajectory led him into management, Selfridge's view of banking has not changed much since his days in San Luis Obispo – stay close to, understand, and grow with the client. Over the past few years, he has observed a shift in importance in larger institutions toward the products or platform and away from the people – both employees and clients. But Selfridge is not worried. First Republic Bank, he said, is "all about the people."[27]

Mike Selfridge joined the Bank's executive leadership team in 2012 as First Republic Bank's Senior Executive Vice President and Deputy Chief Operating Officer.

He was already very familiar with First Republic Bank when he was contacted by the executive recruiter. But his interest in First Republic was in tracking an aggressive and innovative competitor with an outstanding reputation, not in considering a future employer. Compelled by the relationship-banking model, however, Selfridge joined First Republic in March 2012 as Senior Executive Vice President and was later named Chief Operating Officer in February 2014.

BROAD EXECUTIVE EDUCATION PROGRAM

In 2013, as part of succession planning and the senior leadership development process, Herbert started a program of sending over 65 key leaders through various executive education programs at Harvard, Stanford, Dartmouth and Wharton. The objective was to enhance the leadership skills and rejuvenate the entire senior management team simultaneously. Planned to take place over a compressed time period, and inspired by Herbert's experience with the WPO/CEO Executive Education program,

the participants would be able to capitalize on their shared experiences as a cohesive group.

"It caused me to think of ways I can become a better manager," said Chris Coleman, Head of Business Banking, who attended Wharton's Advanced Management Program in 2013. "How can I better promote leadership and foster a culture that inspires innovation, and then drive that through all levels of the organization?"[28]

"The opportunity to interact daily with leaders from around the world broadened my perspective, particularly on areas outside of finance," said Mike Roffler, Chief Financial Officer. "My time at Stanford taught me many things, one of which was not to 'fight the yes.' Let ideas flesh out, continue the conversation. I've committed myself to remaining open to the new, and that is tremendously impactful on how I think about our company and the entire business."[29]

MIKE ROFFLER

Mike Roffler, Executive Vice President and Chief Financial Officer, was one of the first hires to join First Republic as part of the management team's succession planning effort. A former partner at KPMG, an audit, tax and advisory services firm, Roffler was a part of the audit team for First Republic in 2004 and 2005. "I can remember the day, in January 2007, when I saw that First Republic had been sold to Merrill Lynch," recalled Roffler. "My first reaction was 'That's too bad. First Republic would have been a good place to work someday.'"

A little more than two years later, Roffler received a call from a colleague working with First Republic, to ask if he would be interested in reconnecting with the Bank to explore an opportunity. Herbert and August-deWilde were looking to expand the management team. Roffler was interested, but First Republic could not yet make an offer.

"So I waited. It was a leap of faith," said Roffler. He joined First Republic as its Deputy Chief Financial Officer in November 2009, bringing a breadth of experience that included both First Republic as its independent auditor and larger institutions such as Wells Fargo. He was named Chief Financial Officer on January 1, 2015, upon Willis Newton's retirement – a seamless transition on all accounts. "I got even more than I expected. Coming to work every day, you want to get up, look in the mirror and enjoy what you are doing. Every day, I look forward to what challenge is around the corner, what opportunity will come up next." [30]

First Republic's ties to the Silicon Valley area extend deep. George Parker, who has been a member of the Bank's Board of Directors since 2003, is the Dean Witter Distinguished Professor of Finance, Emeritus, for the Graduate School of Business, Stanford University. He previously served as the school's Senior Associate Dean for Academic Affairs, Director of the MBA Program and Director of Executive Education.

"There Are Incredible Growth Opportunities Right Here"

First Republic Bank had mined the San Francisco-area mortgage market since the mid-1980s. But there was no indication that this particular vein of private banking opportunities, or those found in nearby Silicon Valley, were close to being exhausted, said Selfridge, who oversees First Republic's Bay Area regions. The innovation economy that drives economic growth in both San Francisco and Silicon Valley appears as strong as ever.

Many software and Internet-related companies traditionally associated with Silicon Valley have more recently migrated into the San Francisco metro area. The Bay Area, including both San Francisco and Silicon Valley, has increasingly become a global center of innovation and growth, and this economic activity accounted for 46 percent of First Republic Bank's loans originated by year-end 2014. More than 200 venture capital, private equity and other investment management firms, representing approximately 950 funds, were banking clients, and more than one-third of First Republic Bank's deposit offices were in Silicon Valley. "In terms of what's happening now, having come through the financial crisis and watching the innovation sector really blossom for the Bay Area is truly spectacular," Selfridge said. "We have significant opportunity. The economy's doing well, the job creation machine is working well, and we are positioned in a way where our brand has so much positive momentum. The word-of-mouth for First Republic is truly playing out in the Bay Area. There are incredible growth opportunities right here."[31]

San Francisco

Los Angeles

Boston

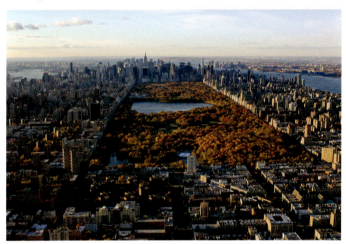

New York

First Republic's Urban, Coastal Footprint

Herbert and the management team had grown the First Republic Bank footprint in a very deliberate fashion. As a high-touch brand, one of First Republic's key growth drivers is the organic, word-of-mouth spread of its exceptional service, which works best within dense urban areas and within defined business segments.

In addition to being the right environment to grow brand recognition, First Republic Bank's urban, coastal, knowledge-based markets continue to outperform the United States as a whole. San Francisco, the Bank's home market, had grown at a rate of almost double that of the U.S. economy at large. And during economic slowdowns,

The Bank's key urban, coastal markets provide an ideal environment for word-of-mouth brand recognition. They also are centered in knowledge-based economies that outperform many other areas in the United States.

First Republic Bank serves the financial needs of a wide variety of nonprofit organizations, including the financing of a new student residence in Northern California for Guide Dogs for the Blind.

the Bank's home markets, with higher than average concentrations of college graduates, had shown evidence that they receded to a lesser extent than the rest of the country.[32]

"Our markets generally outperform the U.S. as a whole. Part of our growth is inherent to the markets we operate in – targeted urban areas, which tend to be housing supply constrained and attract highly educated professionals. Our geographic focus is core to the business model," Herbert said.[33]

Commitment to the Community

"We have made a very important commitment to the community at this Bank," said Carmen Castro-Franceschi, Executive Managing Director – Relationship Management, who was one of the first Relationship Managers to join First Republic in 1986. "That has really reinforced with the client how aligned we are with them."[34] First Republic, while operating in the largest urban areas in the United States, is a community bank at heart, investing in the success of its regions and clients. Rosana Han, who joined the Bank in June 2010 as Vice President, Community Reinvestment Act and Fair Lending Officer, said that in 2013, approximately one-fourth of small business loans made by First Republic were in low- to moderate-income areas, with approximately $643 million in community development loans.[35]

In addition to supporting a variety of different charitable institutions, focused on children, education, community service, health and welfare, and the arts, the Bank also specializes in serving the financial needs of nonprofit organizations. "First Republic's tax-exempt financing helped make our new student residence a reality," said Jane Flower and Bob Burke of Guide Dogs for the Blind in the 2013 Annual Report. "They have been a great partner to us."[36]

"It's part of the DNA of the employees of First Republic Bank – that caring culture is a very important component of who we are," Selfridge said.[37] First Republic employees share their time and skills as an active volunteer corps, providing more than 3,200 hours of community service, most in financial literacy education.[38] "It's a sense of giving back," said David Lichtman, Executive Vice President and Chief Credit Officer. "I've been very fortunate in my life. If I can give back to others, I feel it's my obligation and duty to do so."[39]

"Seamless Across Channels"

First Republic Bank's network of Preferred Banking Offices continues to remain a hallmark of its unrivaled client service. As it set out post-divestiture from Bank of America Merrill Lynch to make up for lost time in adding new professionals to the team, it did the same with new offices. By December 31st, 2014, First Republic had 68 Preferred Banking Offices open across its footprint, up from 56 following the divestiture from Bank of America in July 2010.[40]

These Preferred Banking Offices are vital to serving all of the Bank's clients. In fact, according to Joe Petitti, Executive Vice President – Deposit Sales, Products and Strategy, approximately 40 percent of the transactions that occur in the office network involve business banking clients or remote transactions for clients located elsewhere. "That's a very strong statistic in terms of how we take care of clients, and how we are seamless across channels and locations," Petitti said. "A lot of

A growing number of First Republic Bank's clients have homes in and around Palm Beach, FL, prompting the Bank to open a Preferred Banking Office there in 2013.

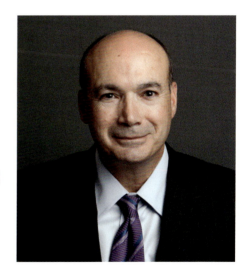

Joe Petitti, Executive Vice President – Deposit Sales, Products and Strategy, joined First Republic Bank in 2007, assuming responsibility for deposit strategies.

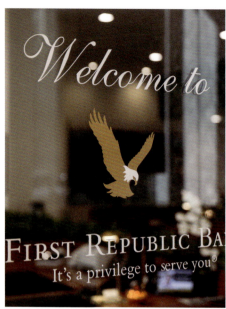

First Republic Wealth Advisor Catherine Evans finds the welcoming atmosphere of a First Republic office resonates with clients.

"Each one of our offices is unique," says Corinna Wan, Senior Vice President – Facilities and Administrative Services, who joined the Bank in 2001. "We really take a 'one-at-a-time' approach in choosing locations, and I take great pride in the transformation of the space we are able to achieve."

organizations talk about delivery channels and being seamless and the service being consistent across all channels. I think we really do a good job of executing that."[41]

The offices are also vital to supporting the Bank's wealth management business. Catherine Evans, Senior Managing Director, joined the Bank in 2002 and a few years later was named the Bank's first Wealth Advisor. She always prefers meeting new clients in one of the Bank's own offices. "They can see the look and feel of the type of entity that they're going to talk to about wealth management," Evans said. "It completely changes the conversation … They realize it's a very special place."[42]

Conversely, some clients sustain excellent long-term relationships with the Bank without ever visiting an office. San Francisco real estate investor Russ Flynn has been banking with First Republic Bank since its inception. But he can count on one hand the number of times he has actually set foot in a First Republic Bank office. In the early years, business was conducted over the phone, and more recently, online. "I'd come to the Bank's parties over the years," Flynn said, "but I'd rarely come to the Bank."[43] As part of First Republic's commitment to providing extraordinary service, the First Republic team will bring the Bank to the client.

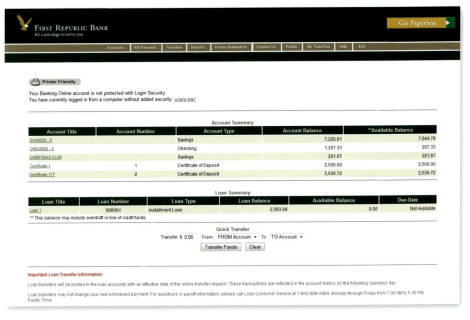

First Republic Bank chooses to focus on relationships over technology, but it continues to serve clients by providing the technological tools they need, including online and mobile banking.

High-Tech Alongside High-Touch

While using technology as much as possible to complement and enhance the client experience, First Republic Bank has not led the industry in terms of technological offerings, choosing instead to emphasize personal relationships. At the same time, the Bank is conscious of the fact that many of its clients live or work in regions such as Silicon Valley and San Francisco, not to mention Century City, Boston and New York, where technological advances help drive the local economies. "Our client base doesn't want us out on the edge, but they do want the new stuff pretty quickly," Herbert said.[44]

Recognizing the shift in technology that took place during First Republic's time inside Merrill Lynch and then Bank of America, the Bank concentrated on enhancing its technological infrastructure and created a new department – Digital Channels – following the divestiture. Focused on enhancing the client's digital experience and engagement with the First Republic brand, this team was tasked with getting First Republic up to speed with certain digital initiatives, including the launch of mobile banking and social media.

Dale Smith, Executive Vice President and Chief Information Officer, joined First Republic in 2000. "In most companies, technology and operations are commodities," he said. "Here, we work in partnership with sales, to better take care of our clients."

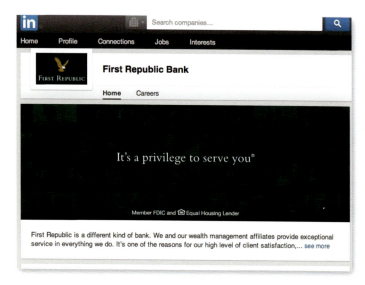

First Republic engages clients through social media sites such as LinkedIn, Twitter and Facebook, to facilitate sharing of financial tips, photos, links and Bank updates.

First Republic, as it has in the past, will continually evolve and innovate in order to enhance the client experience, both in person and online. But Herbert thinks the Bank is well positioned on the technology front. "The environment we are in now is better for someone like us, as long as we stay innovative, because we can change and implement much more rapidly than the big guys can. But we have to do it. We can't just take it for granted," Herbert said.[45]

Net Promoter Score

First Republic experiences growth through a number of drivers, one of the most important of which is word-of-mouth recommendations from current clients to their like/kind friends, colleagues and businesses. In 2013, Selfridge led a study with Greenwich Associates to measure this concept through Net Promoter Score.

Scott Finder, Senior Vice President and Head of Digital Channels, joined First Republic Bank in 2012 to lead its expansion into digital delivery and communication.

The Net Promoter Score, a common metric used for high-touch brands, was developed by the consulting firm, Bain & Company, Fred Reichheld and Satmetrix, and is based on the premise that a company's customers can be divided into promoters, who are enthusiastic supporters of the company and encourage others to support it as well, and detractors, who are unhappy with the company's offerings. Net Promoter Score surveys current customers to ask "What is the likelihood that you would recommend

Company X to a friend or colleague?" It subtracts detractors from promoters to derive a value used to measure positive brand awareness and word-of-mouth recommendation.[46]

The study confirmed what Herbert and the team already intuitively knew to be true: First Republic Bank's customers were very actively promoting the Bank's products and services in the marketplace. While the banking industry in the United States scored 18 percent, First Republic scored 55 percent overall – fully three times greater. When identified by clients as their "lead bank," or the one that they primarily used, First Republic scored an even higher 74 percent, or more than four times greater. These scores place First Republic far above the industry and in alignment with highly regarded brands such as Amazon, Apple and Ritz-Carlton hotels. The already stellar results increased when the study was updated in 2014, with First Republic scoring 77 percent when identified as "lead bank," and 62 percent overall, versus 34 percent for the U.S. banking industry.[47]

"This gets to the heart of the business model," said Selfridge. "Our clients value the products that we offer. That is the tangible element. But the emotional – do I trust my banker, do they deliver on what they say they will – that is key and reflected in these scores."[48]

Andrea Miller, Artistic Director and Founder of Gallim Dance, works with First Republic Bank to provide support for the dance company's worldwide tours and other business needs. "First Republic shares our passion for innovation and world-class performance," said Miller.

Maureen Maginn, Senior Vice President, serves as the leader of the Deposit Services team: a group key to the service proposition at First Republic Bank, able to execute with quick turnaround times ahead of the competition.

"First Republic is a traditional, relationship-based bank with new technology and efficiency," said relatively new business banking clients Sheila and Ron Marcelo of Care.com.

Business Banking at First Republic

First Republic Bank's business banking division grew dramatically as a result of a strategic effort to build out this increasingly important piece of the enterprise post-divestiture. Business banking deposits more than tripled, from $5.7 billion at year-end 2010 to $17.6 billion at year-end 2014, representing 47 percent of total deposits at the Bank. Business loans quadrupled to $4.9 billion during the same time period, equaling 13 percent of the total loan portfolio.[49] It continues to be a very profitable piece of the Bank, with plenty of room to grow. "Business banking is a dominant growth engine inside the Bank," Herbert said.[50]

Business banking and wealth management were two areas of focus in the years following the buyback from Bank of America Merrill Lynch, particularly as it pertained to hiring.

Chris Coleman, Senior Vice President and Head of Business Banking, joined the Bank in 2008, first in credit approval management before transitioning to lead the expansion of its Business Banking platform.

CLIENT

EXTRAORDINARY SERVICE THROUGH PERSONAL & DIGITAL CHANNELS

YOUR FIRST REPUBLIC RELATIONSHIP MANAGER

FULL-SERVICE PRIVATE AND BUSINESS BANKING

PRIVATE WEALTH MANAGEMENT

Residential Lending

Personal Lending

Commercial Real Estate Lending

Checking, Savings, CDs (Deposits)

Private Business Banking

Trust Services

Brokerage Services

Investment Management

First Republic Bank clients still work with a single point of contact, but the lead-in may originate from wealth management solutions or business banking as well as personal banking.

The successful growth of the business banking division was a result of both growing the team by adding new professionals and the maturing of a department that developed from a modest base in 2001. "Business banking grew initially in its first six or eight years from what we call internal referrals, existing clients, personal clients, who wanted us to provide the same service that we provide on the personal side for the business side," said Chris Coleman, Senior Vice President and Head of Business Banking. Coleman joined First Republic as the Deputy Chief Credit Officer in March 2008, working alongside Lichtman. He then shifted to Co-Head of Business Banking in January 2012, with Paul Gardner, as the division grew, and was named Head of Business Banking upon Gardner's retirement in 2014.[51]

"We reached an inflection point a few years ago where more business bankers were sourcing their own business and bringing in new business because the word had spread," Coleman added. "It's what I call the boomerang effect. That's a natural

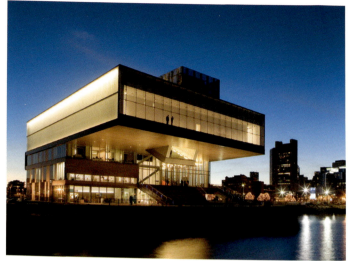

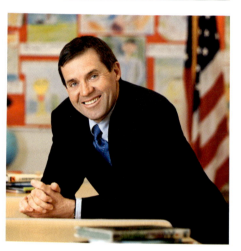

evolution of the business where referrals now are coming from the Business Bankers to the private banking needs of the client. So now it's a much more even flow of business and cross-sell." [52]

"We'd rather go deep and confine ourselves to certain target markets and have greater market share as a result," Coleman said. Schools, private equity, venture capital, doctors, lawyers and professional services are key target markets for business banking, he said. "We'd rather stay in those industries, stay focused, get more market share than be more diffuse. So we very much tell ourselves and tell the marketplace we're not all things to all people. Most banks are highly commoditized in their marketing and branding. This bank is very focused." [53]

The philosophy applied to business banking is the one Herbert has echoed in each of his ventures and with the development of First Republic Bank itself – the belief that there are no businesses, only people. By providing personal banking services to the key decision-makers at a firm, it was a natural progression to then serve the firm as well, along with any nonprofit interests and involvements the people may have. Business banking grew just as the Bank did, by adding one client at a time. "If you understand the individual, and you understand what they're trying to do, then it makes it a lot easier to figure out how to take care of both the personal and business sides," said Paul Gardner, who grew the Business Banking team under his leadership prior to retirement. "That's private banking. Pretty simple – challenging but simple." [54]

Lending to nonprofit institutions is a focus of First Republic's business banking activities. Reynold Levy, former President of Lincoln Center for the Performing Arts, joined the First Republic Bank Board of Directors in 2013 to enhance the Bank's expertise from a leadership perspective in the nonprofit area, as well as further deepen relationships in the New York City region.

Nonprofits, such as The Institute of Contemporary Art/Boston (top), and independent schools, including The Bishop's School (middle, left and center), Chandler School (middle, right) and Head-Royce School (bottom), help make up 40 percent of First Republic Bank's business loans. [55]

"First Republic created an innovative loan program that allows our employees to invest in Blackstone's funds – it's a creative concept, very efficiently executed," shared Laurence Tosi, Senior Managing Director and Chief Financial Officer of Blackstone.

Next Generation of Clients

"We are a bank of entrepreneurs," said Herbert. "Our private banking offices aren't on the 30th floor – they are ground level. Because our clients are busy. They want to walk in, be recognized and have their needs met. Quickly."

When Herbert and Roger Walther founded First Republic Bancorp in 1985, many clients from their previous venture, Westcoast Thrift & Loan, joined the newly formed institution. These clients grew with the Bank, as did the many clients acquired over time. As their needs expanded, First Republic expanded its products and services in lockstep.

"But we always look to the future here," said Herbert. "How do we find the entrepreneurs of today? How do we attract the next generation of clients?"[56]

Following divestiture from Bank of America Merrill Lynch in July 2010, First Republic did just that, by focusing some marketing efforts on its newly formed Professional Lending Program. First Republic, responding to a need for quick decision-making and turnaround times, provided tailored loan programs for professionals looking to buy into a partnership or fund a capital call contribution with their firm of employment. Willing to extend credit to those who meet First Republic's strict standards, not only to the partners of the firm but also the next level of future leaders, the Bank not only met an important banking need but also found a way to seed the institution for future growth.

"This has the same emotional nature as a home loan," said Patrick Macken, Senior Managing Director and Head of Eagle Lending. "You work very hard, you get out of school and go to work at a private equity firm, with an opportunity to invest in your firm's funds. We'll help you do that. We'll help you create your wealth, and then we'll grow with you. That is a powerful partnership."[57]

Wealth Management

The influx of new hires and the addition of new capabilities since 2010 continue to reinvigorate First Republic Bank's wealth management division. "As we've hired people from larger, more prominent competitors, it's made a statement," said Bob Thornton, President, Private Wealth Management. "Now, we are routinely getting approached by people of major firms who frankly wouldn't have considered us five years ago as a place to come and go to work. And that's gratifying to the team and the people who have helped build the business."[58]

The expanding group drove strong organic growth. From its recession low of $14.1 billion in assets under management or administration in 2009, the wealth management division grew to $20.2 billion by year-end 2011. The addition of Los Angeles-based Luminous Capital in December 2012 further augmented the wealth management brain trust by bringing in an extremely highly regarded group of money managers.[59] In 2013, First Republic Private Wealth Management was named by *Barron's* among the Top 40 Wealth Managers in the United States and was ranked #1 on *Forbes'* Fastest Growing RIAs List. By December 31st, 2014, wealth management assets under management totaled $53.4 billion, and by March 2015, were $56.4 billion.[60]

The Bank's open-architecture wealth management platform has evolved over the past few years to enable First Republic Bank to respond to clients' full range of wealth management needs, often with customized solutions. "What you find over time is that clients want tax efficiency. They want customization. They want things that you have to be able to do internally," Catherine Evans said.[61]

Howard Noble, Senior Vice President and Deputy Chief Credit Officer (left) and James Reeve, Vice President and Deputy Head of Human Resources (right), joined First Republic in 2011 and 2012, respectively, as part of the Bank's expansion of the leadership team.

MOLLIE RICHARDSON

Mollie Richardson, Senior Vice President and Deputy Chief Administrative Officer, has worn many hats at the Bank throughout her tenure, having joined as Herbert's Executive Assistant in 2003. As a key leader in the integration with Merrill Lynch and subsequent buyback from Bank of America, Richardson's responsibilities grew exponentially over the years. After establishing and overseeing Investor Relations following the Bank's second initial public offering, Richardson completed the Advanced Management Program at Harvard. In 2013 she joined Jason Bender's team as Deputy Chief Administrative Officer, overseeing numerous initiatives that will help move the Bank into the future while remaining consistent in its founding values.

"First Republic's business model is predicated on providing extraordinary service at all levels of the organization," said Richardson. "This is no easy feat to achieve as a company grows in size, locations and number of employees, yet it's critical to our business that we continue to provide this consistent service experience. A particular focus of the Chief Administrative Office is to ensure that the Bank continues to function in a user-friendly manner, maintaining our critical culture of quick, fully coordinated responsiveness and outstanding client service."[68]

Transparency is the key to developing wealth management, Evans said. "Part of my job is to listen and to hear what clients' touch points are, and to give them my honest advice on what I think is in their best interest, given the goals of the portfolio. Sometimes that's internally managed, and sometimes that's all outside managers, and there's no benefit to me either way."[62] The open-architecture platform, along with absence of proprietary products, allows First Republic to continue to put the client's needs and interests first. Not only is this a powerful draw for clients, but also for wealth management professionals to join the First Republic team.

The Bank's acquisition of Luminous Capital helped bolster its wealth management division. The two companies both favored an open-architecture approach to investment management. Pictured, left to right: Mark Sear, Eric Harrison, Alan Zafran, Kim Ip, David Hou and Robert Skinner.

As word of the Bank's success with wealth management has spread over the past few years, Evans and her colleagues find that they are often the first contact a potential client has with First Republic Bank. They are no longer relying on referrals from other business lines at the Bank. "Clients coming to us first for wealth management or calling their banker to say, 'Hey, my friend just sold a company. You really should talk to him.' That's new," she said.[63]

"The opportunity within our existing client base is very robust," said Herbert. "Our cross-sell capabilities and results continue to grow, but we still have vast opportunity just within our existing banking clients – the urban professionals who have grown with First Republic, many of whom are now entering or planning for their next stage of life."[64]

Luminous Capital

In December 2012, First Republic purchased substantially all of the assets of Luminous Capital, which had $5.9 billion under management at the time. Luminous takes a similar approach to open architecture, and the acquisition added access to alternative investments to First Republic's existing wealth management platform. Culturally, the money management firm, whose operations have been folded into the Bank's wealth management division, was a good fit. Conversely, First Republic, during the integration, had the opportunity to learn from the firm, incorporating ideas such as those on team structure into the larger enterprise.[65]

JASON BENDER

Examples abound of employees at First Republic who have found enormous personal and professional growth at the Bank, including Jason Bender, Executive Vice President and Chief Administrative Officer.

Bender received his undergraduate degree from Swarthmore College and holds an MBA from Stanford University. He was also a participant in the Advanced Management Program at Harvard, as part of First Republic's Executive Education Program.

Bender joined First Republic in 1999, following graduation from Stanford. First working on a variety of projects, including the articulation of First Republic's Values, he was later named Head of Finance for the Bank. In 2013, the role of Chief Administrative Officer was created, which he filled. Tasked with "maintaining

First Republic's critical culture of quick, fully coordinated responsiveness and outstanding client service," Bender's leadership of the Finance team extended into ensuring the full enterprise continues to evolve while staying true to its founders' core principles.[66]

"At First Republic, we are unique in that everyone feels accountable for the Bank's success and everyone worries about taking care of the client," Bender stated in a case study developed for the Bank. "We don't have the silos or same interdepartmental competition for resources that characterize so many large institutions and get in the way of delivering the whole bank to the client. As we grow, we have to be very wary of these 'big bank' approaches, lest they cause us to lose what makes us special and successful."[67]

Pictured, left to right: Stephen Johnson, Alex Herbert, Seta Hanoian, Sharon Ng, Taso Kasaris, Tim Maguire and Hilary Byrde.

"A Willingness to Go Above and Beyond"

Herbert, August-deWilde, Selfridge and the rest of the leadership team at the Bank are constantly focused on developing the next generation of leaders at First Republic Bank. Mentoring across divisions helps junior employees learn from in-house cultural leaders and helps them prepare to fill big shoes in the future.

"If people have a passion for the business, this is a very good place for them," Herbert said. "Our job is to make it a safe, fair place to work, meritocracy-based, and to take very good care of our clients. And if we do a good job in making it a good place to work and get the right people, the clients will be taken care of as well."[69]

Stories of personal professional growth and success abound at First Republic. Fostering a culture of individual responsibility, with a meritocracy-based structure, creates limitless opportunity for those willing to "roll up their sleeves and work hard," said Lichtman.[70] "This is the kind of environment that gives top performers, people who work hard, people who are good at what they do, the ability to rise. And there are no barriers to stop that," said August-deWilde.[71]

"There is an expectation that First Republic wants to be the best," said Hilary Byrde, Relationship Manager at First Republic Bank. "The success of the Bank is due to the hard work of so many. Twenty-five years of success for Relationship Managers, for bankers. You want to carry that on."

A cultural tradition for both First Republic and the Herbert family, each year Jim and Cecilia send a holiday card to the full company. Both the Bank and the Herbert family have grown over time, and by 2013 this tradition had spanned their children's childhood.

Proud parents and San Francisco 49ers fans, Jim and Cecilia welcomed sons-in-law Vance Griffith (far left) and Stephen van Helden (far right) to the family

The younger generation of Bank employees also clearly sees the value in the Bank's unique culture and appreciates the opportunity to take on leadership roles early in their careers. "One thing I feel at the Bank is regardless of where you are on the chain, everyone is kind of in a senior position," said Client Systems Engineer Stephen Johnson. "We can all take ownership of issues, and it's really just a willingness to go above and beyond that I feel embodies First Republic and makes someone a First Republic employee."[72]

Herbert cites another key to the Bank's continuing success that is rarely the focus of business school banking seminars. "It's a lot of fun. We have just tremendous people in the organization. It really is a lot of fun."[73] ❖

Since 1985, exceptional people have come together at First Republic Bank to provide extraordinary service – a legacy that will continue to grow as the Bank goes above and beyond for its clients and communities.

CHAPTER TEN | 2015

THE NEXT CHAPTER:
2015 and Beyond

The Difference is Focus and Simplicity

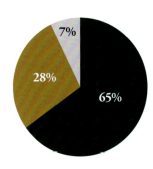
Thirty years since its founding, as First Republic grows past $50 billion in total bank assets, it finds itself in a unique position. "We aren't a complicated institution," says Herbert. "We don't do complicated things. We don't offer complex, transactional products, originate subprime loans, do foreign lending or engage in proprietary trading, amongst many other activities." A bank without a bank holding company and with only four subsidiaries, First Republic is significantly differentiated by its continued focus and simplicity in structure and activities. It is significantly more focused when compared to other institutions of a similar size as well. It is also smaller by other metrics, with less than one-third the number of client accounts when compared with this same group, allowing for greater individual relationship oversight and higher levels of service.[1]

"We stay focused on our core competencies of safe lending and extraordinary service," Herbert continues. While the Bank has grown and evolved over time by following the needs of its clients – to the East Coast, into Private Wealth Management and Business Banking – simplicity as well as consistency in its focus remain hallmarks. In 2004, single-family home loans and HELOCs – First Republic's key lead products – represented about 65 percent of the total loan portfolio. Ten years later, in 2014, they represented 60 percent. "We absolutely have never, nor will we ever, waver on credit

1985

"WE BELIEVE THAT NARROWLY TARGETED OPERATIONS AND STRONG CAPITALIZATION WILL PROVE IN THE LONG RUN TO BE THE PROPER FORMAT FOR A MOST SUCCESSFUL BANKING ENTERPRISE."

Jim Herbert
Chairman and
Chief Executive Officer
(Founding)

Roger Walther
Founding Chairman

First Republic Bank
1985 Annual Report

2014 BANKER OF THE YEAR

"For building First Republic into one of the nation's most profitable banks, while remaining disciplined on credit and exceeding expectation for service, Herbert has been named *American Banker*'s Banker of the Year for 2014," an esteemed award. Herbert entered 2015 as part of a small group of banking luminaries who had received this accolade over the years.[4]

standards," says Herbert. "We stick to what we know. Our growth is not a target we strive to reach. It is simply the result of our primary focus: taking great care of clients."[2]

Always Over-Deliver

"Our responsibility to our shareholders, clients and employees always begins with our most important constituent, our regulators," says Herbert. Crossing the threshold of $50 billion in total assets is the next milestone for the enterprise. This step in First Republic's evolution has brought enhanced regulatory oversight, including certain requirements pertaining to capital structure, enterprise risk management and compliance.

"Our entire team is focused on this inflection point," Herbert states. Substantially increased investment in systems, implementation of procedural changes and a formalization of processes, along with additions to the senior management team are part of this focus as the Bank's balance sheet grows. In 2014, Bill Ward and Gaye Erkan joined First Republic, to enhance its Bank Secrecy Act / Anti-Money Laundering ("BSA/AML"), investment and enterprise risk management functions

"As we mature as an enterprise, we continue to make improvements accordingly," shares Justin Gibson, who joined First Republic in 2012.

Nancy Segreto, (top)
Senior Vice President – Lending Services

Kellie Abreu, (center)
Regional Managing Director –
Relationship Management

Justin Gibson, (bottom)
Senior Vice President and Chief Auditor

and serve in key leadership capabilities. "Our ability to attract top talent who bring with them extensive experience in these areas from larger institutions, is key to our preparation and planning process, as well as our future," shares Herbert.[5]

"I brought a background of having either built or enhanced BSA/AML programs at larger institutions," says Ward, Executive Vice President and Chief BSA/AML and Security Officer, who joined First Republic from Union Bank in 2014. "First Republic takes a proactive approach, to both enhance for today and build to enable future growth ahead."[6]

Erkan, Senior Vice President, Chief Investment Officer and, through mid-2015, Co-Chief Risk Officer, also joined First Republic in 2014 from a larger institution, Goldman Sachs. "While the considerable investments we are making in people and infrastructure lead us to greater risk management procedures and tools, they also create business opportunities. There is an entrepreneurial imperative here, to establish and build deep client relationships by delivering the full bank, which extends to all functions of the enterprise," explains Erkan.[7]

Relationship Banking in a Digital World

"We use technology to enable, not replace, an even greater level of high-touch service," says Hugh Westermeyer, Senior Vice President and Deputy Chief Information Officer, who joined First Republic from The Charles Schwab Corporation in 2011. With that approach, First Republic stays true to its relationship banking model, while adapting to the changing environment and responding to clients' needs. "But we can't wait for the ask. If we do that, we're behind. We look beyond what we do today, to understand the business needs of the future."[8]

In 2014, the Bank announced the development of a new role, Chief Data Officer, to oversee data collection, organization and analysis. Jared Souter, who was named to the position, previously consulted with First Republic before joining the enterprise in 2007. "We are successful at growing with our clients and managing the Bank's risks because of our bankers' intimately close relationships with and knowledge of their

1998

"WE REMAIN DILIGENT IN OUR EFFORTS TO MAINTAIN THE HIGH STANDARD OF SERVICE EXCELLENCE THAT IS THE FOUNDATION OF FIRST REPUBLIC."

Jim Herbert
Chairman and
Chief Executive Officer
(Founding)

Roger Walther
Founding Chairman

First Republic Bank
1998 Annual Report

clients. So how do we support them, complement what they already do, in finding opportunities and mitigating risks?"[9]

First Republic focuses on enhancing service delivery through continuous development and improvement of its online and mobile banking platforms. It focuses on improving internal communications as well, initiating an enterprise-wide online collaboration system. This system, along with the Bank's social media presence, was introduced and led by Alex Herbert, Vice President of Digital Communications and Strategy.

The Bank takes the approach that leveraging technology to create efficiencies for its bankers, through enhanced digital services, will allow them to do what they do best – provide service and advice in partnership with clients. "We only look to build relationships, not just engage in transactions," says Jim Herbert. "We have grown in partnership with and thanks to our clients, with bankers whose goal is to provide exceptional service as lifetime advisors."[10]

Eric Lucero, Deputy Chief Marketing Officer, joined the Marketing team at First Republic in 2014, from Umpqua Bank. "Convenience and user-experience are very important. As we continue to grow, and technology continues to advance, we will certainly adapt. But many of our competitors are moving from people to technology. That's not our model. So we think about how we blend with technology, in the right fashion."[11]

"It's amazing to have experienced the growth over the past 23 years," says Cecelia Mauck, who joined the First Republic team in 1991. "It has been a tremendous honor and great fun, to be a part of the team."

Cecilia Mauck (upper left)
Executive Assistant

Hugh Westermeyer, (bottom left)
Senior Vice President and
Deputy Chief Information Officer

Susie Cranston, (seated left)
Senior Vice President,
First Republic Investment Management

Angela Osborne, (seated right)
Chief Operating Officer,
First Republic Investment Management

"Our business model is so close to the client, across the entire enterprise," shares Scott Finder. Finder joined First Republic in 2012 to lead Digital Channels, which is focused on delivering the Bank through online offerings. "We are a learning-based organization. We proactively put in place tools and processes to constantly question the way we think about our challenges and opportunities. And everyone keeps the client in the center of the conversation."[12]

Focus on the Client

While First Republic has evolved over time to strengthen the delivery of its core competencies, one mantra remains paramount: Focus on the client. "Our people wake up each day thinking about how they can take care of their clients," explains Herbert.

A study conducted by the consulting firm Oliver Wyman in 2014 quantified the Bank's client-centric, one relationship at a time approach, which focuses on taking excellent care of the clients it already has. It confirmed that the majority of the growth in the enterprise comes from the growth of *existing clients*. Fully 50 percent of all growth in checking accounts from 2007 through 2014 came from existing clients. Another 25 percent came from their direct referrals.[13]

"My clients are my sales force," says Julie Harkins, Executive Managing Director – Relationship Management. Harkins joined First Republic Bank in 1993 and has experienced firsthand, within her own book of business, the exponential growth driven by existing clients. "Take care of your client, because that client will grow with you. That client will bring in the next three."[14]

"Our word-of-mouth referral network is key to the growth of the business and something we focus on – through providing extraordinary client service – each and every day, at all levels of the enterprise," states Mike Selfridge, Chief Operating Officer. "It truly is a community banking model, one that stays close to the client."[15]

"We're not product pushers here. We find solutions, to help our clients achieve their goals," says Anna Legio, Senior Managing Director and Manager of the Bank's Park Avenue Preferred Banking office in Manhattan since 2001.[16] "I call our new clients just to ask 'Are we taking good care of you?' It's simple – I teach my team to make each client feel special," shares Nancy Sargent, Senior Managing Director and Manager of the Preferred Banking office in San Mateo, CA who joined the Bank in 2000.[17]

HAFIZE GAYE ERKAN

Gaye Erkan, Senior Vice President, Chief Investment Officer and, through mid-2015, Co-Chief Risk Officer, joined First Republic Bank in 2014 after having consulted with the Bank for a number of years on its capital stress test preparations.

A graduate of Bogazici University in Turkey, her birthplace, Erkan was encouraged by her professors to apply for fellowships in the United States after receiving the honor of Valedictorian. Erkan moved to the United States to attend Princeton University, where she earned a PhD in Operations Research and Financial Engineering. "At the time, I was eager to stay in academia and become a professor," shares Erkan. But she was approached by

The Goldman Sachs Group, Inc. first. In 2005, Erkan joined Goldman Sachs, where, in 2012, as Managing Director and Head of Financial Institutions Group Strats, she was introduced to a new client – First Republic Bank.

Working closely with the First Republic management team while at Goldman Sachs, she grew familiar with the Bank's business model, culture and people. "I thought it could be an exciting opportunity, to join this unique bank with a successful track record." In 2015, less than a year into her tenure as a member of the First Republic team, Erkan is even more excited about what lies ahead. "When you combine all of these things – a strong culture, great people and clients, a well-respected

institution and unique model – and look at the room to grow within our markets, there are great opportunities ahead."[18]

Jonathan Santelli, (upper left)
Senior Vice President and
Deputy General Counsel

Jared Souter, (upper right)
Vice President and Chief Data Officer

Anna Legio, (bottom left)
Senior Managing Director –
Preferred Banking Offices

Stephanie Bontemps, (bottom right)
Senior Vice President and Co-Chief Risk Officer

Ingrid Martinez, (top)
Technical Trainer

Doug Voncannon, (center)
Vice President and
Deputy Director of Client Support

Maria Ascuncion, (bottom)
Vice President, Wire Operations

"When I began my career, as a Preferred Banker in our Park Avenue office," shares Martin Gibson, Senior Managing Director, "I asked my first client why she moved her banking to us. 'Because you called me back,' she stated. I never forgot that. While we have clients with complex needs, sometimes it really can be that simple." Afsaneh Iranpour, Director of Sales – Preferred Banking Offices, also finds client-focus a leading edge. "It's a privilege to serve you. Other banks have the same products. We are different because we aren't focused on the products. We're focused on the client, on serving the client."[19]

Fatema Arande, Deputy Director of Preferred Banking Offices, began with First Republic in Southern California, moving with the firm to help establish Boston and then New York. "Boston was daunting at first – a new market, a small team – but very exciting. So we focused on service, taking care of the client, one at a time, to set us apart. Service delivers business." Amie Stevens, Senior Managing Director – Preferred Banking, was also one of the first to join the Boston team, in 2006. "At First Republic, sales and service are intertwined. At other institutions, those are thought of as separate functions, but here, to keep the client at the center, that is the approach."[20]

Focusing on the client is not limited to the Bank's associates on the front-line of client service, however. This mission permeates throughout the enterprise, at all levels and through all departments. "It's organized around the client, from Day One, from the bottom up. It isn't driven by the products, or services, or business unit," shares Susie Cranston, who joined the Private Wealth Management strategy team from McKinsey & Company in 2013. "The thought process around profitability

BILL WARD

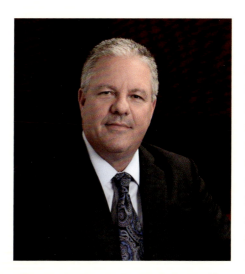

Bill Ward, Executive Vice President and Chief BSA/AML and Security Officer, joined First Republic Bank in 2014 with over 25 years of experience in law enforcement, corporate security, investigations, fraud prevention and Bank Secrecy Act (BSA)/Anti-Money Laundering (AML) compliance. Ward began his career in law enforcement, serving in a variety of divisions including narcotics, organized crime and financial crime during his 18-year tenure. He transitioned into the private sector first with Riggs Bank, and then spent 7 years with Union Bank before joining First Republic.

"Corporate citizenship and personal responsibility are top priorities here," says Ward. "With that you have the proper cultural foundation to protect clients and uphold the responsibilities held as a member of the United States financial system." [21]

then followed suit. It isn't driven by budgets segmented by products, services, units, structures – it is managed at the top, so that the client-facing teams can make decisions best for the client. The client is the number one organizing figure. And that base, that philosophy, it's hard to duplicate." [22]

Angela Osborne joined First Republic from Blackrock in 2013, as the Chief Operating Officer for its Private Wealth Management division. "Are you driven by the client or by the bottom line? There is a firm direction here, that these goals are not in contradiction," she notes. "Clients and shareholders do not need to compete. Everyone looks to do the right thing for the client, and that delivers bottom-line value and growth. The two are not in opposition over time." [23]

With the client at the center of the enterprise, and service at the core of its culture, First Republic Bank increased total enterprise value 25.8 percent per annum from July 1985 to March 2015.

"We share the same values of our long-term shareholders – a focus on quality,

BOARD OF DIRECTORS
Leadership that Looks Ahead

Addressing the needs of a growing enterprise, First Republic Bank's Board of Directors is committed to both providing consistent leadership and guidance over time, while also welcoming new ideas, new members and new perspectives.

With Directors who led the enterprise from the very beginning, in 1985, alongside those who helped lead through the sale to Merrill Lynch and advise during the management-led buyback, plus even newer leaders who joined in recent years, the guidance at the top is well-balanced with extensive institutional knowledge and innovative approaches to challenges and opportunities.

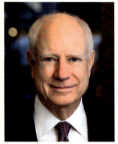

James H. Herbert, II
Chairman, CEO
Director Since 1985

Katherine August-deWilde
President
Director Since 1988

Thomas J. Barrack, Jr.
*Director from 2001 to 2007
and 2010 to date*

Frank J. Fahrenkopf, Jr.
Director Since 1985

L. Martin Gibbs
Lead Outside Director
Director Since 1985

Boris Groysberg
Director Since 2015

Sandra R. Hernández, M.D.
Director Since 2010

Pamela J. Joyner
Director Since 2004

Reynold Levy
Director Since 2013

Jody S. Lindell
Director Since 2003

Duncan L. Niederauer
Director Since 2015

George G. C. Parker
Director Since 2003

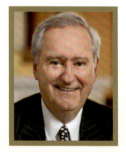

Roger O. Walther
Chairman Emeritus

performance and strong, stable, predictable returns over time," says Shannon Houston, Director of Investor Relations. "We firmly believe that keeping the client at the center of everything we do, and maintaining a culture of extraordinary service, achieves an optimization of shareholder value. There is a symbiotic relationship between delivering safety and stability that serves all key constituent groups: shareholders, regulators, clients and our team."

"Everything starts with the client. How are we going to make our clients' lives better, easier? That permeates throughout the enterprise – everyone is marching to the same beat," says Jonathan Santelli, who joined as Deputy General Counsel in 2013 from Merrill Lynch.[24]

One Bank, One Team

Providing extraordinary service begins with the team. "We will do whatever it takes to service our clients and deliver for them," shares Gaby McNiel, Vice President of Closing and Funding, who joined the Bank in 1989 and leads a key team in supporting the Bank's lending activities. "That extraordinary service is both external and internal. Our colleagues treat one another as they would treat a client. There is a genuine respect and partnership here, and a knowledge that when a client is served well, it brings individual and collective success and reward," adds Angela Osborne.[25]

Stephanie Bontemps first joined the Bank in 2008 to build its Credit Administration function, and then transitioned to lead its Enterprise Risk Management efforts in 2015. "We are very careful here to protect an environment where people can ask questions, and challenge what others are thinking. That collaboration helps us to make better decisions, for our clients and for the Bank."[26]

Opportunity and Diversity

First Republic is committed to an environment of opportunity and meritocracy, where hard work is rewarded and accountability reinforced.

The Bank credits a meaningful share of its success to the diversity of its workforce in all regards as well. Hailing from many geographies, over 50 languages are spoken at First Republic. Additionally, gender diversity is prevalent across the enterprise. 51 percent of the full team is female, with females representing 45 percent of the top producers at First Republic.

Scheba Cius, (top)
Client Services Manager

Tracy Chan, (bottom)
Senior Managing Director – Preferred Banking

Roberto Rivera, (left)
Relationship Manager

Gayatri Brar, (right)
Director of Professional Loan Products

Leadership and an Ever-Changing Future

The quality and depth of the leadership team has never been stronger at First Republic Bank. The combined industry experience of the Bank's top management professionals exceeds 800 years. The approach towards expanding the management team mirrors the Board's expansion, balancing institutional knowledge with newer members who represent a variety of backgrounds and experiences and provide a fresh perspective.

Importantly, to capture the collective experience and knowledge of the team, an Executive Forum was formed by Herbert in early 2015. Meeting monthly, this team of key leaders addresses the challenges and opportunities facing the enterprise in a carefully-coordinated manner, leading change as warranted while upholding the enterprise's core values and maintaining its client-focused, entrepreneurial culture.

As always, banking and financial services, like all industries, face challenges. An extended low-interest rate environment has opened doors for technology disruption through peer-to-peer lending platforms. Rapid innovation in online financial services spans from full online mortgage applications to "robo" investment platforms. Mobile digital delivery remains the fastest growing channel for banking services. All have common goals: to take business away from traditional commercial bank and investment firms, through delivering an improved online, digital client experience and the minimization of human interaction.

But, as Herbert states, "This is First Republic's opportunity."

The Bank strives likewise for improved digital delivery. "We continually invest in improving the client experience and look to gain efficiencies through leveraging technology, at all times," shares Herbert.

Elia Malick, (left)
Team Leader – Eagle Lending

Mohamed Fahmi, (right)
Senior Managing Director –
Relationship Management

"However, we remain focused on our fundamental value proposition – delivering honest, unbiased financial advice through person-to-person relationships built by professionals who genuinely care – for their clients and for one another," he continues. "Delivery channels and structures in banking and financial services will always continue to evolve. Integrity and caring, relationship-based, professional advice are eternally valuable."

Exceptional People, Extraordinary Service

When Herbert envisions the Bank 5 or 10 years into the future, he sees this opportunity – to leverage technology to better serve clients and create efficiencies, while continuing to focus on relationship-based banking with extraordinary service as the Bank's competitive advantage.

"We have evolved over the past 30 years from an uninsured thrift and loan to a full-service commercial bank and private wealth management enterprise, able to fully serve our clients' needs through a wide breadth of offerings," continues Herbert. "We operate in a limited number of targeted urban, coastal, knowledge-based markets, with excellent opportunities to safely expand market share by doing more of the same. And we grow with our clients, because at the end of the day we are a service organization, focused on them. The ability of our professionals to provide thoughtful, honest, caring advice and, through the team, take full care of a client's financial needs, is unequalled. We live and breathe that mission, throughout the enterprise. That is our culture." [38]

The ability to stay humble, stay nimble, adjust for challenges and capitalize on opportunities – all while sticking to a set of fundamental values and principles – has allowed First Republic to evolve and innovate successfully over time. Though things

change, at the core it is still the same operation. As Pamela Joyner, Director of First Republic Bank, describes, "My sense is that it doesn't, on a day-to-day basis, feel internally and operate any differently, really, than it did on Day One. And I also think that is one of the key components of success."[39]

"Why am I successful? Relationships," says Elise Wen, Regional Managing Director – Relationship Management, who joined the Bank in 1997. "You need to establish relationships internally. We may be bigger today than when I joined, but the importance of our culture – the reliance on the team and those relationships – is the same."[40]

From its founding to the present day, First Republic has been built upon several core tenets: Provide extraordinary service to clients. Trust the individual employee to make decisions in order to protect the Bank while providing that service. Foster an environment that encourages and promotes respectful teamwork across all business lines, departments and regions. Ensure an atmosphere of personal responsibility and accountability that joins in a collective success.

And at the end of the day, always remember there are no businesses, only people.

"When banks wake up in the morning and think that the corporate entity with the name on the door is the source of business, they are dead," says Herbert. "When the bank wakes up in the morning and understands that it is Margaret and Mary and Scott and Carmen, and they come in and do a good job for their clients, then it works."[41]

"Bankers used to be part of the community and wanted to be of the community," describes Bill Ford, former Director of First Republic Bank and Chief Executive

2015

"THE CULTURE OF FIRST REPUBLIC IS THE SUCCESS OF THE ENTERPRISE. THERE ISN'T ANYTHING ELSE. WE JUST HAVE SERVICE, AND SERVICE SPRINGS FROM CULTURE, AND CULTURE TRUMPS EVERYTHING ELSE."

Jim Herbert
Chairman and
Chief Executive Officer
(Founding)

The Power of a Client-Focused Heritage and Culture:
Exceptional People, Extraordinary Service

Officer of General Atlantic. "And I think that's what First Republic is going back to – those traditional roots. It's not just a financial transaction. What First Republic has maintained, and frankly is unwilling to abandon, is that personal connection."[42]

Collectively, those personal connections – fostered by the people of First Republic, both those new to the enterprise and those present that first day in July 1985 – developed the rich heritage and culture of the organization. "We wake up each day thinking about how we can build the best banking experience possible, how we can better serve our clients, how we can return value to our shareholders," said Herbert. "And we have the privilege of working with the best professionals in the industry. It really is that simple – excellent credit, a well-capitalized institution, with a team providing extraordinary client service – but extremely hard to execute. Unless you have our culture and people. And that is the key."

Looking back, the experiences that shaped the individuals who formed First Republic Bank can be seen throughout its operations, culture and values today. The next generation will carry the responsibility and have the privilege of moving it into the future. "We've learned a lot over time, from what we've done well and the mistakes we've made. But what is truly astonishing is the entire First Republic team. I'm tremendously proud of them," shares Herbert. "I'm excited to see how they write our next chapter."[43] ❖

FIRST REPUBLIC BANK
It's a privilege to serve you®

Work hard. Stay humble. Keep it simple.
And always focus on the client.

TOTAL ENTERPRISE VALUE

March 2015
$8.1 Billion

+25.8%
Increase Per Annum in Total Enterprise Value

July 2010
Management-Led Buyback from
Bank of America Merrill Lynch
$1.9 Billion

September 2007
Sale to Merrill Lynch
$1.8 Billion

July 1985
Founding
$8.8 Million

Sept. 2007 -
June 2010:
Bank was not
an independent
entity

ACKNOWLEDGMENTS

A true reflection of First Republic's team-based approach, this publication could not have been written without the help of many.

We would like to thank, first and foremost, Jim Herbert, Chairman and Chief Executive Officer (Founding) of First Republic Bank and Katherine August-deWilde. Many members of the First Republic team gave of their time for this project; we extend our sincerest thanks to this full group, listed on the following page.

This publication was made possible with the work, guidance and support of The History Factory: in particular, Bruce Weindruch, Scott McMurray, Michael Leland, Anthony Crews, Ashley Walters and Michelle Witt. In addition, we are tremendously appreciative of the work done by Howry Design, under the leadership of Jill Howry and Chris Cincebeaux.

We would also like to thank those instrumental in the construction of this story, including Dianne Snedaker, Mollie Richardson and Crystal Bryant along with Seta Hanoian and the Marketing team at First Republic. A special thank you to Kimberly Shannon, whose dedication to moving this project forward was invaluable.

Lastly, this publication means to capture the story created by each and every person at First Republic Bank. We are grateful to have the opportunity to share this unique heritage and culture.

Shannon Houston
Vice President, Director of Investor Relations

We extend our deepest gratitude to those interviewed for this publication.

In addition to those interviewed, the following people were key in building First Republic's historical archive, from which this book was constructed, and in acting as a resource for the publication.

Kellie Abreu
Iggie Alferos
Fatema Arande
Katherine August-deWilde
Jason Bender
Dan Ben-Ora
Stephanie Bontemps
Crystal Bryant
Hilary Byrde
Carmen Castro-Franceschi
Chris Coleman
Susie Cranston
Mary Deckebach
Bill Dessoffy
Ed Dobranski
Scott Dufresne
Gaye Erkan
Catherine Evans
Mohamed Fahmi
Scott Finder
Paul Gardner
Bill Ghriskey, Jr.
Justin Gibson
Martin Gibson
Rosana Han
Seta Hanoian
Julie Harkins
Mike Harrington
Alex Herbert
Jim Herbert
Delores Hill
Anna Hirano
Afsaneh Iranpour
Stephen Johnson
Taso Kasaris

Anna Legio
David Lichtman
Eric Lucero
Patrick Macken
Maureen Maginn
Tim Maguire
Margaret Mak
Ravi Mallela
Cecelia Mauck
Scott McCrea
Gaby McNiel
Willis Newton
Sharon Ng
Angela Osborne
Joe Petitti
Mollie Richardson
Mike Roffler
Linda Rohde
Jonathan Santelli
Nancy Sargent
Nancy Segreto
Mike Selfridge
Nick Simpson
Dale Smith
Dianne Snedaker
Jared Souter
Amie Stevens
David Tateosian
Bob Thornton
Dyann Tresenfeld
Corinna Wan
Bill Ward
Karen Weissenbach
Elise Wen
Hugh Westermeyer

Maria Asuncion
Jamal Avery
Tim Bailey
Tina Barton
Greg Berardi
Amy Black
Miguel Borrero
Gayatri Brar
Alex Caropino
Mariette Cesar
Tracy Chan
Joanne Choyan-Yung
Cathy Clarkin
Odette Dayans
Lyle Dean
Glenn Degenaars
Diane Epstein-Porter
Linda Farris
Shannon Flynn
Judy Ann Galvez
Aminta Garcia
Marissa Gilbert
Mika Harrington
Michael Hensley
Joe Hibbitts
Jermaine Jones
Kate Kent-Sheehan

Sonia Knight-Gutierrez
Jessica Kornblum
Allie Kregness
Amy Kyono
Dorey Larsen
Mike Laubenstein
Jennifer Leung
Reynold Levy
Mackenzie Lino
Kristina Low
Regina Lum
Elia Malick
Ingrid Martinez
Manny Medina
Jenny Mendoza
Monica Molina
Lynnette Nerney
Sammy Ng
Grace Nitta
Lorrie Pendleton
Shirin Pirzadeh
Chad Rego
Girlie Rezzetti
Roberto Rivera
Janisha Sabnani
Jessica Schaper
Kirk Schumacher

Marjan Shariat
Renee Simms
Rose Stewart
Jamey Stillings
Ester Trillana
Regina Valladares y Velásquez
Todd Valoff
Mark Van Divner
Doug Voncannon
Jill Whiby
Brittany Whitmer
Clay Williams
Rachel Woldeselasie

Honoring Our Longest-Tenured Professionals

as of March 31, 2015

OVER 25 YEARS

Iggie Alferos
Alex Arnold
Katherine August-deWilde
Jon Bull
Marian Burns
Carmen Castro-Franceschi
Kate Cooper Herzog
Bill Ghriskey, Jr.
Judy Hansen
Jim Herbert
Delores Hill
Jacqueline Kadel
Jeffrey Konover
Robin Kopeikin
David Lichtman
Margaret Mak
Michele McComb
Gabriela McNiel
Patricia Meeder
Willis Newton
Gary Pollock
Bob Schwartz
Christina Sifuentes
Rose Stewart
Todd Sullivan
Dyann Tresenfeld

OVER 20 YEARS

Krista Andrews
Maggie Carnero
Sandra Chacon
Mary Deckebach
Edward Dobranski
Scott Dufresne
Diane Epstein-Porter
Eileen Fong

Julie Harkins
Anna Hirano
Kimberley Hutchinson
Mea Kwon
Paula Lazar
Janine Le
Tina Levonian
Cecelia Mauck
Manuel Medina
Esther Ng
Phil Nonneman
Sandra Page-Wilson
Elizabeth Palomeque
Hector Pereira
Duane Phillips
Linda Rohde
Laurine Smith
Tammy Turner
Valerie Ulrich
Regina Valladares y Velásquez
Karen Weissenbach
Gayle Young

OVER 15 YEARS

Renzi Abedania
Ruth Aronowitz
Jason Bender
Teenia Burris
Joan Calder
Florence Calixto
David Canzano
Pam Cervantez
Tracy Chan
Wendy Chu
Mei Chu
Bill Dessoffy
Hazel Devito

Dianne Devlin
Nya Bertuido-Domingo
Elizabeth Dumlao
Tom Egan
Gloria Esquivel
Linda Farris
Stephen Feller
Liz Fitzpatrick
Aminta Garcia
Kit Jackson
Dennis Joe
John Kai
Jason Kaimer
Gaurav Kapur
Mary Kasaris
Diane Kohler
Joy Kulis
Anna Kwok
Kathryn Lawrence
Eileen Lelia
Lisa Lemons
Kristen Lizcano
Yolanda Lo
Adele Lopez
Scott McCrea
Victor Mena
Joycelyn Morris
Lynnette Nerney
Sammy Ng
Grace Nitta
Athena Palisoc
Rudolf Palma
Stefani Phipps
Shirin Pirzadeh
Devon Porpora
Chad Rego
Lynn Rodriguez

Vikki Siu
Diane Slater
Sunshine Smith
Bob Staples
Joy Suacillo
Lina Susantin
Rita Tuohy
Arnold Veek
Doug Waggener
Elise Wen
Delane Willis-Ysaguirre
Dee Won
Millie Yeung

OVER 10 YEARS

Kellie Abreu
Marilou Abuan
Doug Aiken
Anita Alon
Fatema Arande
Maria Asuncion
Tim Bailey
Bernadette Barairo
Tina Barton
Aubrey Bautista
Dan Ben-Ora
Monica Bent
Daxa Bhakta
Robert Bloom
Daeng Boonmanee
Miguel Borrero
Kymberlie Boston-Keplinger
David Brady
Karen Bratt
Joe Brown
Jeffrey Bruce
Jim Buckley

Hilary Byrde
Cynthia Castillo
Cherie Castle
Joshua Castro
Melody Catalla
Michele Celestino
Mariette Cesar
Charlee Chadaratana
Judy Chan
May Chan
Mobie Chan
Sheri Ann Chang Yamaguchi
Oliver Cheng
Gregg Chorebanian
Paul Chou
Movses Chukhuryan
Timothy Clancey
Roxann Corbin
Monica Corrales
Earl Crawford
Annette Dawson
Amanda Dayan
Karen Decker
Kelny Denebeim
Shelly Dipchand
Luz Duenas
Blaine Dunday
Thomas Ehrhardt
Diana Elton
Jovee Encinas
Catherine Evans
Mohamed Fahmi
Sarina Familetti
Drew Feraios
Bradley Finn
Monica Foy
John Froley

John Fruehe
Cristina Fruto-Palabyab
Alwin Fung
Yva Gallant
Judy Ann Galvez
Paul Gardner
Connie Garvin
Mary Gaspari
Nicolas Gentin
David Giang
Martin Gibson
Hortensia Gittins
Anne Golden
Sujit Govindraj
Karen Griese
Paola Guerra
Jayvee Gulmatico
Richard Halog
Safraz Hamid
Michael Harrington
Michael Hensley
Joe Hibbitts
Pency Ho
Mark Hoffman
Afsaneh Iranpour
Edwin Irizarry
Richard Israel
Evelyn Jankousky
Joanne Jenkin
Cynthia Jenkins
Maryann Jensen
Kathy Jin
Marianne Johnson
Barbara Jones
Jason Jones
Sharon Jones
Guy Joslin

Sungwon Kang
Renuka Karan
Taso Kasaris
Frank Keane
Kathleen Kirk
Jessica Kittel
Julie Klinge
Sonia Knight-Gutierrez
Beth Kothe
Gigi Kubursi
Larry Kuchan
Sara Kurth
Gloria Lai
Kim Lamb
Polly Le
Cynthia Leghorn
Anna Legio
Kay Levis
Po-Chi Lin
Rafael Lopez
Rosanna Lucero
Kim Thien Luong
Patricia Macdonald
Cea Madrigal
Judi Mages
Michael Manneh
Lani Martin
Michael Martini
Brina Mata
Greg Matoba
Steven Mazzella
Douglas McNulty
Bill Merrill
David Moe
Raul Montalvo
Stephen Moore
John Moroney

Maresa Navarro
William Neil
Monita Ng
Connie Nguyen
Nancy Nguyen
Alexandra Nichols
Kristin Nicholson
Matthew Nordahl
Famela Oliva
Don Onia
Scott Opperman
Monica O'Reilly
Marilou Pagal
Ammy Park
Buck Parson
Ramesh Patel
Marijane Paulino
Furman Pearson
Chris Pederson
Arturo Pensato
Carolyn Perkins
Felix Peronilla
Gina Phillips
Brian Plotner
Carolyn Powell
Stacey Powell
Joseph Powers
Rowela Prestosa
Fred Przekop
Janina Pulido
Gregory Quan
Barbara Quartero
Reena Ram
Venkat Ram
Christopher Ramos
Nora Raymundo
Marco Remedios

Maria Renellen Reyes
Mary Jane Reyes
Girlie Rezzetti
Mollie Richardson
Steve Rochlin
Jo-Ann Rose
Isabella Rozman
Anamaria Salmeron-Carr
Nancy San Pedro
William Sapenter
Nicole Saragosa
Nancy Sargent
Carolyn Sarmiento
Sam Schoner
Alison Schweitzer
Jeanne Scungio
Nancy Segreto
Ricki Seto
Bernard Shaw
Jason Shidler
Lauren Shortt
Emily Sidell
Jagroo Singh
Angela Situ
Brian Smith
Dale Smith
Dennis Smith
Dianne Snedaker
Paula Soto
Pachara Stegemann
Jill Strong
Shelley Svoren
Cathy Sweeney
Jennifer Sze-Merrick
Dawn Tague
Jeannie Tam
Rachel Tan

Yvonne Tan
Stan Tankersley
Toni Tartamella
David Tateosian
Francisco Terrizzano
Hayley Thompson
Robert Thornton
Jenny Tien
Danet Tittle
Yvonne Tom
An Na Tran
Ester Trillana
Dinh Truong
Todd Valoff
Jennifer Vaughn
Ana Vega
Deana Vi
Steve Wagner
Christine Waldo
Corinna Wan
Laura Harrison Ward
Art Wardwell
Michelle Watson
Brent Wiblin
Dylan Williams
Jeff Winkel
Jennifer Wong
Linda Workman
Carlson Yee
Bersi Yilma
Hilary Yu
Yan Yan Yu
Michael Zazzara
Chris Zweifel

Publication Notes

CHAPTER 1

[1] "Willard I. Webb." *Toledo Blade*, May 11, 1972; "Bankers Elect Local Man." *The Piqua Daily Call*, May 15, 1972, 15l; "Who's News . . . in Business." *The Daily Reporter*, May 15, 1972, 18.

[2] Jim Herbert, interview conducted by Bruce Weindruch, The History Factory, Washington, D.C., October 4, 2012, transcript, 3.

[3] Ibid., 4-6.

[4] "Sir David Davies." Global Leadership Foundation, http://www.g-l-f.org/index.cfm?PAGEPATH=Organization/Biography_Bin/Biography_Sir_David_Davies&ID=23848. Accessed June 4, 2013.

[5] Jim Herbert, interview, October 4, 2012, 6.

[6] Ibid., 28.

[7] Martin Gibbs, interview conducted by Scott McMurray, September 13, 2012, The History Factory, Washington, D.C., transcript, 4.

[8] Jim Herbert, interview, October 4, 2012, 6-9.

[9] Ibid., 9.

[10] Ibid., 10.

[11] "1975." The Pop Shoppe Story. http://www.thepopshoppe.com/about/in1975/. Accessed April 3, 2013.

[12] Jim Herbert as quoted by Bill Tracy, interview conducted by Bruce Weindruch, September 11, 2012, The History Factory, Washington, D.C., transcript, 9.

[13] Linda Moulds, interview conducted by Scott McMurray, January 8, 2013, The History Factory, Washington, D.C., transcript, 2-3.

[14] Jim Herbert, interview, October 4, 2012, 12-14.

[15] Ibid., 12, 14.

[16] Ibid., 20.

[17] Ibid., 20-21.

[18] "The end of the Bretton Woods System." International Monetary Fund, http://www.imf.org/external/about/histend.htm. Accessed May 30, 2014.

[19] Roger Walther, interview conducted by Bruce Weindruch, December 6, 2012, The History Factory, Washington, D.C., transcript, 6-7.

[20] Ibid.

[21] San Francisco Bancorp 1982 Annual Report, 14; First Republic Bancorp 1986 Annual Report, 15-16.

[22] "WestCoast Thrift & Loan." Business Profiles/California, http://businessprofiles.com/details/westcoast-thrift-and-loan/CA-C0985586. Accessed May 6, 2013.

[23] Jim Herbert, interview, October 4, 2012, 21-22.

CHAPTER 2

[1] Jim Herbert, interview conducted by Bruce Weindruch, October 4, 2012, The History Factory, Washington, D.C., transcript, 25; Jim Herbert, interview conducted by Shannon Houston, January 2014.

[2] Roger Walther, interview conducted by Bruce Weindruch, December 6, 2012, The History Factory, Washington, D.C., transcript, 9.

[3] Robinson, Louis. "The Morris Plan." *The American Economic Review* 21:2 (June 1931), 222-235.

[4] "Morris Plan Banks." Economic History Association. http://eh.net/encyclopedia/morris-plan-banks/. Accessed January 28, 2014.

[5] Ramirez, Steven A. "Federal Home Loan Bank Act (1932)." http://www.encyclopedia.com/doc/1G2-3407400120.html. Accessed April 9, 2015.

[6] Mason, David. "Savings and Loan Industry (U.S.)." Economic History Association. http://eh.net/encyclopedia/savings-and-loan-industry-U-S/. Accessed May 11, 2015.

[7] Bill Tracy, interview conducted by Bruce Weindruch, September 11, 2012, The History Factory, Washington, D.C., transcript, 6.

[8] Jim Herbert, interview, October 4, 2012, 24.

[9] Ibid., 25-26.

[10] Ibid., 35-36; Jim Herbert, interview conducted by Shannon Houston, January 2014.

[11] Steve Weiner, interview conducted by Bruce Weindruch, July 25, 2012, The History Factory, Washington, D.C., transcript, 3-4, 6, 13; North, Oliver. *War Stories II: Heroism in the Pacific.* http://books.google.com/books?id=sgYHvMAgSyAC&pg=PT32&dq=Bellows+Field+communications+shack&hl=en&sa=X&ei=pyAkVIGQBMejyASD_oGACA&ved=0CDIQ6AEwAA#v=onepage&q=Bellows%20Field%20communications%20shack&f=false. Accessed April 9, 2015.

[12] Steve Weiner, interview, July 25, 2012, 8.

[13] "Recession of 1981-82." http://www.federalreservehistory.org/Events/DetailView/44. Accessed April 9, 2015; "Inflation United States 1981." http://www.inflation.eu/inflation-rates/united-states/historic-inflation/cpi-inflation-united-states-1981.aspx. Accessed April 9, 2015; "1980-82 Early 1980s Recession." *Slaying the Dragon of Debt: Fiscal Politics & Policy from the 1970s to the Present.* http://bancroft.berkeley.edu/ROHO/projects/debt/1980srecession.html. Accessed January 28, 2014; "The Volcker Recession: Who beat inflation?" *The Economist*, March 31, 2010. http://www.economist.com/blogs/freeexchange/2010/03/volcker_recession. Accessed January 28, 2014; Silber, William L., ed. "Volcker: The Triumph of Persistence." http://people.stern.nyu.edu/wsilber/ VOLCKER%20COMPILATION%20OF%20REVIEWS.pdf. Accessed January 28, 2014.

[14] Steve Weiner, interview, July 25, 2012, 5-8.

[15] Jim Herbert, interview, October 4, 2012, 36-37.

[16] Roger Walther, interview, December 6, 2012, 26-27.

[17] Jim Herbert, interview, October 4, 2012, 37.

[18] San Francisco Bancorp Form S-1, June 3, 1983, 4.

[19] Jim Herbert, interview, October 4, 2012, 39; Barth, James R., Tong Li and Wenling Lu. "Bank Regulation in the United States." *CESifo Economic Studies.* Oxford University Press, November 5, 2009.

[20] Frank Fahrenkopf, interview conducted by Bruce Weindruch, January 14, 2013, The History Factory, Washington, D.C., transcript, 2-8.

[21] Jim Herbert, interview, October 4, 2012, 39.

[22] Ibid., 40.

[23] Ibid., 39. San Francisco Bancorp 1982 Annual Report, 11.

[24] Jim Herbert, interview, October 4, 2012, 42; San Francisco Bancorp 1982 Annual Report, 2, 16.

[25] Jim Herbert, interview, October 4, 2012, 26.

[26] Ibid., 33

[27] Ibid., 27; San Francisco Bancorp 1982 Annual Report, 15.

[28] Roger Walther, interview, December 6, 2012, 11.

[29] Jim Herbert, interview conducted by Shannon Houston, December 2013.

[30] Jim Herbert, interview, October 4, 2012, 27.

[31] San Francisco Bancorp, Prospectus, July 25, 1983, 1.

[32] Linda Moulds, interview conducted by Scott McMurray, January 8, 2013, The History Factory, Washington, D.C., transcript, 8.

[33] Linda Moulds, interview, January 8, 2013, 5.

[34] Ibid., 5.

[35] Jeanne Forster Gutsche, interview conducted by Scott McMurray, February 23, 2013, The History Factory, Washington, D.C., transcript, 3.

[36] San Francisco Bancorp, Prospectus, July 25, 1983, 1.

[37] Based on a 3,396,560 total shares at $7.50 price per share. San Francisco Bancorp Form S-1 Registration Statement, June 3, 1983; San Francisco Bancorp, Prospectus, July 25, 1983.

[38] Roger Walther, interview, December 6, 2012, 14.

[39] "Thrift Unit Merger." Reuters, May 10, 1984.

[40] Martin Gibbs, interview conducted by Scott McMurray, September 13, 2012, The History Factory, Washington, D.C., transcript, 6.

[41] "San Francisco Bancorp Says It Will Be Bought By Atlantic Financial." *Wall Street Journal*, May 10, 1984; Jim Herbert, interview, December 2013.

[42] Gilpin, Kenneth. "Atlantic Financial Picks Successor to Late Chief." *The New York Times*, September 11, 1984, D2.

[43] Roger Walther, interview, December 6, 2012, 15; Jim Herbert, interview, October 4, 2012, 31.

CHAPTER 3

[1] Roger Walther, interview conducted by Bruce Weindruch, December 6, 2012, The History Factory, Washington, D.C., 15.

[2] Ibid., 16

[3] First Republic Bancorp 1985 Annual Report, 8.

[4] Ibid., 1, 10.

[5] Jim Herbert, interview conducted by Bruce Weindruch, October 4, 2012, The History Factory, Washington, D.C., 43.

[6] Ibid., 43.

[7] Roger Walther, interview, December 6, 2012, 16.

[8] First Republic Bancorp 1985 Annual Report, 1.

[9] Jim Herbert, interview, October 4, 2012, 32.

[10] Ibid., 32-34.

[11] Katherine August-deWilde, interview conducted by Bruce Weindruch, September 7, 2012, The History Factory, Washington, D.C., 3.

[12] Jim Herbert, interview, October 4, 2012, 30-34, 43.

[13] Katherine August-deWilde, interview, September 7, 2012, 5.

[14] Ibid., 13.

[15] Jim Herbert, interview October 4, 2012, 61-62.

[16] Kinsman, Michael. "El Camino Thrift Sold by S.D. Bancorp." *The San Diego Union-Tribune*, January 14, 1986.

[17] Jim Herbert, interview, October 4, 2012, 47.

[18] Willis Newton, interview conducted by Bruce Weindruch, July 27, 2012, The History Factory, Washington, D.C., transcript, 11.

[19] First Republic Bancorp 1985 Annual Report, 10.

[20] Jim Herbert, interview, October 4, 2012, 48.

[21] First Republic Bancorp 1986 Annual Report, 3.

[22] Jim Herbert, interview, October 4, 2012, 48.

[23] Ibid., 47.

[24] "First Republic Bancorp Announces New President and CEO for El Camino Thrift and Loan Association." *Business Wire*, December 1, 1988.

[25] Jim Herbert, interview, October 4, 2012, 48-9.

[26] Hayes, Thomas C. "Depositors in Limbo in California Case." *The New York Times*, December 19, 1984. http://www.nytimes.com/1984/12/19/business/depositors-in-limbo-in-california-case.html. Accessed April 9, 2015.

[27] First Republic Bancorp 1989 Annual Report, 4; First Republic Bancorp 1986 Annual Report, 3.

[28] Katherine August-deWilde, interview, September 7, 2012, 35-36; First Republic Bancorp 1986 Annual Report, 2; "Fannie Mae Charter." http://www.fanniemae.com/portal/about-us/governance/our-charter.html. Accessed April 9, 2015.

[29] First Republic Bancorp 1986 Annual Report, 2, 11.

[30] Jim Herbert, interview conducted by Shannon Houston, April 3, 2014; Jim Herbert, interview, October 4, 2012, 55-56; First Republic Bancorp 1985 Annual Report, 13; First Republic Bancorp 1987 Annual Report, 3.

[31] San Francisco Bancorp 1983 S-I, 3, 8; First Republic Bancorp 1986 Annual Report, 2-3; First Republic Bancorp 1985 Annual Report, 2.

[32] Jim Herbert, interview, October 4, 2012, 59-60.

[33] Dyann Tresenfeld, interview conducted by Bruce Weindruch, July 26, 2012, The History Factory, Washington, D.C., transcript, 40-41.

[34] Ibid., 8.

[35] Ibid., 6-7.

[36] David Lichtman, interview conducted by Bruce Weindruch, July 27, 2012, The History Factory, Washington, D.C., transcript, 4-5.

[37] Margaret Mak, interview conducted by Bruce Weindruch, July 26, 2012, The History Factory, Washington, D.C., transcript, 3.

[38] Ibid., 4.

[39] Carmen Castro-Franceschi, interview conducted by Bruce Weindruch, November 20, 2012, The History Factory, Washington, D.C., transcript, 14.

[40] Ibid., 26-27.

41 Katherine August-deWilde, interview, September 7, 2012, 32-34; Jim Marver, interview conducted by Bruce Weindruch, November 20, 2012, The History Factory, Washington, D.C., transcript 7-8, 30.

42 Jim Marver, interview, November 20, 2012, 6-8.

43 First Republic Bancorp 1986 Annual Report, 2, 13; 1986 First Republic Form 10-K, 16-17; *Consistently Profitable for Twenty-Eight Years: 1985 / 2013*. First Republic Bank, 2014.

44 Margaret Mak, interview, July 26, 2012, 8.

45 First Republic Bancorp 1986 Annual Report, 2.

46 Katherine August-deWilde, interview conducted by Bruce Weindruch, November 19, 2012, The History Factory, Washington, D.C., transcript, 14.

47 "First Republic Bancorp Inc." *The Wall Street Journal*, September 23, 1987; "First Republic Bancorp Announces Private Placement of Stock." *Business Wire*, September 11, 1987; First Republic Bancorp 1987 Annual Report, 21.

48 Willis Newton, interview, July 27, 2012, 3-4.

49 First Republic Bancorp 1988 Annual Report, 20

50 First Republic Bancorp 1987 Annual Report, 3.

51 David deWilde, interview conducted by Bruce Weindruch, January 3, 2013, The History Factory, Washington, D.C., transcript, 3.

52 First Republic Bancorp 1988 Annual Report, 4-6.

53 Ely, Bert. "Savings & Loan Crisis." Library of Economics and Liberty. http://www.econlib.org/library/Enc/SavingsandLoanCrisis.html. Accessed August 5, 2013; Curry, Timothy and Lynn Shibut. "The Cost of the Savings and Loan Crisis: Truth and Consequences." *FDIC Banking Review*. https://www.fdic.gov/bank/analytical/banking/2000dec/brv13n2_2.pdf. Accessed April 9, 2015.

54 Weiss, N. Eric. "Government Interventions in Financial Markets: An Economic and Historic Analysis of Subprime Mortgage Options." Congressional Research Service. Order Code RL34423. March 25, 2008.

55 "Resolution Trust Corporation." *The New York Times*. http://topics.nytimes.com/topics/reference/timestopics/organizations/r/resolution_trust_corporation/index.html. Accessed June 18, 2013; Davison, Lee. "Politics and Policy: The Creation of the Resolution Trust Corporation." *FDIC Banking Review*. Vol. 17, No. 2, 2005.

56 First Republic Bancorp 1988 Annual Report, 4-5.

57 First Republic Bancorp 1989 Annual Report, 4.

58 First Republic Bancorp 1988 Annual Report, 4.

59 Ibid., 10

60 First Republic Bancorp 1989 Annual Report, 12.

61 Ibid., 4.

62 First Republic Bancorp 1989 Annual Report, 6-9.

63 Katherine August-deWilde, interview, November 19, 2012, 37.

64 Carmen Castro-Franceschi, interview, November 20, 2012, 28-29.

65 Jim Herbert, interview, October 4, 2012, 77.

66 Carmen Castro-Franceschi, interview, November 20, 2012, 29-30.

67 Jim Herbert, interview, October 4, 2014, 70-74.

68 "Who We Are." Young Presidents' Organization. http://www.ypo.org/about/. Accessed April 8, 2014; "About WPO." World Presidents' Organization. http://www.wpo.org/about.html. Accessed December 26, 2014; Jim Herbert, interview, October 4, 2012, 72. "Mission and Principles." http://www.ypo.org/about-ypo/mission-and-principles/. Accessed April 9, 2015.

69 First Republic Bancorp 1989 Annual Report, 5.

70 Jim Herbert, interview conducted by Bruce Weindruch, June 25, 2013, The History Factory, Washington, D.C., transcript, 44-46.

CHAPTER 4

1 Gerber, James. "Recession and Restructuring in the California Economy, 1990-1995." *Frontera Norte*, vol. 7, no. 14, July-December 1995, 1-3.

2 First Republic Bancorp 1990 Annual Report, 2.

3 Ibid., 4.

4 Ibid., 3.

5 First Republic Bancorp 1992 Annual Report, 3.

6 First Republic Bancorp 1991 Annual Report, 4.

7 David Lichtman, interview conducted by Bruce Weindruch, July 27, 2012, The History Factory, Washington, D.C., transcript, 12.

8 First Republic Bancorp 1991 Annual Report, inside cover; 1991 First Republic Form 10-K, 17.

9 Jim Herbert, interview conducted by Bruce Weindruch, March 6, 2013, The History Factory, Washington, D.C., transcript, 2.

10 First Republic Bancorp 1991 Annual Report, 3-4.

11 First Republic Bancorp 1992 Annual Report, 4.

12 Katherine August-deWilde, interview conducted by Bruce Weindruch, September 7, 2012, The History Factory, Washington, D.C., transcript, 31.

13 First Republic Bancorp 1992 Annual Report, inside cover.

14 First Republic Bancorp 1992 Annual Report, 4.

15 Jim Herbert, interview, March 6, 2013, 5.

16 Edward Dobranski, interview conducted by Bruce Weindruch, September 27, 2012, The History Factory, Washington, D.C., transcript, 4-7; First Republic Bancorp 1992 Annual Report, 4.

17 First Republic Bancorp 1992 Annual Report, 3, 32, 37.

18 Carmen Castro-Franceschi, interview conducted by Bruce Weindruch, November 20, 2012, The History Factory, Washington, D.C., transcript, 34.

19 Edward Dobranski, interview, September 27, 2012, 8.

20 First Republic 1992 Annual Report, 34; Jim Herbert, interview conducted by Shannon Houston, February 2014.

21 First Republic Bancorp 1992 Annual Report, 2.

22 Russ Flynn, interview conducted by Scott McMurray, December 6, 2012, The History Factory, Washington, D.C., transcript, 4-5.

23 First Republic Bancorp 1990 Annual Report, 3-4.

24 Willis Newton, interview conducted by Bruce Weindruch, July 27, 2012, The History Factory, Washington, D.C., transcript, 7.

25 Gray, Madison. "The L.A. Riots: 15 Years After Rodney King." *TIME*. http://www.time.com/time/specials/2007/la_riot/article/0,28804,1614117_1614084_1614831,00.html. Accessed July 9, 2013.

26 Weinstein, Henry. "Riot Areas Receive $2.8 Million in Irvine Grants." *Los Angeles Times.* December 5, 1992.

27 First Republic Bancorp 1993 Annual Report, 14.

28 Ibid., 17.

29 Ibid., 18.

30 Ibid., 3.

31 First Republic Bancorp 1995 Annual Report, 3.

32 "First Republic Acquires Silver State Thrift." *The American Banker*, January 10, 1994, 6; First Republic Bancorp 1993 Annual Report, 2.

33 First Republic Bancorp 1995 Annual Report, A Ten Year Perspective.

34 Anna Hirano, interview conducted by Bruce Weindruch, August 13, 2013, The History Factory, Washington, D.C., transcript, 7-8.

35 Ibid., 13-15; Sang, Larry. *The Principles of Feng Shui: Book One*. The American Feng Shui Institute, 1995, 2-3.

36 Jim Herbert, interview conducted by Bruce Weindruch, June 25, 2013, The History Factory, Washington, D.C., transcript, 55.

37 Anna Hirano, interview, August 13, 2013, 13-16.

38 Anna Hirano, interview conducted by Shannon Houston, February 2014.

39 Anna Hirano, interview, August 13, 2013, 14.

40 Ibid., 16-17.

41 Jim Herbert, interview, June 25, 2013, 17.

42 "Southern California Earthquake – Jolted Again: Quake in Los Angeles Kills Dozens, Leaves Commerce in Chaos – With Busy Highways Cut, Often-Battered Region Faces Another Challenge – The Big One? 'Big Enough.'" *The Wall Street Journal*, January 18, 1994, A1.

43 Mary Deckebach, interview conducted by Bruce Weindruch, November 14, 2012, The History Factory, Washington, D.C., transcript 10.

44 Jim Herbert interview, March 6, 2013, 3.

45 Ibid., 6.

46 First Republic Bancorp 1994 Annual Report, 3.

47 Jim Herbert interview, March 6, 2013, 4-7.

48 First Republic Bancorp 1994 Annual Report, 25;

Jim Herbert interview, March 6, 2013, 6; First Republic Bank 1995 Annual Report, 25.

49 First Republic Bancorp 1995 Annual Report, 2, 48.

50 Katherine August-deWilde, interview conducted by Bruce Weindruch, November 19, 2012, The History Factory, Washington, D.C., transcript, 20-21.

51 Ed Dobranski, interview, September 27, 2012, 9.

52 First Republic Bancorp 1995 Annual Report, 4.

53 "Consolidation in the U.S. Banking Industry." *FDIC Banking Review*, 2005, Vol. 17, No. 4; Rhoades, Stephen A. "Bank Mergers and Industrywide Structure, 1980-94." Board of Governors of the Federal Reserve System, Washington DC, January 1996, 27-29.

54 Scott Dufresne, interview conducted by Bruce Weindruch, The History Factory, Washington, D.C., September 13, 2012, transcript, 13.

55 Jim Herbert, interview, March 6, 2013, 7.

56 DeLong, Erin. "Minutes of the Assembly Committee on Commerce: Sixty-ninth Session." May 14, 1997. http://leg.state.nv.us/Session/69th1997/97minutes/AM/CM/am5-14CM.htm. Accessed July 9, 2013; First Republic Bank 1997 Annual Report, 57.

57 1997 Statutes of Nevada. No. 286

58 Ed Dobranski, interview, September 27, 2012, 11-12.

59 First Republic Bancorp 1996 Annual Report, 3-4.

60 Jim Baumberger, interview, March 18, 2010, First Republic Bank archives.

61 Ibid.; "First Republic Acquires Silver State Thrift." *The American Banker*, January 10, 1994, 6.

62 David Lichtman, interview conducted by Shannon Houston, February 2014.

63 First Republic Bank 1994 Annual Report, 18-19.

64 First Republic Bancorp 1995 Annual Report, 14.

65 Jim Herbert, interview, March 6, 2013, 10-11; "Luxury Home Values Rise in the First Quarter." First Republic Bank. http://www.firstrepublic.com/aboutus/newsroom/luxury-home-values-rise-in-the-first-quarter. Accessed August 8, 2013.

66 Dianne Snedaker, interview conducted by Bruce Weindruch, November 19, 2012, The History Factory, Washington, D.C., transcript, 7.

67 Bill Tracy, interview conducted by Bruce Weindruch, September 11, 2012, The History Factory, Washington, D.C., transcript, 9-11.

68 Jim Herbert, interview March 6, 2013, 12-13.

69 Paul Gardner, interview conducted by Bruce Weindruch, September 6, 2012, The History Factory, Washington, D.C., transcript, 32-33.

70 First Republic Bancorp 1996 Annual Report, inside cover.

CHAPTER 5

1 Dyann Tresenfeld, interview conducted by Bruce Weindruch, July 26, 2012, The History Factory, Washington, D.C., transcript, 11-12.

2 Jim Herbert, interview conducted by Shannon Houston, March 2014.

3 Jim Herbert, interview conducted by Bruce Weindruch, March 6, 2013, The History Factory, Washington, D.C., transcript, 14-16.

4 First Republic Bank 1997 Annual Report, 3.

5 Margaret Mak, interview conducted by Bruce Weindruch, July 26, 2012, The History Factory, Washington, D.C., transcript, 11.

6 First Republic Bank 1998 Annual Report, 5.

7 First Republic Bank 1997 Annual Report, 1, 4.

8 Taylor, Dennis. "First Republic Bank Invades Valley." *Business Journal*, August 10-16, 1998; First Republic Bank 1999 Annual Report, inside cover; First Republic Bank 2000 Annual Report, inside cover.

9 Jason Bender, interview conducted by Bruce Weindruch, December 6, 2012, The History Factory, Washington, D.C., transcript, 10-11.

10 First Republic Bank 1999 Annual Report, 8.

11 Jim Herbert, interview, March 6, 2013, 17-18.

12 Sullivan, Joanna. "Calif. Bank Catering to Rich Eyes Investment Firm Stake." *The American Banker*, July 1, 1997, 10; First Republic Bank 1998 Annual Report, 2.

articles/293954-the-bull-market-turns-five?type=old_article. Accessed January 15, 2015; Proxy Statement for First Republic Bank Special Meeting, June 22, 2007, 35, 45-46; Jim Herbert, interview with Shannon Houston, April 2012.

[16] Proxy Statement for First Republic Bank Special Meeting, June 22, 2007, 35-36.

[17] Ibid., 45; Jim Herbert et al. interview, January 24, 2013, 37-38.

[18] Jim Herbert et al. interview, January 24, 2013, 37-38; Proxy Statement for First Republic Bank Special Meeting, June 22, 2007, 35-36.

[19] Roger Walther, interview conducted by Bruce Weindruch, December 6, 2012, The History Factory, Washington, D.C., transcript, 43.

[20] Martin Gibbs, interview conducted by Scott McMurray, September 13, 2012, The History Factory, Washington, D.C., transcript, 21-22.

[21] Tom Barrack, interview conducted by Bruce Weindruch, November 13, 2012, The History Factory, Washington, D.C., transcript, 16.

[22] Proxy Statement for First Republic Bank Special Meeting, June 22, 2007, 36.

[23] Jim Herbert et al interview, January 24, 2013, 40-41.

[24] Schroeder's group interview: Jim Herbert, Katherine August-deWilde, Mollie Richardson, Willis Newton, Ed Dobranski, David Lichtman and Jason Bender, interview conducted by Bruce Weindruch, December 7, 2012, The History Factory, Washington, D.C., transcript, 7-11; Proxy Statement for First Republic Bank Special Meeting, June 22, 2007, 39.

[25] Jim Herbert et al. interview, January 24, 2013, 44-46.

[26] Ibid.; Jim Herbert, private correspondence, January 28, 2007, 1-2.

[27] Proxy Statement for First Republic Bank Special Meeting, June 22, 2007, 37-38.

[28] Ibid., 8; Jim Herbert et al. interview, January 24, 2013, 39-44.

[29] The IFA Index Calculator, https://www.ifa.com/calc ulator/?i=sp500&g=100000&s=8/1/198 6&e=9 /30/2007&gy=true. Accessed January 20, 2015; Growth in Enterprise Value chart, courtesy First Republic Bank/Bloomberg.

[30] First Republic Bank 2007 Annual Review, 3-4; "Merrill Lynch and First Republic Bank Successfully Close Merger." *Business Newswire*, September 21, 2007.

[31] Jason Bender, interview conducted by Bruce Weindruch, December 6, 2012, The History Factory, Washington, D.C., transcript, 30.

[32] Carmen Castro-Franceschi, interview conducted by Bruce Weindruch, November 20, 2012, The History Factory, Washington, D.C., transcript 36-38.

[33] Dyann Tresenfeld, interview conducted by Bruce Weindruch, July 26, 2012, The History Factory, Washington, D.C., transcript, 24.

[34] Margaret Mak, interview conducted by Bruce Weindruch, July 26, 2012, The History Factory, Washington, D.C., transcript, 22.

[35] Bill Dessoffy, interview conducted by Scott McMurray, September 13, 2012, The History Factory, Washington, D.C., transcript, 27.

[36] Bob Thornton, interview conducted by Bruce Weindruch, October 4, 2012, The History Factory, Washington, D.C., transcript 21-22.

[37] Katherine August-deWilde, interview conducted by Bruce Weindruch, November 19, 2012, The History Factory, Washington, D.C., transcript, 12.

[38] Russ Flynn, interview conducted by Scott McMurray, December 6, 2012, The History Factory, Washington, D.C., transcript, 12.

[39] "425 1 y29734e425.htm FILED PURSUANT TO RULE 425." http://www.sec.gov/Archives/edgar/data/65100/000095012307001057/y29734e425.htm. Accessed January 20, 2015.

[40] "Merrill Lynch and First Republic Bank Successfully Close Merger; Final Results of Election Regarding Merger Consideration Announced." Merrill Lynch & Co., Inc. News Release, September 21, 2007.

[41] Jim Herbert, interview conducted by Shannon Houston, April 2014.

[42] Tully, Shawn. "Wall Street's Money Machine Breaks Down." *Fortune Magazine*, November 12, 2007; Morgenson, Gretchen. "The Reckoning: How Merrill Lynch Faltered and Fell." *The New York Times*, November 9, 2008. http://www.nytimes.com/2008/11/09/business/09magic.html. Accessed January 15, 2015.

[43] Hamilton, Walter. "NYSE chief Thain to lead Merrill Lynch." *Los Angeles Times*, November 15, 2007, C4.

[44] Thomas Jr., Landon. "2 Executives Are Ousted at Merrill." *The New York Times*, October 4, 2007. http://www.nytimes. com/2007/10/04/business/04merrill. html. Accessed August 19, 2013.

[45] David Lichtman, interview conducted by Bruce Weindruch, July 27, 2012, The History Factory, Washington, D.C., transcript, 22-23.

[46] David Lichtman, Schroeder's group interview, December 7, 2012, 13.

[47] Dyann Tresenfeld, interview, July 26, 2012, 25.

[48] Willis Newton, Schroeder's group interview, December 7, 2012, 12.

[49] Jason Bender, interview, December 6, 2012, 40.

[50] First Republic Bank 2010 Annual Report, 6.

[51] Jason Bender, interview, December 6, 2012, 40.

[52] First Republic Bank 2010 Annual Report, 6-13; Jim Herbert, interview conducted by Shannon Houston, June 2014.

[53] Jim Herbert, Schroeder's group interview, December 7, 2012, 16.

[54] Ibid.

[55] Bill Dessoffy, interview conducted by Bruce Weindruch, September 13, 2012, The History Factory, Washington, D.C., transcript, 25.

[56] Herbert, Jim and Katherine August-deWilde. "First Republic Culture Maintenance Council." Memorandum, July 15, 2008.

[57] Jim Herbert, interview conducted by Shannon Houston, April 2014; Mollie Richardson, interview conducted by Shannon Houston, August 2013.

[58] Jim Herbert et al. interview, January 24, 2013, 24-26; Mollie Richardson, Schroeder's group interview, December 7, 2012, 19.

[59] Jim Herbert, Schroeder's group interview, December 7, 2012, 20.

[60] Tully, Shawn. "Wall Street's Money Machine

Breaks Down."

61 Ibid.

62 Sidel, Robin, Dennis Berman and Kate Kelly. "J.P. Morgan Busy Bear in Fire Sale, As Fed Widens Credit to Avert Crisis." *The Wall Street Journal*, March 17, 2008. http://online.wsj.com/ article/SB120569598608739825.html. Accessed January 15, 2015; "Bear Stearns, JPMorgan Chase, and Maiden Lane LLC." Board of Governors of the Federal Reserve System. http://www.federalreserve.gov/newsevents/reform_bcarstearns.htm. Accessed August 19, 2013.

63 Jim Herbert, Schroeder's group interview, December 7, 2012, 22-23.

CHAPTER 8

1 Sorkin, Andrew Ross. "Lehman Files for Bankruptcy; Merrill Is Sold." *The New York Times*, September 15, 2008. http://www.nytimes.com/2008/09/15/business/15lehman.html?_r=1&. Accessed May 15, 2014.

2 "Subprime Crisis: A Timeline." *CNN Money*, September 15, 2008. http://money.cnn.com/2008/09/15/news/economy/subprime_timeline/index.htm. Accessed May 15, 2014; Applebaum, Binyamin, and Zachary A. Goldfarb. "Weekend Merger Struck with Bank of America." *The Washington Post*, September 15, 2008. http://www.washingtonpost.com/wp-dyn/content/article/2008/09/14/AR2008091401468.html. Accessed January 16, 2015.

3 Lipton, Josh. "Bank of America to Buy U.S. Trust." *Forbes*, November 20, 2006. http://www.forbes.com/2006/11/20/bank-of-america-markets-equity-cx_jl_1120markets12.html. Accessed January 16, 2015.

4 Moore, Heidi N. "Bank of America-Merrill Lynch: A $50 Billion Deal from Hell." *The Wall Street Journal*, January 22, 2009. http://blogs.wsj.com/deals/2009/01/22/bank-of-america-merrill-lynch-a-50-billion-deal-from-hell/tab/print/?mg=blogs-wsj&url=http%253A%252F%252Fblogs.wsj.com%252Fdeals%252F2009%252F01%252F22%252Fb

ank-of-america-merrill-lynch-a-50-billion-deal-from-hell%252Ftab%252Fprint. Accessed January 16, 2015; Kouwe, Zachery. "Thain's the Man." New York Post, November 15, 2007. http://nypost.com/2007/11/15/thains-the-man/. Accessed April 30, 2015.

5 Ed Dobranski, Schroeder's group interview conducted by Bruce Weindruch. December 7, 2012, The History Factory, Washington, D.C., transcript, 27-28.

6 Scott Dufresne, interview conducted by Bruce Weindruch, September 13, 2012, The History Factory, Washington, D.C., transcript, 38.

7 Mary Deckebach, interview conducted by Bruce Weindruch, November 14, 2012, The History Factory, Washington, D.C., transcript, 22.

8 Scott Dufresne, interview, September 13, 2012, 36.

9 Bill Dessoffy, interview conducted by Bruce Weindruch, September 13, 2012, The History Factory, Washington, D.C., transcript, 32.

10 Dyann Tresenfeld, interview conducted by Bruce Weindruch, July 26, 2012, The History Factory, Washington, D.C., transcript, 23-24; First Republic Bank Form 10-K 2010, 12, 49; First Republic Offering Circular, December 8, 2010, 1-3.

11 Schroeder's group interview, transcript, 24-25.

12 Ibid., 25-26.

13 Ibid., 33.

14 Jim Herbert, Willis Newton, Schroeder's group interview, December 7, 2012, 34-36.

15 Ibid., 43-44.

16 Ibid., 46.

17 Ibid., 46-47.

18 Jim Herbert, interview conducted by Shannon Houston, April 2014.

19 Tom Barrack, interview conducted by Bruce Weindruch, November 13, 2012, The History Factory, Washington, D.C., transcript, 25.

20 William Ford, interview conducted by Bruce Weindruch, October 16, 2012, The History Factory, Washington, D.C., 9.

21 Roger Walther, interview, December 6, 2012, 49.

22 Ed Dobranski, Schroeder's group interview, 54; Report No. AUD-12-004, December 11, 2011,

Officer of Inspector General, I-6.

23 David Lichtman, Schroeder's group interview, 56; Jim Herbert, interview conducted by Shannon Houston, April 2014.

24 Jim Herbert, interview conducted by Shannon Houston, April 2014.

25 First Republic Bank Offering Circular, December 8, 2010, 5.

26 First Republic Bank Offering Circular, December 8, 2010, F4-F5.

27 First Republic Bank Offering Circular, December 8, 2010, 10.

28 First Republic Bank Offering Circular, December 8, 2010, ii.

29 Bill Dessoffy, interview, September 13, 2012, 28-30.

CHAPTER 9

1 Jim Herbert, interview conducted by Bruce Weindruch, June 25, 2013, The History Factory, Washington, D.C., transcript, 2-3.

2 Ibid., 3-7; First Republic Bank Press Release, July 1, 2010; Merrill Lynch Press Release, January 30, 2007; First Republic Bank Investor Presentation, March 5, 2012, 29.

3 Jim Herbert, interview, June 25, 2013, 4-5.

4 Ibid., 4.

5 First Republic Bank Form 10-K, 2010. First Republic Bank Form 10-K, 2013.

6 Katherine August-deWilde, interview, September 7, 2012, 37-38.

7 Jim Herbert, interview, June 25, 2013, 4-5. Trotter, Daniel. "Bank Stocks Ignite Big Rally." CNNMoney, July 7, 2010. http://origin.tampabays10.com/news/topstories/story.aspx?storyid=135780. Accessed April 30, 2015.

8 "First Republic Bank Named Best Private Bank in North America." *Wall Street Journal*, February 13, 2013. http://online.wsj.com/article/PR-CO-20130213-908966.html. Accessed August 26, 2013.

9 Jim Herbert, interview, June 25, 2013, 4-5.

10 First Republic Bank Press Release, December 8, 2010.

11 Jim Herbert, interview, June 25, 2013, 5.

12 Ibid., 5.

13 Jim Herbert, interview, June 25, 2013, 5-7.

14 First Republic Bank Investor Presentation, March 5, 2012, 29. First Republic Bank 2012 Proxy Statement, 17-18.

15 First Republic Bank 2013 Proxy Statement, 18-19.

16 First Republic Bank Investor Presentation, August 14, 2013, 33.

17 First Republic Bank Investor Presentation, August 14, 2013, 32-33.

18 Jim Herbert, interview, June 25, 2013, 7-9.

19 Jim Herbert, interview, June 25, 2013, 7-8.

20 Ibid., 8.

21 *Institutional Investor* magazine, December 2013/ January 2014. www.iimosthonoredcompanies. com/default.php. Accessed July 8, 2014.

22 Jim Herbert, interview, June 25, 2013, 9-11.

23 Ibid., 9.

24 Ibid., 12; "First Republic Bank Names Mike Selfridge Chief Operating Officer." First Republic Bank Press Release, February 26, 2014.

25 Jim Herbert, interview, June 25, 2013, 10-13.

26 Mike Selfridge, interview conducted by Bruce Weindruch, January 3, 2013, The History Factory, Washington, D.C., transcript, 3.

27 Ibid., 4-10, 43.

28 Jim Herbert, interview conducted by Shannon Houston, June 2014. Chris Coleman, interview conducted by Crystal Bryant, February 2014.

29 Mike Roffler, interview conducted by Shannon Houston, February 2014.

30 Ibid.; First Republic Bank Press Release, November 17, 2014.

31 Jim Herbert, interview, June 2014. Mike Selfridge, interview, January 3, 2013, 22-23; First Republic Bank Investor Presentation, February 13, 2015, 17.

32 Jim Herbert, interview, June 2014. First Republic Bank Investor Presentation, August 14, 2013, 8-9; First Republic Bank Investor Presentation, February 13, 2015, 6.

33 Jim Herbert, interview, June 2014.

34 Carmen Castro-Franceschi, interview conducted by Bruce Weindruch, November 20, 2012, The History Factory, Washington, D.C., transcript, 57.

35 Rosana Han, interview conducted by Shannon Houston, February 2014; First Republic Bank Investor Presentation, February 13, 2015, 11.

36 First Republic Bank Annual Report, 2013, 64.

37 Mike Selfridge, interview, January 3, 2013, transcript, 40.

38 Rosana Han, interview, February 2014; First Republic Bank Investor Presentation, February 13, 2015, 11.

39 David Lichtman, interview conducted by Bruce Weindruch, July 27, 2012, The History Factory, Washington, D.C., transcript, 33-34.

40 First Republic Bank Form 10-K, 2010, 45. First Republic Bank Form 10-K, 2014, 47.

41 Joe Petitti, interview conducted by Bruce Weindruch, August 14, 2013, The History Factory, Washington, D.C., 19.

42 Catherine Evans, interview conducted by Bruce Weindruch, August 13, 2013, The History Factory, Washington, D.C., transcript, 26.

43 Russ Flynn, interview conducted by Scott McMurray, December 6, 2012, The History Factory, Washington, D.C., transcript, 6.

44 Jim Herbert, interview, June 25, 2013, 27.

45 Ibid., 30.

46 Mike Selfridge, interview conducted by Shannon Houston, February 2014; Net Promoter System. http://netpromotersystem.com. Accessed July 1, 2014.

47 First Republic Bank Investor Presentation, May 23, 2014, 7; First Republic Bank Investor Presentation, February 13, 2015, 10.

48 Mike Selfridge, interview, February 2014.

49 First Republic Bank Investor Presentation, Investor Presentation, February 13, 2015, 18, 24, 27.

50 Jim Herbert, interview, June 25, 2013, 19-20.

51 Chris Coleman, interview conducted by Bruce Weindruch, August 13, 2013, The History Factory, Washington, D.C., transcript, 6.

52 Ibid.

53 Chris Coleman, interview, August 13, 2013, 9-10.

54 Paul Gardner, interview conducted by Bruce Weindruch, September 9, 2012, The History Factory, Washington, D.C., transcript, 21.

55 First Republic Bank Investor Presentation, February 13, 2015, 28.

56 Jim Herbert, interview by Shannon Houston, July 2014.

57 Patrick Macken, interview conducted by Shannon Houston, February 2014.

58 Bob Thornton, interview conducted by Bruce Weindruch, October 4, 2012, The History Factory, Washington, D.C., transcript, 33.

59 First Republic Bank Investor Presentation, August 14, 2013, 25.

60 First Republic Bank Investor Presentation, April 16, 2015, 27. First Republic Bank Press Release, April 10, 2013; First Republic Bank Press Release, October 10, 2013.

61 Catherine Evans, interview, August 13, 2013, 20.

62 Ibid., 21.

63 Ibid., 22.

64 Jim Herbert, interview conducted by Shannon Houston, June 2014.

65 Jim Herbert, interview, June 25, 2013, 21-22; First Republic Investor Presentation, August 14, 2013, 25.

66 Jim Herbert, interview, June 2014; First Republic Bank Press Release, January 28, 2013.

67 Donnellon, Anne. Case study on First Republic Bank, Babson College, 2013.

68 Mollie Richardson, interview conducted by Shannon Houston, May 2014.

69 Jim Herbert, interview, June 25, 2013, 44-45.

70 David Lichtman, interview, July 27, 2012, 32.

71 Katherine August-deWilde, interview conducted by Bruce Weindruch, November 19, 2012, The History Factory, Washington, D.C., transcript, 42.

72 Next Generation Roundtable, interview conducted by Bruce Weindruch, June 25, 2012, The History Factory, Washington, D.C.,

transcript, 9.

73 Jim Herbert, interview, June 25, 2013, 56.

CHAPTER 10

1 Jim Herbert, interview conducted by Shannon Houston, February 2015; First Republic Bank Investor Presentation, April 16, 2015, 24.

2 "Q2 2014 First Republic Bank Earnings Conference Call." *Fair Disclosure Wire,* July 16, 2014.

3 First Republic Bank Investor Presentation, February 13, 2015, 18-19.

4 Kline, Alan. "Banker of the Year: First Republic's James Herbert." American Banker, December 21, 2014.

5 Jim Herbert, interview, February 2015.

6 Bill Ward, interview conducted by Shannon Houston, February 2015.

7 Gaye Erkan, interview conducted by Shannon Houston, February 2015.

8 Hugh Westermeyer, interview conducted by Shannon Houston, February 2015.

9 Jared Souter, interview conducted by Shannon Houston, February 2015.

10 Jim Herbert, interview conducted by Shannon Houston, February 2015.

11 Eric Lucero, interview conducted by Shannon Houston, February 2015.

12 Scott Finder, interview conducted by Shannon Houston, February 2015.

13 First Republic Bank Investor Presentation, February 13, 2015, 7.

14 Julie Harkins, interview conducted by Shannon Houston, February 2015.

15 Mike Selfridge, interview conducted by Shannon Houston, February 2015.

16 Anna Legio, interview conducted by Shannon Houston, February 2015.

17 Nancy Sargent, interview conducted by Shannon Houston, February 2015.

18 Gaye Erkan, interview conducted by Shannon

19 Martin Gibson, interview conducted by Shannon Houston, February 2015; Afsaneh Iranpour, interview conducted by Shannon Houston, February 2015.

20 Fatema Arande, interview conducted by Shannon Houston, February 2015; Amie Stevens, interview conducted by Shannon Houston, February 2015.

21 Bill Ward, interview, February 2015.

22 Susie Cranston, interview conducted by Shannon Houston, February 2015.

23 Angela Osborne, interview conducted by Shannon Houston, February 2015.

24 Jonathan Santelli, interview conducted by Shannon Houston, February 2015.

25 Angela Osborne, interview, February 2015.

26 Stephanie Bontemps, interview conducted by Shannon Houston, February 2015.

27 Crystal Bryant, interview conducted by Shannon Houston, February 2015.

28 Karen Weissenbach, interview conducted by Shannon Houston, February 2015; Mohamed Fahmi, interview conducted by Shannon Houston, February 2015.

29 Alex Herbert, interview conducted by Shannon Houston, February 2015.

30 Nancy Segreto, interview conducted by Shannon Houston, February 2015.

31 Nancy Sargent, interview, February 2015.

32 Jim Herbert, interview, February 2015.

33 Mike Harrington, interview conducted by Shannon Houston, February 2015.

34 Kellie Abreu, interview conducted by Shannon Houston, February 2015.

35 Maureen Maginn, interview conducted by Crystal Bryant, February 2014.

36 Dale Smith, interview conducted by Shannon Houston, February 2015.

37 Willis Newton, interview conducted by Bruce Weindruch, July 27, 2012, The History Factory, Washington, D.C., transcript, 41; Katherine August-deWilde, interview conduced by Bruce

Houston, February 2015.

Weindruch, November 19, 2012, The History Factory, Washington, D.C., transcript, 58.

38 Jim Herbert, interview, February 2015.

39 Pamela Joyner, interview conducted by Bruce Weindruch, December 13, 2012, The History Factory, Washington, D.C., transcript, 4

40 Elise Wen, interview conducted by Shannon Houston, February 2015.

41 Jim Herbert, interview conducted by Bruce Weindruch, June 25, 2013, The History Factory, Washington, D.C., transcript, 46.

42 Bill Ford, interview conducted by Bruce Weindruch, October 16, 2012, The History Factory, Washington, D.C., transcript, 31.

43 Jim Herbert, interview, February 2015.

Index

Italicized page numbers indicate illustrations and captions.

Image Credits

CHAPTER 1

Pages 10-14, 17
Morning Journal / Sam Greene

Page 16
Coshocton National Bank

Page 17, bottom left
Nyttend

Page 17, bottom center
Nyttend

Page 17, bottom right
Henryk Sadura / Shutterstock.com

Page 18, left
Jim Herbert

Page 18, right
Specimen/Alamy

Page 19, left
© Charles E. Rotkin / Corbis

Page 19, right
Bernard Gotfryd / Getty Images

Page 21, left
© Bettmann / Corbis

Page 21, right
Sam Falk / The New York Times / Redux Pictures

Page 24, left
Israeli Defense Forces

Page 24, right
National Archives at College Park - Still Pictures (RD-DC-S)

Page 25, left
© R. Krubner / ClassicStock / Corbis

Page 25, right
Warren Reed

Page 28, left
Bill Ray

Page 28, bottom right
Griff Durant

Page 29
Billy Hathorn

Page 30
The Pop Shoppe

Page 32
Carol M. Highsmith Archive, Library of Congress, Prints and Photographs Division

Page 33, top
Jon Sullivan

Page 33, bottom
Noah Clayton / Getty Images

Page 34, left
Mark Coggins / Getty Images

Page 34, center
© Ed Young / Corbis

Page 34, right
Michael Layefsky / Getty Images

CHAPTER 2

Page 45
Andrew Sacks / Getty Images

Page 48, right
Steve Weiner

Page 51
Fior d'Italia Restaurant, San Francisco

Page 63, left
Carol M. Highsmith Archive, Library of Congress, Prints and Photographs Division

Page 63, right
Carol M. Highsmith Archive, Library of Congress, Prints and Photographs Division

Page 64
From reuters.com, May 9, 1984 © 1984 reuters.com. All rights reserved. Used by permission and protected by the Copyright Laws of the United States. The printing, copying, redistribution, or retransmission of this Content without express written permission is prohibited.

CHAPTER 3

Page 79
Dlw415

Page 82, right
mikeledray / Shutterstock.com

Page 84
Federal Deposit Insurance Corporation

Page 101
Carol M. Highsmith Archive, Library of Congress, Prints and Photographs Division

CHAPTER 4

Page 117
Federal Home Loan Bank System

Page 125, top left
Sanfranman59

Page 125, top right
Sanfranman59

Page 127, right
Mike Smith / Flickr

Page 135, top left
© David Butow / Corbis

Page 135, top right
Federal Emergency Management Agency

Page 135, bottom left
Federal Emergency Management Agency

Page 135, bottom right
Federal Emergency Management Agency

CHAPTER 5

Page 160, bottom
Cambridge International Partner LLC

Page 171
© Reuters / Corbis

CHAPTER 6

Page 188
MaxFX / Shutterstock.com

Page 202, bottom left
Boston Globe / Getty Images

CHAPTER 7

Page 213
© Seth Wenig / AP / Corbis

Page 226
Securities and Exchange Commission

Page 229
Schroeder's Restaurant, San Francisco;
San Francisco History Center, San Francisco
Public Library

Page 233
© James Leynse / Corbis

Page 234, top left
Colin Robertson

Page 234, top right
Olivier Le Queinec / Shutterstock.com

Page 234, bottom
© Mark Lennihan / AP / Corbis

CHAPTER 8

Page 241, left
David Shankbone

Page 241, top right
Alex Proimos

Page 241, bottom right
© Bebeto Matthews / AP / Corbis

Page 244
Museum of American Finance, NYC

Page 246, right
justasc / Shutterstock.com

Page 252
Sahajesh Patel

Page 254
Matthew G. Bisanz

Page 255
Used with permission of The Associated Press
Copyright © 2015. All rights reserved.

CHAPTER 9

Page 266
Peter Lockwood

CHAPTER 10

Page 303
From *American Banker,* December 22,
2014 © 2014 SourceMedia, Inc. All rights
reserved. Used by permission and protected
by the Copyright Laws of the United States.
The printing, copying, redistribution, or
retransmission of this Content without express
written permission is prohibited.